The
Middle
Generation

The Middle Generation

The Lives and Poetry of

Delmore Schwartz
Randall Jarrell
John Berryman
and
Robert Lowell

BRUCE BAWER

Archon Books

1986

First published 1986 as an Archon Book,
an imprint of The Shoe String Press, Inc.
Hamden, Connecticut, 06514

Printed in the United States of America

The paper in this book meets the guidelines
for permanence and durability
of the Committee on Production Guidelines
for Book Longevity of
the Council on Library Resources.

Acknowledgment of permission to quote protected material
is made to The Estate of Delmore Schwartz,
for unpublished poetry, and to Farrar, Straus & Giroux and Faber & Faber
for quotations from poetry in *Day by Day* by Robert Lowell

It should be understood that the high cost of permission
fees have made frequent quotation of poetry impossible.

Library of Congress Cataloging-in-Publication Data

Bawer, Bruce, 1956-
The middle generation.

Bibliography: p.
Includes index.
1. American poetry—20th century—History and
criticism.   2. Alienation (Social psychology) in
literature.   3. Poets, American—20th century—Biography.
I. Title.
PS310.A44B39   1986   811'.5'09   86-14016
ISBN 0-208-02125-6 (alk. paper)

Contents

Acknowledgments

I must thank Ruth Miller, whose extensive and incisive critique of the original version of this study improved it immeasurably, and whose course in American literary criticism helped me to orient myself as a critic. I extend my thanks as well to Thomas Flanagan and Louis Simpson for their comments and encouragement, and for providing inspiring examples of the creative mind as critical mind. I thank David Sheehan for his helpfulness, and Krin Gabbard for his suggestions. I am grateful for the use of the facilities of the New York Public Library, the Mid-Manhattan Library, the Bobst Library at New York University, the Beinecke Library at Yale University, and the Delmar T. Oviatt Memorial Library at the California State University at Northridge.

I also wish to acknowledge the following debts: Leonard Gross shared his recollections of Delmore Schwartz; the late R. H. Deutsch shared his memories of John Berryman; Martha Sherrill and Eugenio Villacaña shared their memories of Robert Lowell. Stacey Olster and William J. Harris provided helpful advice at an early stage. My parents, Nell and Ted Bawer, provided solace and sanctuary. Robert Cohen and Dorothea Matthäus listened patiently and offered wise observations. Chronologies of the lives and works of John Berryman and Randall Jarrell prepared by Gail Smith and Paula Uruburu proved very useful. I was inspired beyond measure by the example of John Mascaro, who approaches the act of criticism with a keenness and an enthusiasm that few critics could equal.

Lastly, I would like to thank John Thompson, friend and mentor, who taught me "how grown-ups talk about literature," whose own literary criticism served me as a model of wit, perception, and clarity, and who first drew my attention to the four tragic figures whose lives and work form the subject of this study.

PART ONE
"The Generic Life"

Prologue

. . . really we had the same life,
the generic one
our generation offered
                    Robert Lowell

The generation to which Lowell refers in these lines is the so-called Middle Generation, a group of American poets that consisted of Delmore Schwartz, Randall Jarrell, John Berryman, and Lowell himself.[1] They were all born between 1913 and 1917, three of them within an eleven month period. To a fascinating degree, Lowell is right when he suggests that they shared a generic life. That they shared the distress of deep and disruptive psychological problems is generally known. They were erratic, driven to pathological excesses in behavior by an assortment of secret agonies. Profound pain filled much of their lives and informed much of their work.

Yet few people seem really to know or understand those lives. Even critics familiar with the details, who have read the biographies and memoirs, often fail to comprehend the true nature of those poets' mutual affliction. Clayton Eshleman, reviewing the 1982 biography of John Berryman by John Haffenden, writes:

> There are those who do find John Berryman's life compelling. I don't. Undermining his ability to throw his whole being into his poetry was a buffoonish web of compulsive personal habits, cute or maddening, depending from what angle, and at what hour, they came at you. Not only did he read poetry to women's feet and meow at them over the telephone, he defecated in university corridors and urinated in hotel beds. As a young man, he slapped himself, beat himself and hid in his mother's closet, snarling. As an older man, he roared and barked at his doctors. In an awful way, Haffenden's "life" makes one realize that Berryman's last decade resembled the last few years in the life of Elvis Presley.[2]

This description of Berryman's behavior characterizes the Middle Generation as a whole. The destructiveness; the self-punishment; the hostility; the testing of other people's love, patience, and devotion; the frenetic all-hours activity; the unorthodox way of relating to women in general and one's mother in particular—every aspect of Berryman's aberrant behavior is repeated in the lives of the other poets. Why? For the same reason that all patients with measles develop rashes. The poets had more in common than a vocation and a period in time; they shared an affliction. Eshleman appears to ignore this fact, to deny its ineluctable significance; he speaks of Berryman's "compulsive personal habits . . . undermining his ability to throw his whole being into his poetry," as if those habits were frivolities extraneous to the creative act. They were not. On the contrary, both his obsessive devotion to the writing of poetry and his "compulsive personal habits" were tricks of the mind, defenses of an embattled psyche struggling against the inimical forces within itself. To an unusual and unfortunate degree, then, it might be said that Berryman's poetry and his "buffoonery" were in fact twin symptoms of a single malady. Had he been "cured" of one of these symptoms, he would almost certainly have been "cured" of the other.

It was no different with the others. All of them were disabled by emotions upon which they could muse eternally and with great eloquence, but which they were powerless to control. Here lies the ultimate irony of their lives: the very conditions which so tragically crippled them as men also provided their poetry with its greatest beauty and strength. James Atlas's observation that Schwartz's "most moving poems were invariably and unmistakably autobiographical" could easily be applied to the works of all four Middle Generation poets.[3] They were, to the end, obsessed with their art. They took poetry as seriously as life, and their lives, in the fullest sense, were dedicated to it. Their compulsive habits, "cute or maddening, depending at what hour, and from what angle, they came at you," reflected anxieties directly related to that dedication. Since those anxieties are largely responsible for the power and freshness of some of the Middle Generation's finest works, among them Lowell's *Life Studies* and Berryman's *Dream Songs,* it is desirable that they be understood as fully as possible.

Turbulent Childhoods

Hail Childhood! . . . / . . . Hail the immortal Past
Delmore Schwartz

O childhood, O images gliding from us
Randall Jarrell

Just as much of the best poetry of the Middle Generation had its roots in their lives, so the roots of their lives lay in their turbulent childhoods. The Middle Generation poets recognized this, and devoted a good deal of their poetry to an exploration of their upbringings. Schwartz's book-length verse epic titled *Genesis: Book One*, a veritable *Bildungsgedicht*, was based on his New York childhood. Jarrell's volume *The Lost World* is dominated by his sense of the irretrievability of his boyhood in Los Angeles. Berryman and Lowell, who once said that his life may have been entirely the result of his relationship with his parents, likewise intently examined their earliest years in verse. Retracing their steps, one is struck by a startling pattern of similarities. They might all have been born under the same star. None of them grew up in anything even remotely resembling a stable, solid home. Each was estranged from his father, and three of the four had destructively close ties to overly possessive mothers. All developed an early sense of rootlessness and alienation. Guilt over feelings of resentment toward the parents plagued each of them well into adulthood.

The first-born of the Middle Generation poets was Schwartz, the older of two sons of a Jewish immigrant couple. Harry Schwartz was successful in both real estate and extramarital affairs, and wanted no children. His wife Rose, however, wanted a family and hoped that once he became a father Harry would settle down and be dependable. Unable to conceive owing to a surgically correctable physical problem, Rose, like the heroine of a Shakespearean comedy, played a trick on her husband; she sold a French war bond and had the necessary operation while Harry was out of town on business. She was soon pregnant, and for a while Harry seemed pleased with the idea. These events, which culminated in Delmore's birth on December 8, 1913, in Brooklyn, became key elements in his personal mythology. Atlas records that

> In later life, when Delmore learned that he owed his birth to a deception, he came to look on his very existence as problematic, the result of a devious struggle between his parents—two "egodoms," as he later referred to them, doomed forever to oppose each other. With an Aristotelian eye for the turning points in the drama of his life, he regarded certain episodes as bearers of such "pity and terror" that the whole of his experience stood revealed in them. Vergil's *Felix qui potuit rerum cognoscere causas* ["Happy is he who can know the causes of things"] was one of his favorite axioms, from which it followed that he should consider his birth the most crucial episode of all.[1]

Atlas further notes that "Like his friend Robert Lowell, who at nearly the same age had observed [or, more correctly, *would* observe, being four years younger] his family's unfolding tragedies, the five-year-old Delmore couldn't help but notice the deepening crisis of his parents' marriage."[2] When the Schwartzes were together, they fought; when they were separated by one of Harry's frequent business trips to Florida, the grief-stricken Rose tortured Delmore with her loneliness. The central event of Schwartz's childhood occurred late one night when his parents had been fighting. As he remembered it, they woke him up and insisted that he choose between them. This event, the memory of which would haunt Schwartz for the rest of his life, may help to explain the insomnia that plagued him during his adult years.

The tension between Harry and Rose Schwartz finally led to a permanent separation. Harry left New York for Chicago, where he continued to prosper in business. The passage of years did not bring Harry and Delmore any closer. The businessman and the poet were simply different types of men, with little to say to each other. When Harry died from a heart attack, the teenage Delmore was disturbed to find that he felt nothing; later, when the estate that the erstwhile millionaire had left him turned out to be worthless, the shock of that discovery so preoccupied Delmore that he was unable to mourn. He did write about the death in a poem (quoted in Atlas's book) which seems to demonstrate, in Atlas's words, that "the only image of stability he knew had been wiped out, never to be recovered." In this poem Schwartz recounts a dream in which he sees his father in a coffin but feels nothing, and realizes that he himself "was in a hold, a coffin and a morgue."[3]

Schwartz's feelings about his father's passing were still unresolved ten years after the fact when, guilt-ridden over his failure to mourn, Schwartz imagined that he had bought himself a cemetery plot beside his father's grave. He also imagined, in his words, "a story in which a young man is in the bathroom and when he is called, he does not answer, permits them to think something has happened to him, until the whole family is greatly disturbed, the door is broken down by the police or the janitor, young man and family mutually denounce each other." Atlas observes that this story

> was, in its own way, a commonplace fantasy of retribution, in which the child resorts to dramatic and punitive means to gain the attention of his family; but in this instance it had special meaning. It was as if Delmore had to repress his urge to "denounce" his father for dying and his mother for her selfish conduct by means of these parables; and that impulse was in turn converted to guilt.[4]

If the absence of the father constituted a lifelong trauma, the continued presence of his mother was equally painful. She did not die until 1962, a mere four years before Schwartz's own death, and remained an emotional burden on him throughout his life. Her possessiveness was extreme. When he told her that he was engaged to be married to his first wife, Gertrude Buckman, she threatened suicide. At the wedding she collapsed and had to be carried up to the synagogue steps. In later years, when Schwartz was working at the *Partisan Review*, she would call the offices of that quarterly to complain to whoever answered the phone that Schwartz was neglecting her. Her suspicious, pessimistic view of life molded Schwartz's own character. She taught him at a very early age to trust no one. Her maxim that all relationships between men and women are based on selfishness warped his view of sex. And her failure to respect his vocation because he made so little money caused him to become obsessed, in middle age, with financial success.

In his childhood, then, lay the seeds of Schwartz's adult personality and, more to the point, the seeds of much of his mature poetry. True, the human mind does not develop neatly, in the manner of an Aristotelian syllogism; but it is surely apparent that Schwartz's chaotic, confused, and eventually psychotic adult personality—his insomnia, sense of alienation, suspiciousness, mania for success, and sexual problems—may be understood, at least in part, as growing out of specific events in his childhood. That Schwartz was acutely aware of his mother's effect on his psychological evolution is manifest in his lifelong resentment of her, and the guilt which that resentment engendered. When Rose died, Delmore sent flowers to her grave, with a card bearing an altered quotation from Joyce: "Oh mother forsaken, forgive your son."[5]

There are other factors that were responsible for the psychological disturbances of Schwartz's mature years. His sense of alienation, which he shares with the other Middle Generation poets, stems also from his sense of Jewishness; more accurately, from the personal meaning that Jewishness held for him. In *Genesis*, he describes his alter ego Hershey Green as a Jew, and therefore an heir of pain and alienation.[6]

John Berryman's life began in guilt. It was not his guilt, but his mother's, although in their lifetimes there would be enough between them for both. Martha Smith, the wife of John Allyn Smith, a bank employee in McAlester, Oklahoma, gave birth by Caesarian section to her son John Allyn, Jr., on October 25, 1914, less than a year after Delmore Schwartz's birth. Martha had wanted her son as desperately as Rose had wanted hers, and from the moment of his birth the child was everything in the world to her. Having waited all her life for someone to lavish with affection, she loved her son obsessively. Yet she felt guilty over the manner of his delivery, fearing neurotically "that I had been guilty of some sin or fault that I could not bear my sons in agony."[7] Although Berryman was not as obsessed with his birth as Schwartz was, he and his mother apparently discussed and corresponded about it more than once.

John Allyn Smith, like Harry Schwartz, was not so enthusiastic about parenthood as was his wife. Martha's excessive love for the baby isolated him, and when she became pregnant again he proposed an abortion on the grounds that he couldn't afford another baby. Martha refused.

Like young Delmore Schwartz and young Robert Lowell, young John Allyn Smith, Jr., looked on helplessly while his parents' marriage disintegrated. Writes Eileen Simpson, Berryman's first wife, of Berryman and Schwartz: "The similarities between their situations were striking. Each was the older of two boys. Each was intellectually precocious, observing, inquisitive. Each overheard his parents' terrible disputes and suffered from divided loyalties."[8] The terrible disputes began, in the Smith household, soon after the family moved to Tampa, Florida, where Smith hoped to profit from the Florida land boom. But the economic tide turned, and Smith fell into the worst financial difficulties of his career. It was then that, as Berryman later told Simpson, "They began to quarrel. At night I'd hear them in the next room. Or, braced for the angry voices about to begin, I couldn't fall asleep." Simpson comments: "Was this the beginning of his insomnia? I wondered."[9]

At about this time, both husband and wife became romantically involved with other parties. Martha filed for divorce, and the day the divorce was to become final, John Smith committed suicide. Just as Harry and Rose's noctural disturbance would stay with Schwartz forever, so the sound of the gunshot that killed his father would haunt Berryman's life. His feelings over the death were never resolved. Haffenden writes:

> He believed that he had gone through an agony of grief after his father's death, but it seems probable that his mother and other kin grievously agitated and confused his natural feelings. . . . Later in life Berryman believed that he had been stunned by his loss, and took it as the *point d'appui* of his psychological problems. Convinced that his father's self-serving action had broken his own peace of mind, he swung between compassion and loathing for the man.[10]

Berryman's inability to feel grief after his father's death is strikingly similar to Schwartz's reaction to his own father's death. His resentment of his father for dying is also reminiscent of Schwartz. Like his friend from Brooklyn, Berryman felt a need to denounce his father for dying; in "Dream Song 384" he spits on his father's grave and wonders when indifference will take the place of his moaning, raving self-torture.[11] As with Schwartz, his father's death helped make Berryman an unstable, insecure adult.

But his mother was an even more formidable influence. After Smith's suicide, she married the man who gave Berryman his name, but, overprotective and domineering, she centered her life on her son. Her love, comments Haffenden, was "often less that of a parent than of a girlfriend,"[12] She reacted to the news of Berryman's first engagement to be married with resentment. She constantly manipulated his emotions, particularly his sense of guilt, and alternately gratified and oppressed him with her love. Eileen Simpson suggests that the power of Martha's love ruined his adult sexual relationships, and that her description of Smith to his son, shortly after the suicide, as an unsatisfactory breadwinner and lover inflicted upon the small boy "a damaging view of his father's manliness and, by extension, his own."[13]

Berryman's adult feelings of resentment and guilt toward his mother were as strong as those he felt toward his dead father. Their arguments were frequent, explosive, and mutually wounding, and often led to fainting spells or suicide threats on the part of Berryman. The attempt to punish his mother by threatening suicide cannot but bring to mind Schwartz's imagined scenario in which a young man locks himself in a bathroom in order to make his parents think that something has happened to him.

Unlike Schwartz, Berryman did not have to deal with a mother who considered him a failure. It was from Martha, in fact, that he learned to love literature and got the idea of becoming a writer. Yet Martha, like Rose Schwartz, was no less jealous of her son's literary career than she was of his wives and girlfriends. Martha also shared with Rose a gift for deceit, and both women passed it on to their sons. Rose had used it to get pregnant; Martha used it years later, when Berryman was of college age, to introduce him to her coworkers as a younger brother.

It was not until middle age that Berryman realized the effect that his "unspeakably powerful possessive adoring MOTHER" had on him, and admitted to feeling that he could get away with anything because of the knowledge that she would always forgive him.[14] These observations represent a genuine awakening to reality on Berryman's part; yet even here he seems not completely enlightened as to his own subconscious motives. For no one tests a love in which he is fully confident; he only tests that which he doubts. And there is good reason to believe that Berryman subconsciously doubted his mother's love. After all, it was she who had filed for the divorce from his father—the divorce which might indeed have been Smith's reason for killing himself. Eileen Simpson records that for a time after the suicide the boy did in fact blame his mother for it. One imagines Berryman's subconscious thinking that if his mother could fall out of love with her husband, even drive him to suicide, couldn't she do the same to her son? This may account for the many suicide threats and the episodes of flirting with death that occurred throughout Berryman's adult years. It is also possible that Berryman's self-destructive behavior represented an effort to discourage his mother's smothering adoration, to force her to love him less. These motives may seem mutually contradictory, but since we are dealing not with logic but with the motives of the subconscious, both may well have existed simultaneously.

Berryman, in his comments on his mother, goes on to cite her as the cause of his intense ambition. Eileen Simpson makes essentially the same connection when she says that Berryman picked up from Martha the tendency to "overburden his system." Berryman seems to have grasped the essential fact of the matter; the ultimate effect of his relationship with his mother, he writes, was to "block . . . my development."[15]

Like Schwartz's childhood, then, Berryman's early years contain the seeds of several of his more prominent adult characteristics. His insomnia, his sense of insecurity, his combativeness, his mania for success, and his problems with women can all be explained, at least in part, by childhood events and by various elements of his relationship with his parents. As with Schwartz, there was an unusual amount of guilt and resentment involved in this relationship. And as with Schwartz, the thought of a parent's death brought to mind the question of forgiveness. Berryman, in the guise of Henry, wrote of his father, in "Dream Song 145," that he was "trying to forgive" the man who, unable to persevere a moment longer, "left Henry to live on."[16] The obsession with mortality in the poetry of both Schwartz and Berryman can be traced, in part, to their fathers' deaths, deaths after which both sons, for one reason or another, were unable to go through the normal process of grief and recovery.

The young Robert Lowell also lost a father, in a sense. Lowell was born on March 1, 1917, in Boston, into one of the first families of New England. His father, Robert Traill Spence (Bob) Lowell III, however, was personally undistinguished, a meek and foolish navy man— virtually a cipher. His wife, the former Charlotte Winslow, had married him because she knew she could control him. Even in their wedding photographs she was the center of attention, and Bob a willing part of the background. Yet, almost from the start, she was restless and unhappy. She hated being a navy wife, resented having to follow Bob's career to Washington and Philadelphia. When her nagging forced him to transfer back to Boston, she refused to live in the house provided by the navy. This resulted in separate households. Every night, Bob had dinner with his family in Charlotte's house on Revere Street, then repaired to the navy house to be on call during the night. Eventually Charlotte managed to pressure him into quitting the navy altogether, after which he drifted from job to job. In the eyes of his son, Bob declined in dignity and substance during these aimless years. Berryman and Schwartz had suffered the deaths of their fathers; Lowell's father died a metaphoric death. Later the poet would say: "Father's soul went underground."[17]

Just as Schwartz and Berryman were unable in their adulthood to cultivate indifference to their fathers' deaths, so Lowell in his middle age would find his father's spinelessness difficult to accept. His prose reminiscences and poetry alike refer to Bob Lowell in a tone of condescension tinged heavily with bitterness. His poem "Commander Lowell" begins by saying that a father who was an officer in the navy was "nothing to shout about" among the wealthy summer resort crowd.[18] Nearly every detail in the poem seems designed to present something contemptible in Bob Lowell's character. He is childish, playing with ships in the bathtub; he is incompetent, losing job after job. He is a prodigal father, who squandered sixty thousand dollars in three years.

Clearly, the poet harbored deep resentment for his weakling father. Like Martha Berryman, Charlotte Lowell may unwittingly have damaged her son's own sense of masculinity with her derisive remarks about her husband. The boy's behavior at school, where he developed a reputation as a horrible bully, would certainly seem to bear out this notion. For boys generally do not become bullies because they are confident of their masculinity, but because that confidence has been shaken, and they feel a need to demonstrate, to the world and to themselves, that they are men. By being a petty tyrant, Robert Lowell seems to have been determined to prove that he was the very opposite of his meek, subservient father. Naturally, the person to whom he wanted to prove it most of all was his mother. As an adult, Lowell still remembered that once, when he was eleven years old, one of his battle wounds scarred over and his mother called him "old soldier." Clearly this was what he longed for, the recognition from Charlotte that he was the soldier that his father was not.

What his father was not, at least in the eyes of his young son, is summed up in an image in the "Commander Lowell" poem. Describing the Commander's golf game, the speaker remarks that he "took four shots with his putter to sink his putt." The image, suggestive of some sexual dysfunction on the part of the father, conveys the essence of his son's perception of him. He is an impotent weakling.

The notion that Bob Lowell was, to his son, as dead as Schwartz's or Berryman's father seems to be supported by the poem. The mother in it is "still her Father's daughter"; her voice has "a hysterical, unmarried panic"; her teeth newly capped, she is "born anew" at the age of forty; at night, she sleeps alone. It is as if her husband does not even exist.

In the poem "Dunbarton," also in *Life Studies*, the speaker finds a father substitute in his grandfather: "He was my Father. I was his son." The poem is rife with positive phallic imagery, forming a distinct contrast to the negative putting image in "Commander Lowell." The poet, moreover, derives from the grandfather that which is not forthcoming from the father, a sense of his own manhood. His grandfather's cane, "more a weapon than a crutch," is an obvious phallic image. Yet there is, in that childhood sense of sexual identity, more than a hint of confusion; he writes of cuddling in his grandfather's bed "like a paramour."[19]

If his father, who in reality lived until 1950, was more or less dead for Lowell during most of his life, his mother was a constant, overwhelming presence. From Lowell's early boyhood, Charlotte, like Rose Schwartz and Martha Berryman, tried to monopolize her son's love; Blair Clark, a friend of the poet, insisted that she was fixated on dominating the boy. In describing Charlotte, those who witnessed her dealings with Lowell at various stages in his life paint a picture of an irresistible force. Jean Stafford, Lowell's first wife, referred to Charlotte as "my inimitable mother-in-law who . . . would stop a clock." Elizabeth Hardwick, Lowell's second wife, called Charlotte "impossible."[20] Indeed, his mother intimidated the poet to such a degree that until her death in 1954 he was unable to live in the same city; his adult life to that date reads like the chronicle of some extended, self-imposed exile from the city of his birth.

Like Berryman, then, Lowell was cursed by an "unspeakably powerful possessive adoring MOTHER." Yet, also like Berryman, there was a part of Lowell which saw her not as a curse but as a blessing. From birth, he was fascinated by Charlotte; the two of them were really very much alike, and like Berryman and his mother they had huge fights of the sort that lovers have. Charlotte herself saw Lowell's first engagement, to a woman several years older than himself, as a symptom of his attachment to her. In later years, Stafford would say much the same thing, asserting that Lowell had turned her into a version of Charlotte.

In short, as with Schwartz and Berryman, there is a good deal in Lowell's childhood and in his relationship with his parents to explain the man and the poet. Lowell resented his father, not, like Schwartz and Berryman, for dying, but for living a death-in-life. His mother he resented for being too close, too strong. Like his two contemporaries, Lowell did not escape guilt, writing in "Middle Age" a plea to his father to forgive the poet his injuries, and noting that, even though his father never was a great man, he nonetheless left behind dinosaur-sized steps in which the poet must walk.[21]

Randall Jarrell was born on May 6, 1914—five months after Schwartz, five months before Berryman—to Owen and Anna Jarrell of Nashville, Tennessee. Like Harry Schwartz, John Allyn Smith, and Bob Lowell, Owen Jarrell was not a constant presence. Some editions of the Nashville city directory list the family home only in the mother's name, and once she is described as a widow, though Owen lived throughout the 1970s. The directory also shows that the Jarrells, like the Schwartzes and Berrymans, changed addresses frequently. Like Schwartz and Berryman, moreover, Jarrell was the older of two children, both boys. Psychologists generally recognize boys in this position, along with only sons, like Lowell, as being the most likely candidates for "mama's boy."[22]

Sometime in the early 1920s, the Jarrells moved to Long Beach, California. Soon afterward—about the time of the Schwartzes' separation, the suicide of John Allyn Smith, and the descent "underground" of Bob Lowell's soul—the Jarrells separated. Anna returned to Tennessee, and Randall was sent to live in Hollywood with his father's parents. Apparently the boy was happy with these arrangements. Like Lowell, he soon began to think of his grandfather as father, and called his doting grandparents Mama and Pop. It was during his residence in their household that young Randall had a profound experience, memorialized in his poem "The Lost World," which introduced him to death and taught him, as Rose Schwartz taught Delmore, to trust no one. The poem features a child, clearly Jarrell, who is sitting in a yard with his grandfather, Pop, and his great-grandmother, Dandeen, another figure from Jarrell's Hollywood childhood. The boy is holding his pet rabbit, whose soft ears and "crinkling nose" give the child a sense of security. "Mama," his grandmother, comes outside to hang up some clothes and looks lovingly at them. Like the mothers of Lowell and Berryman, the grandmother here is young-looking, her face girl-like. Entering the chicken coop, she finds a chicken and wrings its neck. The boy is stunned; suddenly feeling distrust where none had been before, he half asks, half pleads with his grandmother not to kill his pet rabbit. "You won't ever, will you?"[23] She attempts to reassure him on this score, but he is unable to believe her completely. Never again will he be able to trust her, or anyone, absolutely. Like the young Delmore, then, Jarrell learned at a tender age to suspect those who loved him— indeed, to suspect the very idea of love itself. Like Berryman, Jarrell was vouchsafed a profound awareness of death which he was incapable of coming to terms with. To a child, after all, the strangling of a chicken can create the same emotional reverberations as the suicide of a father. Having been certain only moments before "who takes care of him, whom he takes care of," Jarrell, like young Delmore, young John, and young Cal, learned to distrust those closest to him, and, in spite of himself, began to feel separated from them in some irreparable way. The world, which formerly seemed so well-ordered, suddenly appeared full of the most chaotic possibilities. His life, his health, his happiness, which had seemed inviolable, revealed themselves to be terribly vulnerable.

After his sojourn in Hollywood, Randall returned to Nashville to live with his mother, apparently because Mama and Pop could no longer care for him. But Jarrell doubtless felt rejected by his grandparents. It is not unreasonable, I think, to suggest that the child must at the very least have developed a strong sense of rootlessness and confusion as a result of all these shifts and seeming abandonments by one set of parental figures after another.

After leaving California, Randall would never call anyone Pop again. His mother had a second husband named Eugene Regan, but there is no indication that anything approaching a father-son relationship developed between Randall and this man. Indeed, Anna's brother Howell Campbell, Jr., who helped put Randall through school, was more of a father to the boy than Regan. Even Campbell, however, never really took the place of either of the fathers Randall had known. By the time Randall reached adolescence, then, the only two men that he would ever think of as Pop were forever a part of the past. Like the other Middle Generation poets, he lived through his teenage years without the real presence of a father.

If the history of Jarrell's confused childhood demonstrates anything, it is that he shared with the other Middle Generation poets an emotional basis for feeling insecure, distrustful, and alienated. In consequence, he had equal reason to remember his dead with guilt and to seek their forgiveness. He wishes, in "The Lost World," that he could see them all once again, and thinks of them dying "Forgiving me. . . ."

Estrangement, insecurity, resentment, guilt. The parallels scar the early years of all four poets. All came from unstable environments; all, by one means or another, were separated from the father and out of the stress of abandoment grew the sense of an unpardonable loss, the crippling absence seeming like an ineffable injustice; then arose the hate, and, in each of them, the illogical, disabling guilt that only a child's pain can produce. In each of them, the problem of the absent father was compounded by the omnipresent mother. Lowell's personal recognition of this parallel is recorded in a poem written after Berryman's death. The poem alludes to an article about Berryman which he reads "as if recognizing my own obituary." He reads that Berryman's mother loved him obsessively, but was not truly affectionate, and so "he always loved what he missed." Lowell has to remind himself that "This was John Berryman's mother, not mine."[24] The mother-son parallels do not stop here. Any study of the lives of the four poets will provide a long list of abnormal maternal influences. We find the mothers encouraging narcissism in their sons, while at the same time damaging the young men's self-images. Repeatedly we find the mothers poisoning their son's views of women and of the man-woman relationship, and confusing their general sense of sexual self-esteem and gender identification. Clearly, the defeatist attitudes toward love, the problems with heterosexual relationships, and the suggestions of homosexual tendencies that characterize the adult lives of the Middle Generation poets may all be traced in part to these aspects of the poets' relationships with their mothers.

There is more, of course. Fighting between the parents till all hours of the night was likely responsible in more than one instance for the poets' lifelong problems with insomnia; while frequent changes of address during childhood, in combination with poor emotional support, undoubtedly contributed to the sense of rootlessness and alienation that all four poets were to feel as adults.

For two of the poets, Berryman and Jarrell, a lifetime of psychic trauma ended in suicide. A. Alvarez, in his authoritative study, *The Savage God*, clearly considers all four Middle Generation poets as suicides of one kind or another. His observations about the childhood histories of people who take their lives are particularly pertinent to the Middle Generation poets. He quotes from the memoir of a failed suicide, whose experiences he believes to be representative of the type of events that start a child on the path to self-destruction. The memoir could conceivably have been written by any of the Middle Generation poets. "Both my parents . . . were very unhappy together, and I think this sunk in very much. Like my father, I have always demanded too much of life and people and relationships—far more than exists, really. And when I find that it doesn't exist, it seems like a rejection." Alvarez discusses the Italian writer Casare Pavese, who, like the Middle Generation poets, lost his father when he was a child and had a "mother of spun steel, harsh and austere." Writes Alvarez, "A suicide of this kind is born, not made"—meaning born out of the environment in which he grew up, out of the atmosphere created by abnormal parental personalities. "Each child who loses a parent," writes Alvarez,

> must cope as best as he can with a confusion of guilt, anger and an outraged sense of abandonment. And since in his innocence he does not understand this, his natural grief is made doubly painful. In order to relieve himself of this apparently gratuitous and inappropriate hostility, he splits it off from himself and projects it onto the lost figure. As a result, it is possible that when the fantasied identification finally takes place, it is invested with all sorts of unmanageable horror. Thereafter, hidden away in some locked cupboard of the mind, he carries the murderous dead thing within him, an unappeased Doppelgänger, not to be placated, crying out to be heard, and ready to emerge at every crisis.

The mind of a child may, therefore, convert confused feelings arising from the death of a parent into suicidal impulses. Alvarez's statistics indicate that some such mechanism is responsible for most suicides.

> On the evidence of fifty attempted suicides, two New York psychiatrists made an interesting discovery: in 95 percent of all their cases there had been "the death or loss under dramatic and often tragic circumstances of individuals closely related to the patient, generally parents, siblings, and mates. In 75 percent of our cases, the deaths had taken place before the patients had completed adolescence."[25]

If we accept the authority of Alvarez and his sources in these matters, it becomes apparent that the Middle Generation poets were high-risk candidates as children for the self-destructive impulse. Their exposure to continued marital discord, loss of the father, and domination by the mother during the most vulnerable period of personality development was deeply traumatic. These disturbing environmental influences deformed not only the structure and quality of their lives, but, in a very real sense, also set the tragic pattern for their deaths.

Yet no stress is entirely without positive effects. In the early alienation of the poets from their fathers may be found the key to many of their ideological and artistic attitudes. Each of them was impelled to a frenetic lifelong search for values, knowledge, truth, an answer-to-it-all. The need for these intellectual journeys, which moved them through the demesnes of religion, philosophy, psychology, and poetry may be explained largely by the precarious position in which their early recognition of human frailty and mortality placed them. Moreover, it is of particular significance that their early poetry almost slavishly followed the critical dictates of T. S. Eliot, whom the Middle Generation poets admired almost beyond belief. The combination of reverence and resentment with which they regarded him was, for a time, so intensely personal that it is difficult not to see in it an unconscious attempt to replace with Eliot the fathers they had lost and still longed for.

Alienated Adulthoods

It is terrible to be alive
Randall Jarrell

O Life is terror-full
Delmore Schwartz

. . . *[the] gravity of be*ng *alive*
Robert Lowell

The world is lunatic. This is the last ride
John Berryman

The four boys who learned at an early age what it meant to be insecure grew up into adults who found life nearly impossible to deal with. Schwartz and Lowell found shelter from its pain in psychosis; Berryman and Jarrell, in suicide. It is not easy to understand such devastating alienation. Its seeds, sown very early in the lives of the Middle Generation poets, were fertilized by many different factors, and their growth took widely varied forms. In what is possibly one of its most severe forms, alienation blooms into the type of paranoia expressed in Schwartz's poem, "Do the Others Speak of Me Mockingly, Maliciously?", in which he worries whether his friends are talking about him behind his back, discussing his clumsiness, imitating his gestures.[1] This notion that the speaker is alone in a hostile world also appears in Berryman's "Dream Song 74," in which the poet says that "Henry hates the world" because the world has done him in.[2] At times there is the sense of alienation from one's own body. The dichotomy between soul and flesh set up by Jarrell in "The Knight, Death, and the Devil" is not unusual. What is remarkable is the degree to which the soul feels disconnected from the flesh. The poem speaks of "The flesh of his soul, set up outside him—."[3]

Schwartz, similarly, writes of his body in "The Heavy Bear Who Goes With Me" as "A stupid clown of the spirit's motive."[4]

In a more muted vein, we find the Middle Generation poets' sense of alienation emerging in their manifestos on the alienation of the poet. Berryman:

> Of course Americans do not read anything. Some poll lately suggested that only one college graduate in four had read a book—any book— during the past year; the populace at large, as one would expect, reads a little more, but not much. Poetry is only read *less* than other sorts of writing. "The poet is like one who enters and mounts a platform to give an address as announced. He opens his page, looks around, and finds the hall—empty."[5]

Jarrell:

> One of our universities recently made a survey of the reading habits of the American public; it decided that forty-eight percent of all Americans read, during a year, no book at all. . . . The poet lives in a world whose newspapers and magazines and books and motion pictures and radio stations and television stations have destroyed, in a great many people, even the capacity for understanding real poetry.[6]

Schwartz:

> As soon as the student leaves school, all the seductions of mass-culture and middlebrow culture, and in addition the whole way of life of our society, combine to make the reading of poetry a dangerous and quickly rejected luxury. . . . As soon as [the poet] departs from the pleasant confines of the university, he discovers that it is more and more true that less and less people read serious poetry.

Though these quotations are, on the surface, sensible, insightful, well-meant pieces of social criticism, implicit in each of them is the author's profound sense of alienation from his own national culture. And indeed Jarrell concludes the essay from which the above remarks of his are taken with the sentiment that, since no one is listening, the "poet writes his poem for its own sake, for the sake of the order of things in which the poem takes the place that has awaited it." And Schwartz's remarks conclude with the determination that

> In the unpredictable and fearful future that awaits civilization, the poet must be prepared to be alienated and indestructible. He must dedicate himself to poetry, although no one else seems likely to read what he writes; and he must be indestructible as a poet until he is destroyed as a human being. In the modern world, poetry is alienated; it will remain indestructible as long as the faith and love of each poet in his vocation survives.

The species of alienation that cries out "Henry cannot bear the world" is less common in the writings of the Middle Generation than that which cries out "Henry cannot bear America in the nuclear age." Usually the idea, whether explicit or implicit, is that Henry cannot bear it because Henry is a poet. Significantly, when the 1952 *Partisan Review* symposium, "Our Country and Our Culture," demonstrated that "most writers no longer accept alienation as the artist's fate in America," Schwartz, the only one of the Middle Generation poets who took part, was the lone dissenter.

> As things are and as they are likely to be in any near future, the highest values of art, thought and the spirit are not only not supported by the majority of human beings nor by the dominant ways of modern society, but they are attacked, denied or ignored by society as a mass. . . . In the past, there was a genuine choice between exile in Europe, which was a kind of non-conformism, and the attitude exemplified in America in every period and in a variety of ways from Emerson to Mencken. Now that there is no longer a choice, the tradition and the vitality of critical nonconformism is more important than ever.[8]

In the poetry of each of the Middle Generation poets may be found abundant evidence of their disaffection from contemporary America. There is Lowell's "Memories of West Street and Lepke," a poem based on the author's period of confinement as a conscientious objector in the West Street Jail in New York during World War II. Czar Lepke, a leader of organized crime, was a fellow inmate. The speaker remembers that he was a "fire-breathing" Roman Catholic conscientious objector, in lines that manage to define sharply his alienation from his country. He is not a Protestant, like the typical American or, more to the point, like Lowell's family, which had been Protestant since the Mayflower. Lowell had, at the time described by the poem, left the church of his birth for Roman Catholicism. He is not a GI but a CO; he is not sane but manic; he is not patriotic, at least not in the sense understood by the majority of his countrymen. Then there is the murderer Lepke, who keeps in his cell a radio, a dressing table, two small American flags bound together by a ribbon made of Easter palm. These furnishings all represent ways in which the speaker is estranged from his national environment. The radio symbolizes the harmony with mass culture which he is unable to feel; the flags remind us of the un-American act which put him here; the Easter palm that is wrapped about the flags is emblematic of the Christinity that binds together the America from which the speaker feels hopelessly distanced.[9]

Louis Simpson has rejected the contention that this is "a great political poem" on the grounds that

> to take writing seriously as political one must believe the statements in it to be true, and only paranoia could see two convicted criminals, Bioff and Brown [who also appear in the poem], as representative of the American middle class, or Murder Incorporated as representative of American foreign policy. The poem expresses the despair that many of us, at one time and another, have felt about conditions; this is perfectly understandable as an expression of the narrator's point of view, but it cannot be taken seriously as a picture of life.[10]

Can "Memories of West Street and Lepke" be taken seriously as a picture of life? Not if by "picture of life" one means something objective and utterly realistic. But objective and utterly realistic is exactly what "Lepke" is not intended to be. Simpson recognizes the paranoia in the poem as belonging to the narrator, but he knows that the distance between the narrator of "Lepke" and the poet is a hair's breadth. And because of this, apparently, he views the paranoia as extrinsic to the poem, and considers the poem thereby distorted and robbed of credibility. But a poem is not courtroom testimony. That Lowell's narrator is not as much of an objective creation as the equally unreliable narrator of *The Good Soldier* should not detract from the poem's ability to demonstrate a point. The psychological state of the narrator, far from being extrinsic to "Lepke," is as much a part of the poem, is indeed as much the point of the poem, as it is in *The Good Soldier*. By having his speaker equate Lepke with America, Lowell establishes how terribly alienated that speaker truly is. It is the alienation of the narrator which, in the end, gives the poem its force.

This desperate sense of being an outsider, disturbed by and at odds with those on the inside, is to be found throughout Middle Generation poetry. R. K. Meiners writes of the poems in Berryman's 1948 volume *The Dispossessed* that

> It is interesting to compare these early poems . . . with the earliest work of Robert Lowell on the one hand and Delmore Schwartz on the other. It makes one realize how much they were of a generation. . . . There is *an extraordinarily strong sense of harassment* in all three, and this quality remains throughout their work and develops in quite different ways. . . . One would have to look far to find a richer range of talent than those of these three poets, or a greater capacity for anguish.[11]

Meiners' oversight, of course, is that he leaves Jarrell out of his discussion. For Jarrell's writings record as powerful a sense of the

suffering outsider as the work of any Middle Generation poet. The female speaker of "The Woman at the Washington Zoo" is typical of the speakers in many Jarrell poems, lamenting that "The world goes by my cage and never sees me," feeling that it is she and not the zoo animals who lives behind bars, isolated from the foreign-seeming world around her. The woman speaker of "Next Day," the lead poem in *The Lost World*, is also invisible, wishing that the boxboy notice her. "It bewilders me he doesn't see me."[12]

As for Jarrell's essays, the titles alone point up his feeling of alienation from twentieth-century American society: "The Intellectual in America," "The Taste of the Age," "The Schools of Yesteryear," "A Sad Heart at the Supermarket," "The Obscurity of the Poet." The inordinate concern in his war poems with prisoners of war, particularly German ones, and his own postwar fascination with the German language, suggest a deliberate, if subconscious, identification with a people who were, to Jarrell's countrymen, the most abominably alien of nations.

Much the same process was no doubt largely responsible for the early attraction of all four Middle Generation poets to poets of the British isles: Eliot, Yeats, and Joyce. Their strong attachment can be explained partially by their need for father figures, but that they chose not American but foreign writers is well worth noting, particularly since the most highly esteemed of them was an American who had rejected his homeland and was magically transformed into a Britisher. Interestingly, the self-exiled but still very American Ezra Pound did not hold much attraction for the Middle Generation poets early in their careers; the same is true for such stateside innovators as Stevens and Williams. Other major American literary figures of the period, Allen Tate, Mark Van Doren, and John Crowe Ransom, might properly be called the mentors of the Middle Generation poets, but they were not in any sense their idols. That status was reserved exclusively for poets who practiced their trade on the other side of the Atlantic. In fact, to one of the Middle Generation poets, at least, the major attraction of such figures as Tate and Ransom was that they "connected America with the exhilaratingly convinced narrowness of European modernism."[13] So enthusiastic were the Middle Generation poets about aligning themselves with foreign literary figures that the major writers of their own land represented simply a means of making that connection.

Within their sense of alienation from America lurked the suspi-

cion of a possibility of change. Perhaps one of the major motivating forces behind the art of all four Middle Generation poets was a desire to help shape America's conception of itself. Schwartz's *Genesis: Book One*, based on his boyhood, is equally a story of America and of the boy's growing realization of the degree to which his fate is tied to that of his country. In this relatively early poem one finds passages whose vatic tone and strong sense of the poet's obsession with America anticipate the Whitmanesque quality which was to become more and more a component of Schwartz's work as he came to realize his ties to the nineteenth-century bard. In long, rhythmic, repetitive lines, he refers to America as "the deity," a god to praise and criticize, and says that in America, "the world and Life begin afresh." "O what a piercing power nations have!" Schwartz writes elsewhere in this poem; and in parts of *Genesis: Book One* the word America is repeated almost like an incantation.[14] James F. Knapp, in writing about Schwartz's preoccupation with the theme of America, reiterates not only the Middle Generation view of their native land, but the challenge it presented to them: "The idea of America is important to Schwartz: it is the place where stone grey cities have left no magic in the world, and the place where escape is easier than honesty in the lonely room—but it is also a new place and still to be defined. In a sense it is an empty world which must be charged with myth and meaning, and this is the poet's task."[15]

Few poems by the other Middle Generation poets share the bombastic tone of the above lines from *Genesis: Book One*. All share, however, the ambition to charge America with meaning. Although usually their instrument was poetry, at times they engaged in some form of political action. Doubtless they would have professed indifference to the middlebrow machinations of national politics. But they did experience intermittent enthusiasms, as for example in the 1952 presidential election campaign, during which all four poets strongly supported the candidacy of Adlai Stevenson. Stevenson was the candidate of artists and intellectuals; but to the Middle Generation poets, he seems to have represented some golden opportunity for a renaissance-in-a-day, a shift of political and cultural authority from the philistines to the seekers of truth. The Democratic senator from Illinois was treated with the kind of hero worship, extreme and unrealistic, which the Middle Generation poets had earlier focused on T. S. Eliot. Schwartz, Atlas says, "was convinced that Stevenson's election would pave the way to power for intellectuals, and that he

himself would be among the first to benefit. . . . He took to signing all his letters 'Long live Adlai!' " Saul Bellow's character Von Humboldt Fleisher, based largely on Schwartz, is certain that as soon as Stevenson is elected, he, Humboldt, will be called to Washington. " 'And you can see for yourself, Charlie,' said Humboldt . . . 'how important it is for the Stevenson administration to have a cultural adviser like me.' " One party given by the Schwartzes seems to have been devoted to an exchange of words of praise for their candidate. " 'I don't want Stevenson to be President,' Berryman shouted, 'I want him to be King.' " Even in his last years, more than ten years after the Eisenhower landslide in 1952, Schwartz was still Stevenson-crazy, sending telegrams to the sometime candidate at the United Nations, where he was serving as the United States' permanent representative.[16]

For his part, Lowell, on the occasion of Eisenhower's 1952 victory, felt "too hurt to laugh." He wrote a poem about the event; it was not to be the last reference in his poetry to Eisenhower, whom he considered "a symbol . . . of America's unintelligent side—all fitness, muscles, smiles and banality."[17] The major political enthusiasm of Lowell's life, of course, was not Stevenson but Eugene McCarthy; the weird progress of his joint campaigning with that candidate in 1968 is ably chronicled by Ian Hamilton. It is interesting that the candidates the Middle Generation poets supported tended to be nearly as idealistic, as unable to understand and be understood by middle America, and as unaware of cold, hard political realities, as the Middle Generation poets themselves. In fact, Eugene McCarthy may have come closer than any politician in history to the Middle Generation state of mind.

Part of the point here is that the Middle Generation poets' political enthusiasms did not operate in the same manner as those of the intellectuals and artists among whom they moved. These enthusiasms were not, in a word, entirely rational. They were not based on sensible, level-headed appraisals of the true political, social, and cultural status quo. They were, instead, founded on an unrealistic, somewhat pathetic, sometimes desperate, and, indeed, even mad set of notions of what a victory in an American election could accomplish.

For, in truth, none of them wanted to be outsiders in their own country, their own culture. Karl Shapiro has written perceptively of Jarrell that he "was very much an insider. There was a terrible conflict in his soul between his instinct for freedom and his desire for cultural asylum." Lowell's biographer calls his subject "a born joiner." And Schwartz, as we have seen, wanted nothing more than to be called to Washington to join the administration. The delusions of grandeur that accompanied Schwartz's periods of madness often took the form of his being appointed to some significant position in the very government whose apparent ignorance of his existence dismayed him. Tearing up a hotel room in Washington, he bellowed that he was doing so "on the orders of the Chief Executive." An acquaintance recalls Schwartz complaining, "Last week they put me in the crazy house and this week they ask me to be Secretary of Education!" Significantly, Lowell too imagined that he had been appointed to the cabinet.[18]

Throughout this century there have been writers who seem to enjoy, and indeed artistically thrive upon, the tension between their personalities and the American cultural situation. The Middle Generation poets were not like this. Their alienation disturbed them; it hurt rather than enhanced their writing. In *The Armies of the Night*, Norman Mailer records his participation with Lowell in the 1967 anti–Vietnam War demonstrations in Washington. He says of Lowell, who stood on a podium beside him, that

> physical strength or no, his nerves were all too apparently delicate. Obviously spoiled by everyone for years, he seemed nonetheless to need the spoiling. These nerves—the nerves of a consummate poet—were not tuned to any battering. The squalls of the mike, now riding up a storm on the erratic piping breath of Dwight Macdonald's voice, seemed to tear along Lowell's back like a gale. He detested tumult—obviously.[19]

It has been suggested more than once that Mailer's involvement in such events is primarily for the purpose of massaging his ego and finding something to write about. No one could ever ascribe the same motives to the Middle Generation poets. Where politics brought Mailer to life, it tore them to shreds. Mailer could lose and go home and write about it; when the Middle Generation poets lost, it left a painful wound that remained long after Mailer had forgotten the whole thing. Shapiro has written that Jarrell's one great failing was the lack of a sense of power. This might be said of all four Middle Generation poets. None of them truly shared the sense of power, the sense (which Mailer is gifted with) that one is or can be a genuine force within his own culture.

Another literary figure who had that gift was Lionel Trilling.

Trilling and Schwartz, even more than Mailer and Lowell, represent an instructive contrast between literary man as dynamic, smoothly functioning member of society and Middle Generation misfit. The contrast is particularly interesting because of the number of similarities between the two men, similarities of which Schwartz, for one, was painfully aware. Both Trilling and Schwartz were sons of Jewish immigrants, both aimed for success in the New York literary establishment, and both were the victims of English department anti-Semitism, Trilling at Columbia and Schwartz at Harvard. But while Trilling weathered bigotry with apparent ease and ultimate success, Schwartz left Harvard after a short, bitter tenure and spent years pouring the agony he had suffered at the hands of Cambridge anti-Semites into a novel that he never published. What made the agony of alienation more acute for Schwartz was the fact that Trilling, in so many ways Schwartz's alter ego, succeeded so well where Schwartz failed so miserably. For Trilling seemingly had no trouble fitting in. If Schwartz was the premier outsider, Trilling was the insider of insiders. He was everything that Schwartz longed to be but, congenitally, could never be. Thus one can understand why Schwartz's attitude toward Trilling was, as Barrett puts it, one of "consuming hostility."[20]

One can also understand the controversy Schwartz ignited in 1953. Five years earlier, Trilling had argued in an essay, "Manners, Morals and the Novel," that manners and society were the novel's proper subjects. Schwartz, in a piece called "The Duchess' Red Shoes," charged that by manners Trilling meant polite manners and by society he meant high society. Atlas comments that "what Delmore found most oppressive was Trilling's exclusive concern with 'the ideas and attitudes and interests of the educated class, such as it is and such as it may become: it is of this class that he is, at heart, the guardian and the critic.' "[21] But what galled Schwartz was something more than Trilling's defense of the values of the educated class. For Schwartz had written his share of essays in defense of those values. Rather, what irritated Schwartz was that Trilling was such a well-adapted, highly respected member of the educated class. Although he came from the same middle-class Jewish world as Schwartz, Trilling had integrated himself comfortably into what Schwartz saw as high society. And Trilling's tone reflected that integration. It was the tone of an insider, a man who seemed to write every sentence with the confidence that it would be respected by its readers as a major cultural pronouncement. When Schwartz said of Trilling, "I wish he would not make the most obvious remarks in the tone of one who has just discovered a cure for cancer," he was merely demonstrating the envy of the hopeless victim of alienation for the insider's easy sense of authority. Significantly, both the tone and subject matter of "Manners, Morals and the Novel" are very Eliotic; Schwartz may well have resented Trilling's easy ability to mimic Eliot, whose secure, commanding position at the center of his culture Schwartz coveted.

Although the only Jew in the Middle Generation group, Schwartz was not the only one of them to identify his sense of alienation with the idea of being Jewish. Berryman considered becoming Jewish because it meant being "alone with God." Lowell too was obsessed with the figure of the Jew, although in a less attractive manner. Jean Stafford said bluntly that Lowell was anti-Semitic, and many of the anecdotes in Hamilton's biography would seem to confirm this. Louis Simpson notes that at least once in Lowell's poetry "we find him sharpening a knife for the Jew"; the poem is "Christ for Sale," and it refers to "four hog-fatted Jews."[22] Lowell was fascinated with Hitler, who not surprisingly represented to him the archetype of the distant, cruel, omnipotent tyrant. Lowell was apparently never able to exorcise this obsession completely. Identifying with Hitler and writing anti-Semitic poems doubtless were part of a single defense mechanism which has been observed in young Jewish people who scrawl swastikas on synagogues. In identifying with the aggressor rather than the victim, these young people seek to eliminate their fears. It is ironic that, when one is suffering from a syndrome of this type, the more acutely one senses oneself to be the threatened outsider, the more fervently one is likely to declare one's solidarity with the tyrannical insider.

Many critics have observed that the Middle Generation poets lusted inordinately after fame, but few have asked why. The simple truth is that they wanted fame because they felt it would deliver them from alienation. It would make them a part of the world, of their country and their culture; it would give them identity. One of Berryman's *Dream Songs* recalls a time in the early forties when he and Schwartz waited for celebrity to descend upon them "and tell us who we were."[23] William Barrett has written of Schwartz that, in his early years, he followed the careers of contemporary poets "as intently as a stock broker watching the ups and down of the market."

The Wall Street analogy is an apt one. Lowell too, "in 1947, wanted to arrive, to be 'major,' to be '*the* poet,' and he was always to keep a shrewd eye on the fluctuations of rank in the poetry world."[24]

For Lowell, fame came in a big way; Berryman, too, in his later years, received wide recognition, though on a smaller scale. Jarrell remained a respected force in poetry, although his name did not carry the weight of either Lowell's or Berryman's; only Schwartz, who had arrived before any of them, died neglected and nearly forgotten, in a hotel off Times Square. For the successful Berryman, fame, once achieved, seems to have lost its importance; he writes in "Dream Song 133," "ah, but what is fame?"[25] Certainly fame did not bring any greater sense of belonging. The sense of alienation that haunted Lowell and Berryman in their days of obscurity remained with them, as their biographies show, in their years of renown. Fame likewise became less important for Schwartz in his later years, when it was replaced by a growing desire for financial reward.

The Middle Generation poets also shared the hope that love would lead them out of alienation. Desperate for an escape from their pathological sense of isolation, they made unreasonable demands on love. Berryman wrote once that "More and more, with the decay of the family as a social unit, and the world what it contemptibly is, love and friendship must take on the burdens that the Church and State and general hopefulness once bore and bear no more." One of his *Dream Songs* begins with the words "love me" repeated five times. Lowell yearned for love no less fervently. "Cal had to be 'in love,' " a friend of Lowell's told Hamilton. A Lowell poem contains the line, "*Inasmuch as I am loved I am.*" Schwartz expressed much the same sentiment, writing that "To be is to be in love" and defining love as "the fullness of being." Halio's observation that "Love is the single most important abstraction in Delmore Schwartz's poetry, an almost obsessive concern for him," might be applied with equal justice to any of the other Middle Generation poets. Like Berryman and Lowell, Schwartz feels that he needs love to escape a life of alienation, in which night will soon arrive, cold and desolate, "unless Love build its city."[26]

But love was no more effective a salve than fame for the poets' psychic wounds. For love dies, and the pain of alienation returns, worse than ever. All four poets wrote poems bewailing this fact. "Where did it all go wrong?" asks the speaker of *The Dream Songs*, who is "full of the death of love." Schwartz writes, "Love love exhausts"; Lowell speaks of "Love, O careless love"; and Jarrell observes that "Love is dangerous as a mirror." The latter is a curious sentiment, but we find Berryman saying much the same thing in "Sonnet 73," which asserts that falling in love is equivalent to meeting one's soul. To say that love is equivalent to seeing oneself in a mirror or meeting one's soul is to say that love is no permanent solution to alienation. It is only, at best, a temporary respite from the existential dilemma and, ultimately, a return ticket to what Schwartz calls "the lonely room where the self must be honest." In the end, love makes alienation worse, for it gives one a momentary taste, which will haunt one forever, of the alternative. As Schwartz writes, to love is to stand on a promontory overlooking "the promised / land."[27]

Out of what experiences did such poetic reflections grow? There is no point in chronicling the love lives of the four poets, a job which has been done by others, but I do wish to suggest some of the more significant aspects of their experiences with and attitudes toward love, sex, and romance.

First, some statistics on their marriages: among the four of them, they had ten wives. Schwartz and Jarrell each had two; Berryman and Lowell three. Seven of these marriages ended in divorce; an eighth, Lowell's third marriage, to Lady Caroline Blackwood, ended in an estrangement which was in effect at the time of Lowell's death. It is perhaps presumptuous to place blame for the failure of other people's marriages, particularly ones that ended thirty years ago; however, one does notice in examining the histories of these marriages that, as a rule, the wives of the four poets were unusually loyal, devoted, sensitive, understanding, compassionate, and levelheaded, while their husbands, as a rule, were unusually disloyal, suspicious, insensitive, and wildly erratic in behavior. Typical was Berryman's third wife Katherine, who was known to Allen Tate and his wife Isabella Gardner as "Saint Kate." Even Schwartz, in his better moments, realized what he was guilty of; referring to his and Berryman's first wives, he wrote (in a poem published in Atlas's biography) about the miserable lives led by the wives of poets, whose husbands are "knife-throwers" who use their spouses "to prove their will." Gertrude Buckman, Schwartz's wife, did her own share of versifying. In a poem printed in Atlas's biography, she wrote of the "strife" and "hate" that infect marriages.[28] Gertrude was lucky to get off with hate. Schwartz terrorized his second wife, Elizabeth Pollet; and Jean Stafford, Lowell's first wife, had her nose broken.

Many of these marriages didn't even begin well. Far more than the average nervous bridegroom, Berryman was tormented by doubts over his first marriage, to Eileen Mulligan (later Simpson), and after the ceremony declared that "God was not there." Schwartz had a similarly unhealthy view of his first marriage; he saw Gertrude's consent to marry him as a "premonition of doom" and compared the enduring memory of their honeymoon trip up the Hudson to "an incurable disease."[29] Even Jarrell, who seems to have had a comparatively normal and happy home life, is reported to have said that he shared Hamlet's view of remarriage.

As Gertrude Buckman's poem suggests, there was, at least in the lives of Schwartz, Berryman, and Lowell, an extensive series of sexual involvements both during and between marriages. Yet all four poets have been called prudes or Puritans, or described as inhibited. In fact, despite the appearance of promiscuity, the picture beneath the surface is less clear. Lowell, for one, is said to have forsworn sex with his first wife after his conversion to Catholicism, and most of his mistresses seem to have indicated that their affairs did not involve a great deal of actual intercourse. Allen Tate, writing to Elizabeth Hardwick before she became Lowell's second wife, told her that her fiancé "has got himself boxed into the corner that he has always wanted to be in; that is, the inescapably celibate corner. (1) he can't marry again as a Catholic (2) as a strict Catholic, he can't commit adultery. He has been trying to get himself in this dilemma.[30] Schwartz, who once noted in his journal that "It would have been easier to be a homosexual," might conceivably have been pleased with "the inescapably celibate corner" himself.

What does seem probable is that in all the Middle Generation poets' lives, except for that of Jarrell, there was a good deal of repressed homosexuality. The index to Atlas's biography even contains the straightforward entry: "homosexuality." The index to Haffenden's biography of Berryman contains the less straightforward "homoeroticism, concern with." In the lives and writings of Schwartz, Berryman, and Lowell, there is substantial evidence indicating an intemperate fear of, hostility towards, and obsession with homosexuality. One of the friends of Schwartz's adolescence, Julian Sawyer, was homosexual, and Schwartz is said to have broken off the friendship out of fear that the neighborhood boys would think him to be homosexual as well. In the early years of his career, Schwartz became friends with Paul Goodman, who was the center of an openly bisexual circle of intellectuals, and this friendship ended with a denunciatory letter from Schwartz the conclusion of which went something like this: "No doubt, you will go on as you have been doing, corrupting young boys and turning them into fags like yourself." Schwartz also referred to André Gide once as "just another faggot," the latter word, according to Atlas, being "his favorite term of derogation."[31]

It seems manifest that the fear of homosexuality which these anecdotes illustrate was part of a fascination with homosexuality, indeed a natural attraction to it, with which Schwartz could not come to terms. "Delmore," writes Atlas, "was given to postulating the hidden presence of homosexuality in just about everyone," as clear an indication as possible of his own natural inclinations. Parents, Schwartz felt, had children in order to prove that they were fertile and heterosexual. Most interesting of all, he theorized that homosexuality resulted from a child's forced involvement in his parents' emotional relationship, which, as Atlas observes, is exactly what had happened to the young Delmore. "It would be surprising," wrote a doctor who examined the poet's answers to a Rorschach test, "if he had not acted out his homosexual impulses, since he communicated that fact at so many different levels." Yet, comments Atlas, "it seems most unlikely that Delmore ever did have any such experiences, given the labor of sublimation that went on for so many years."[32]

Berryman apparently did a great deal of sublimating as well, but under certain circumstances his defense mechanisms seem not to have worked as well as usual. "Made homosexual advances drunk, 4 or 5 times," he recorded as part of an Alcoholics Anonymous treatment in the late sixties; the incidents themselves apparently had occurred in the middle fifties, between his first and second marriages. If his last novel *Recovery* is to be taken as autobiographical, Berryman's first suicide attempt, at prep school, took place on the heels of a homosexual encounter. "I'm a homosexual, damn you," says the Berryman-like narrator of *Recovery*. "I just don't do anything about it."[33]

Like Berryman, Lowell seems to have been profoundly affected by his adolescent homosexual encounters. His poem "First Love" is about one "Leon Straus, sixthgrade fullback." The poem ends by observing that Flaubert, "the supreme artist," was a boy before his heart was enlarged by "the mania for phrases."[34] The last line of the poem originally contained the word "dried" instead of "enlarged";

supposedly, Lowell changed it because the latter sounded better. "Enlarged," of course, reverses the poem's meaning, making it seem to reject his boyish impulses in the end; with the word "dried," however, the poem concludes with a nostalgic longing for what the speaker appears to believe was a happier, wiser, and more natural (for the artist, anyway) way of feeling.

There are the usual anecdotes about Lowell. A congressional aide who conducted him on a tour of Argentina during the sixties remembered that "for about a week he insisted I was homosexual. I think this was because he had a suitable component himself and was simply transferring it. . . . He kept on saying, 'You're saying that because you're queer.' " Lowell himself remembered railing against "devils and homosexuals" during one of his manic periods. Berryman, likewise, in an Iowa jail cell during one of his manic episodes, accused the policemen of being "*homosexual criminals*." Finally, Lowell spent several weeks announcing that he was going to marry Elizabeth Bishop, a confirmed lesbian. At the very least, this is evidence that Lowell was a man confused about his sexuality.[35]

If we are to understand the Middle Generation poets, we must not fail to recognize the homosexual element in their psyches. If indeed they spent all their lives sublimating their natural sexual inclinations, that would go a long way toward explaining the powerful sense of alienation which they shared. It would also help to explain their distrust of their wives. Berryman, Lowell, and particularly Schwartz continually suspected their wives of infidelity, and the partners in these imagined affairs were often the poets' own friends. Such fantasies on the part of the husband, according to classic psychoanalytic theory, usually represent the husband's defense against his own attraction to his male friend. "The delusion," writes A. A. Brill, "represents an effort to defend oneself against strong homosexual tendencies, and in the male it is expressed in the formula 'I do not love him; she loves him.' "[36]

As they turned to lovers in the hope of escape from alienation, the Middle Generation poets also turned to friends. Friendship was very important to all of them; indeed, the histories of their friendships were, in some cases, even more peculiar than those of their love affairs. Haffenden writes of Berryman that "Despite the heavy demands he always made, his close friends remember him with unmitigated love."[37] The same might be said of any of the four poets. Although each left in his wake a few people who would never speak to him again, each also seems to have had a gift for keeping friends in spite of everything. Atlas writes that

> All his life, Delmore entangled his friends in relationships laden with unnatural ardor. He had a way of demanding their unqualified allegiance and then turning that allegiance into a powerful weapon with which to dominate their lives. His attachments were at times hysterical in their intensity; they resembled love affairs more than friendships. It was as if his immense need for solace and affection could express itself less guardedly with men than with women, since friendship circumscribed the limits of intimacy.[38]

They were, of course, not merely each other's friends. They were special friends. Throughout their mature lives, they provided for one another an all but unique consolation in the face of alienation; just knowing that there was a handful of other people in the world who felt exactly the same way was a comfort. And so when they started to die off, those that remained reacted with a degree of pain and horror far beyond what might have been expected. The poems they wrote in remembrance are not stately elegies along the lines of *Lycidas* or *Adonais*, or even Lowell's own "Quaker Graveyard at Nantucket." Each is a tortured cry of pain, a cry born of the poet's knowledge that he has lost a rare soulmate. Moreover, each poem reflects the poet's fear that his friend's horrid death forebodes another death—his own.

Jarrell was the first of the four to die, on October 14, 1965. By this date Schwartz was well into his final madness, so it is understandable that his reaction to Jarrell's death remains unrecorded. Berryman and Lowell, however, were crushed by Jarrell's suicide, and Berryman poured his distress into "Dream Song 90," wherein he pleads with himself to stop his self-torture over Jarrell's death, and notes that he also is "headed west."[39] The poem is one of Berryman's "Opus Posthumous" songs, published not after his death but after Jarrell's. Haffenden refers to this cluster of morbid verses as a series of "suicide notes," of which he sees this poignant lament for Jarrell as the most explicit. The observation is clearly valid. Berryman makes an unmistakable connection in this poem between Jarrell's death and his own approaching end; one gathers that Jarrell's passing has made the other side of the Mystery somehow more natural, less unacceptable, and has made this world more alien and hostile than ever. Indeed, in another Dream Song written about Jarrell's death, Berryman says that his air is full of the souls of his dead, among whom hangs one soul, not yet dead, which "refuses to come home."[40] Berryman seems to be saying that the souls of his dead, Jarrell's soul included, linger, and that his own soul, as always with Jarrell's, is loath to return to its now-empty shell. With Jarrell's death, not only has Jarrell's soul departed, but Berryman's as well. Not yet dead, Berryman notes that his soul already shuns life.

Lowell, too, was traumatized by Jarrell's death. For years afterwards, he would not accept the fact that Jarrell had killed himself. Lowell's poem to Jarrell, like Berryman's, sees the poet and the deceased as being involved in a common fate. The poem quotes Jarrell as inquiring of Lowell why he was so driven by ambition and by the need to rewrite endlessly, and asks Lowell "why did we live? Why do we die?"[41] The poem, by suggesting that the poets lived for a common purpose, even if that purpose was obscure, anticipates the theme of a "generic life" which becomes explicit in Lowell's elegy for Berryman. It was in fact to Berryman that, after Jarrell's death, Lowell wrote: "This is really just to say that I love you, and wonder at you, and want you to take care. . . . Let me beg you to take care of yourself. You must be physically fragile. If anything happened to you, I'd feel the heart of the scene had gone."[42] It is an odd, desperate-sounding letter. The anxious repetition of the plea to "take care of yourself," the pointed concern about Berryman's fragility, make it clear that losing "the heart of the scene" refers less to any loss to the world of poetry than to a critical emotional dependence. The letter is, in truth, a confession of need. The "scene" is the world that Lowell and Berryman share, and Berryman is the "heart," the force that sustains them both. The tone of the letter is that of a plea, full of the fear of a man with a tenuous hold on life, who senses that the only reason for continuing to maintain his grip on it is apt to be lost if Berryman should die.

But before Berryman died, Schwartz was taken. On July 11, 1966, he succumbed to a heart attack in a hotel near Times Square, where he had lived for several months, isolated by his psychosis. Lowell, writes Hamilton, "had for some time been nervous of the *idea* of Delmore Schwartz, of his decline from early promise, of the ways in which he had wasted his real talent." He had suffered over Jarrell's passing; now he was crushed by Schwartz's death. Hamilton tells us that by this time "The notion of there being a sort of generic curse on the poets of his generation was recurring time and again in Lowell's letters."[43] Lowell's anguish over Schwartz went into three poems, which appear in his book *History*. The third, "Our Dead Poets," although it avoids names, seems to refer to both Schwartz and Jarrell, whose deaths have plunged the poet into a deathlike ennui wherein he cannot bring himself to dress, brush his teeth, or open his mail. "Sometimes for days I only hear your voices."[44] Berryman, for his part, wrote no fewer than fourteen Dream Songs in Schwartz's memory. In the most beautiful of these, "Dream Song 147," Schwartz's death has left his mind black, his life broken, his love nearly dead, "the world . . . lunatic."[45] Schwartz's death, it is clear from this elegy, has intensified the poet's sense of alienation. The world is now uglier and more inhospitable than ever. In this poem, perhaps even more a "suicide note" than was his elegy to Jarrell, the poet tells us he can no longer love, no longer sing. "This is the last ride," he cries, and one senses that Berryman has moved through death with Schwartz, so sharp is the pain. In Schwartz's *Genesis*, "America" is repeated like an incantation; here the word "Delmore" is reiterated, echoing like a litany, a kabbala, a mantra. It is as if the atheist Berryman's only article of faith was Schwartz's friendship. What the poem tells us about Berryman and Schwartz is true of all four. In a way, the only religion any of them had was one another.

On January 7, 1972, Berryman committed suicide by jumping from a bridge in Minneapolis. A joke made the rounds that Berryman had left a note reading, "Your move, Cal." Lowell's reaction to the death is found in several poems; in one, he imagines that he and Berryman are taking their lives together on a bridge. There is also, of course, "For John Berryman," in which Lowell declares that

> . . . really we had the same life,
> the generic one
> our generation offered.[46]

The poem appears in the collection *Day by Day*, where it is surrounded by poems about age, time, and approaching death. That Lowell's interest in these themes grew into an obsession in that late volume can be attributed largely to the cumulative power of the deaths of Jarrell, Schwartz, and Berryman upon Lowell's fragile psyche.

Obsession, in fact, is a good word to use in reference to the Middle Generation poets' relationships with one another, whether in death or in life. In one of his elegies for Schwartz, Berryman writes that, in all the years of his life, he doesn't suppose a day passed "without a loving thought for him."[47] "I can't get him out of my mind," writes Berryman in another one of his songs to Schwartz. Not only were they constantly on each other's minds, but they knew each other's minds better than has been recognized; in a poem written to Berryman, Lowell says that he feels each of them knows what the other has "worked through."[48] One of Lowell's finest *Life Studies* poems is "To Delmore Schwartz," which is about a time in 1946 when the two poets shared a flat in Cambridge, Massachusetts. The poem, though written during Schwartz's lifetime, is notable for sounding like an elegy; it evokes a powerful sense of nostalgia for the unspoken understanding of one another that the two poets shared, the sense of the two of them standing alone against "the chicken-hearted shadows of the world." Alienated from all others on the six continents of earth, they are "Undersea fellows, nobly mad." Their only company, in this contemporary world to which they do not belong, is the dead—Freud, Joyce, Coleridge.[49] The central point of the poem is that the two poets are soulmates in a world of walking shadows. Alienated from the whole world, they find their only real solace in one another. Clearly, these elegies demonstrate that all four poets felt this way. So powerful was their mutual need that when they began to die off, the living grew to feel increasingly out of place in the world, and felt their own deaths to be perilously near.

Indeed, I would go so far as to say that, in addition to everything else that contributed to Berryman's early death, this final factor should be seriously considered: that watching Jarrell and Schwartz die so early may have made his decision to end his life easier to reach.

Perhaps the ultimate symbol of this tragic sense of alienation is the insomnia which all four poets shared. Schwartz once remarked to Berryman that they would be known to future students of their work as "the sleepless school of poets." It is a good name. Sleepless, they were in their most characteristic position: helpless, suffering, alone, trying to combat and survive the dark night of the soul. While everyone else slept, became refreshed, worked out the conflicts of their conscious lives in dreams, the Middle Generation poets waited out the darkness in utter solitude, meditating upon the fact of the passing hours and the dreams that were denied them.

Insomnia was more of a problem for some of the poets than others. Perhaps Schwartz had it worst. "Insomnia," writes William Barrett, the friend of his youth, "hit him early in his life and brutally."[50] Schwartz's most famous poem, "In the Naked Bed, in Plato's Cave," powerfully evokes the insomniac's experience of night and early morning. Berryman's "At Chinese Checkers" also refers to Schwartz's insomnia, his inability to sleep in "the unfriendly city" and "the unsteady night."[51] These lines suggest a connection between insomnia and the subject's sense of alienation from the world. For it seems to be insomnia that makes the city unfriendly, the night unsteady. Atlas calls this stanza "cruel in its reference to the insomnia that tormented [Schwartz] all his life," and indicts the poem as vindictive.[52] On the contrary; Berryman wrote these lines not out of vindictiveness but out of empathy. The Delmore of this poem was to Berryman not a comic but a tragic figure, for Berryman suffered from insomnia himself, and knew well the painful sense of alienation that insomnia intensified. He wrote about Schwartz as if he were writing about himself. This is true of all four Middle Generation poets: their torments being shared torments, they wrote about one another's agonies as if they were writing about their own. Far from ridiculing Schwartz, Berryman was performing what was, for him, the ultimate act of sympathy. And as he wrote about Schwartz's long, unsteady nights, he wrote about his own, testifying in "Dream Song 137," for instance, that Henry has seen in many a dawn, and that "things are going to pieces."[53] The poem is not entirely comprehensible. Indeed, the lines at the beginning of the second stanza ("I don't understand this dream . . .") are in part a comment upon the poem's unintelligibility. And that unintelligibility is, perhaps, a comment on the insomniac's confused state of mind, his aggravated sense of alienation from a chaotic world.

In Jarrell's "Eine Kleine Nachtmusik," the speaker's sense of alienation, resulting from a failed love affair, is complicated by insomnia. The memory of his lost love's "sleep-swollen face, secure and huge," mocks the speaker in his sleepless insecurity, and he prays for sleep to deliver him from the waking world which only he seems to inhabit. "What world I have sleeps on," he observes; alone, he faces "the night, the real night." Similarly, Lowell's "Myopia: A Night" presents a speaker who, unable to sleep, feels confused, fragile, and lost in his "dull and alien room."[54]

Both "Eine Kleine Nachtmusik" and "Myopia: A Night" conclude with a profound awareness of night. Jarrell's speaker sees, as if for the first time, "the night, the real night." In Lowell's poem, "morning comes, saying 'This was a night!'" To all four Middle Generation poets, life was indeed a lonely, painful night from which they desperately sought an escape. But the supposed joys of fame, love, and friendship proved unable wholly to vanquish the pain of alienation.

There were, however, other means by which the Middle Generation poets sought to overcome alienation. For the poets held the hope that if the mind could understand the way the pieces of life fit together, then the soul might be delivered from its painful sense of not fitting. This is where the Middle Generation poets' preoccupation with truth and knowledge comes in.

3

The Dream of Knowledge

Knowledge and belief devour the mind of man
Delmore Schwartz

O knowledge ever harder to hold fast to . . .
Randall Jarrell

All through their lives, the Middle Generation poets attempted to vanquish the sense of alienation which they shared by seeking the light of knowledge. The triteness of the metaphor perfectly matches the naive intensity, the self-conscious but sincere heroism, of their dedication to this goal. In order to achieve the profound perception into the meaning of life which they craved, the poets were willing to suffer greatly. In fact, they felt one had to suffer. For in order to understand the pain of life, one must live with a continuous and intense awareness of that pain. One had to live, in other words, at the edge. This of course made one's suffering even worse than it would ordinarily be, but to their mind there was no other way. Only through pain could one hope to achieve salvation from pain. And naturally, only by suffering could one write great poetry. Each of them expressed such a notion at one time or another. Schwartz wrote, "Into the Destructive Element . . . that is the way." Berryman said, "The poet has got to know pain." Lowell observed, "poetry is . . . a sensuous, passionate, brutal thing." Jarrell felt that "poetry should be worth a life."[1] All of these are different ways of saying the same thing.

In a sense, the Middle Generation poets' hunger for knowledge was nothing more or less than a wish to find God. They wanted God to stand up and say "Here I am." Throughout their work one finds evidence of this. In one of Berryman's *Dream Songs*, for example, "god howled 'I am.' " In an explanatory note to one of his *Selected Poems*, Jarrell says that

> I put into "A Game at Salzburg" a little game that Germans and Austrians play with very young children. The child says to the grown-

up, *Here I am*, and the grown-up answers, *There you are;* the children use the same little rising tone, and the grown-ups the same resolving, conclusive one. It seemed to me that if there could be a conversation between the world and God, this would be it.[2]

All of the Middle Generation poets lived, in a sense, to know, first, that there was a God, and, second, where they stood in relation to him; they wanted to be able to say, "Here I am," and to have God say, "There you are."

The frantic quest for a God, of course, is equivalent in Freudian psychology to the quest for the father. Indeed, Maurice Zolotow once made just this connection in conversation with Schwartz, suggesting that Schwartz's belief in God represented his desire for a father. Schwartz himself felt that he believed in God "because it made life seem important."[3] Significantly, perhaps, his own father was cynical about the existence of God. But Harry sent Delmore to Hebrew school anyway, and in high school the young man made an impression for his interest in metaphysical questions and the importance he placed on loving God. At college Schwartz prayed fervently and sincerely, and thought of ideas for short stories about God.

But while he prayed, he studied philosophy as well. It was his undergraduate major, and reportedly he was both deeply absorbed in it and extremely well versed in its technicalities. The major influence on Schwartz at New York University was his teacher Sidney Hook, the Marxist author of *From Hegel to Marx*, but Schwartz identified himself during these years not as a Marxist but as a logical positivist. Although Marx became, with Freud, one of his two nonliterary heroes, the Communist thinker interested him not so much for what he had to say but for how he said it; Marx had "the poetry of passion."[4] Similarly, Schwartz admired Trotsky mainly for his literary knowledge, and like Lowell was intrigued by Catholicism largely for aesthetic reasons. Predictably, both religion and philosophy figure prominently in Schwartz's early poetry. His autobiographical poem *Genesis*, originally titled *Having Snow*, began during his undergraduate years as a work of epistemology, its theme "the difficulty of knowledge." It was with this poem that Schwartz turned his philosophical interests from the utterly objective logical positivism to its almost exact opposite, the intensely subjective phenomenology of Husserl. This was a critically important step for Schwartz, for it indicates that he came to realize that he was interested in philosophy because he wanted to attain metaphysical knowledge; logical positivism and existentialism were useless to him, for Schwartz did not need to be told that he was alone. He needed to find out how he fit in, how everything fit together. He wanted, in his own word, unity. As Atlas puts it, "He had urgent metaphysical questions to resolve."[5] Thus it is not surprising that, upon graduating from New York University, Schwartz spent a year at Harvard Graduate School with the intention of becoming a professional philosopher, and, during his time there, fell into the habit of making fun of the logical positivists and existentialists who dominated Harvard's philosophy department. This state of affairs can only have made Schwartz feel more isolated than ever.

Genesis did more than turn Schwartz from a positivist into a Husserlian; it in fact marks the decline of his interest in religion and the increasing sophistication of his involvement not only in philosophy but in psychology. By the time he wrote the final version of *Genesis: Book One* (published in 1943, seven years after the year at Harvard) he was already conceiving of God more as a poetic device than as anything else.

Perhaps it was in his early essay on "The Two Audens" that the nature of Schwartz's interest in Freud was most clearly established. Schwartz sees Auden as having two poetic voices, one associated with the ego, the other with the id. The former voice is that of "the clever guy, the Noel Coward of literary Marxism," which "springs from the conscious motives of the poet." It is the latter voice, however, that is the more valuable, a "sibyl who utters the telltale symbols in a psychoanalytic trance," producing "many images of the greatest import and power." Schwartz congratulates Auden for his natural talents, and for the poetry of the id, but warns him against heeding "the solicitations of the ego."[6] Taken unconditionally, this is nothing less than a call for automatic writing. The essay, in warning against the danger of Marxism to the artist and metaphysician, demonstrates how far Schwartz had come from ideological harmony with Sidney Hook, if in fact such harmony had ever existed. It also demonstrates that even at this early stage, Schwartz quite firmly identified the poetic act with the psychoanalytic act, an identification which all the Middle Generation poets would eventually make.

During the 1940s, the decade in which Schwartz aged from his mid-twenties to his mid-thirties, he stopped studying philosophy and began to read Freud in earnest. Indeed, it was during the late Forties, as Barrett says, that "the figure of Freud loomed larger" for everyone in the United States. "We were perhaps the first generation in America," writes Barrett, "to take Freud and psychoanalysis seriously." The Middle Generation poets were certainly the first generation of American poets upon whose work Freud exerts a major influence. Unfortunately, "Freud was a disaster for Delmore," Barrett explains.

> Freudian therapy, particularly in the wrong hands . . . can turn the patient's attention away from his current life problems and fix it on the years of his childhood. Delmore's self-absorption was such that his mind was already excessively riveted on the "family romance" of his own childhood; and he needed no encouragement that way. He had picked up the collected works of Freud at a Cambridge bookshop, and as he pored relentlessly over the pages, he was absorbed more and more into his own diagnosis of his childhood.[7]

From that time on, Schwartz was addicted. He immersed himself in Freud, professed himself a disciple of the great physician, and wholeheartedly embraced the words Freud had coined to explain the workings of the human mind. More than anyone else, perhaps, Freud helped Schwartz to approach the sought-for understanding of himself, his world, his times, and the way in which they all interrelated. Sadly, however, Schwartz derived no comfort from his knowledge; Freudian psychology, ironically, seems only to have aggravated his sense of being chained to the past. "The mind possesses and is possessed by all the ruins / Of every haunted, hunted generation's celebration."[8]

Like Schwartz, Jarrell greatly admired Freud; his devotion may indeed have been as fanatical as Schwartz's, although it appears not to have been as much of a disaster for him as it was for his New York friend. Like Schwartz, Jarrell began with a greater interest in religion than in psychology. He was brought up a Protestant, and some of his poems about childhood record a precocious wrestling with the problems of faith. However, he seems never to have been deeply involved in religion at any time in his life, and his poetry, though full of Biblical imagery, is surprisingly short on Christian themes. Ferguson identifies one book, *Losses*, as treating of Christian themes at length, but indicates that the poems in that volume generally dismiss Christianity as a solution to the questions of life.[9]

Rather, Jarrell's quest for knowledge seems to have begun in earnest with philosophy, an interest he came to about the same time as Schwartz. During the year he took off between high school and college, Jarrell "continued to study in depth, concentrating on *Prin-*

cipia Mathematica, an abstruse book by Bertrand Russell and Alfred North Whitehead with a thesis that mathematics is reducible to logic."[10] Like Schwartz at the same age, the young Jarrell seems to have been at ease with such complexities. According to a friend, Jarrell not only completed the book but understood it. At this time Jarrell also read Russell's *Philosophy,* whose distinction between the possible and the real appears to have had a profound effect on him. His interest in Russell seems to have been contemporary with his heavy reading in the equally rational, ethical, and mathematical Spinoza. Jarrell's alignment of himself with such paradoxically unpoetic philosophers seems to have continued well into his adult years; in the late forties, he told William Barrett that he was a positivist, and declared death to be meaningless.

What are we to make of this? How can we explain someone whose life and poetry illustrate his obsession with metaphysical questions, but who stubbornly adheres to a philosophy which asserts, in essence, that the only real knowledge is scientific knowledge?

My sense is that, unlike Schwartz, Jarrell performed a balancing act between his poetry and his philosophy. In his poetry, he gave free rein to his metaphysical questions and speculations. But philosophy he saw as a science—after all, he had learned it from Bertrand Russell—and so in his philosophy he behaved like a scientist. As a philosopher, in other words, he played a sort of devil's advocate to his poetry-writing self. His method of arriving at knowledge was thus dialectical. Jarrell the philosopher and Jarrell the poet squared off, and between them attempted to arrive at the truth.

This is not simply idle speculation. The records indicate that Jarrell was much more involved in, and had a much clearer understanding of, science than any of the other Middle Generation poets. This fact would seem to predispose him, more than the others, to the way of thinking outlined above. Moreover, Jarrell was the most well-adapted member of the group. This adaptation had to be achieved somehow; a solid devotion to positivism, as a balance to what Alvarez would call his Extremism, might well have been a subconsciously founded contrivance, designed to provide a rational base upon which to construct a life more stable than that of Schwartz or Berryman or Lowell.

At any rate, despite his enduring interest in philosophy, Jarrell chose to study psychology at Vanderbilt University. While Schwartz, at New York University, was planning a life as a professional philosopher, Jarrell, in Nashville, looked forward to a career as an analyst. Like Schwartz, Jarrell revered Freud, and read him avidly. "His knowledge of the father of psychoanalysis," writes Eileen Simpson, "was broader and deeper than that of many analysts. He knew pages of Freud the way he knew Yeats, Proust, and Tolstoy—by heart."[11] When, during his second marriage, he discovered that Freud's birthday was the same as his, he gave up celebrating the day as his own and celebrated it as Freud's instead. His interest in Freud, like Schwartz's, seems to have exceeded, in the end, his interest in either religion or philosophy.

The same is true of Berryman. Berryman was brought up a devout Catholic—but, when his mother remarried, he adopted his stepfather's religion. The elder Berryman was an Episcopalian, and Haffenden says that the teenager was "smoothly assimilated."[12]

This seems highly unlikely, if only because no part of Berryman's religious life appears ever to have gone smoothly. Throughout his life, Berryman was obsessed with the question of the existence of God. Although, like Schwartz, he studied philosophy as an undergraduate, and names like Kierkegaard, Hegel, and Wittgenstein dance across the pages of his poetry, he never really subsumed his theological questions into a fundamentally philosophical framework. Or, to put it another way, he never really stopped believing that there might be a First Cause, in the person of the Judeo-Christian God. His faith, however, was no rock. Haffenden's biography charts a constant shifting back and forth between, on the one hand, the belief that religion is mere superstition and, on the other hand, fervent faith in God and the calming conviction that God's will is central to the meaning of life.[13] Particularly in his last years, the question of the existence of God was supremely important to him.

In his early years, though, philosophy and psychology probably held greater significance. In fact, during his college years, and the decade or two afterward, the history of Berryman's quest for knowledge looks a great deal like that of Schwartz's. One good reason for this is that it was during the early forties that these two poets were closest, and Berryman idolized Schwartz so intensely that the latter found it annoying. It is known that Berryman imitated poems by Schwartz during this period; doubtless he also followed Schwartz's lead in his intellectual pursuits.

However, the similarity of their meanderings through philosophy and psychology predates their first meeting. Like Schwartz, Berryman was quite young when he began a lifelong habit of intensive self-analysis. Barrett would have said of Berryman, as he did of Schwartz, that Freud was a disaster for him; being, as Haffenden writes, "dedicated to atomising his own mind," Berryman "tended to intellectualise his feelings with an intensity that compounded the problem."[14] As with Schwartz, Berryman's religious beliefs appear to have waned during the early forties, a period of profound disbelief for him, and his serious reading in Freud and the other authorities in psychoanalysis to have begun later in that decade. Like Schwartz, Berryman went to Freud to understand his childhood; and as Schwartz used Freudian terms to explain the creative art of Auden, Berryman did the same for Stephen Crane when he came to write his book about that author. The last chapter of the Crane study, titled "The Color of This Soul," was almost universally condemned by critics for what they saw as an excessively Freudian analysis.[15]

Finally we come to Lowell, who also eventually became a devout Freudian. Lowell's experience with religion is perhaps the most peculiar of all the Middle Generation poets. In his early twenties he rejected the Episcopalianism of his parents, which he now saw as his enemy, and joined the Roman Catholic Church, which until a short time before had been, according to Lowell's derisive jokes, "a religion for Irish servant girls." Now, suddenly, Catholicism was the answer to Lowell's prayer—a prayer for a religion "whose disciples could be seen as different from those of Boston in their antiquity, their opulence, their intellectual distinction: rules for a better life, not rules made to protect the mediocre, rules that would engender art, not view it with suspicion."[16] Note the aesthetic, not doctrinal, criteria by which Lowell chose his new denomination; clearly, however genuine his faith, Lowell saw God, as Schwartz did after a certain age, largely as a poetic device.

This, of course, is not to say that there were no other reasons for Lowell's decision to abandon "Boston-styled Calvinism" for Rome. Hamilton writes that one motive for Lowell's inquiry into Catholicism was that he craved order; we have already observed that Schwartz turned from positivism to metaphysics because he sought unity. Interestingly, through Catholicism, Lowell learned a good deal of metaphysics. He identified himself not merely as a Catholic, but as an adherent of the philosophy of St. Thomas Aquinas, who believed that the rational and the religious perspectives could be seen to be utterly compatible. In particular, Aquinas attempted to use reason to demonstrate the existence of God, to use logic to prove the truth of faith. This rigorous, difficult system of philosophy developed into a constant obsession for Lowell, a fanaticism that made his conversations "so 'insanely illogical' that they could be written into a case history of religious mania."[17] Day by day he buried himself in sacred texts, including the works of Aquinas himself, and such fellow Thomists (more accurately, neo-Thomists) as Jacques Maritain and Etienne Gilson. These studies occupied him to the exclusion of virtually every other activity, including, apparently, sexual relations with his wife at the time, Jean Stafford. I have already discussed Allen Tate's theory that Lowell became involved with Catholicism primarily to avoid sex, to work himself into "the inescapably celibate corner." This, in addition to the need for order and for a poetic theme, gives us three possible reasons for Lowell's fascination with Catholicism. These three reasons indicate the degree to which Lowell's philosophical, religious, psychosexual, and aesthetic motivations and interests were bound together.

During the late forties, Lowell fell away from Catholicism, eventually coming to see religious orthodoxy as destructive. By the late fifties, Lowell was by his own admission an agnostic. During these years of waning religious fervor, Lowell's interest in Freud, like that of the other Middle Generation poets, grew rapidly. In 1953 he described himself as "gulping" Freud, and declared himself "a slavish convert" to the father of psychoanalysis.[18]

Indeed, all of the Middle Generation poets were, in the end, slavish converts. For each of them, the last stop on the road to knowledge turned out to be Vienna. Granted, there was no miracle. The clouds did not open; the Angel of Truth did not descend from heaven; God never stood up and said "Here I am." But Freud did. It is perhaps pointless to observe that, for the most part, the Middle Generation poets would doubtless have been better off had the great doctor remained seated. It would hardly be fair to Freud, either. He was not responsible for the way these four poets made a habit of quarrying the id; he was only responsible for providing them with newer and better tools for the job—tools which, in the end, they misused. It is undeniable that "Freud was a disaster for Delmore," and for each of the Middle Generation poets; his writings clearly encouraged what was, for men in their state of mind, a dangerous tendency. But the fundamental truth of the matter is that it was

Delmore who was a disaster for Delmore; and Randall who was a disaster for Randall; and so on. They were already headed into the destructive element when Freud came along; he merely handed them a map.

Yet they followed it avidly. One cannot understand the Middle Generation without recognizing the degree to which they relied on Freud, in the latter part of their lives, for their understanding of their world, their time, and themselves. This interest in Freud quite naturally coincides with the writing of their later poetry, which is predominantly subjective. One demonstration of Freud's influence is the prominence, particularly in their later poetry, of the dream motif. One need only glance at the titles of their works to establish this prominence. Schwartz wrote *In Dreams Begin Responsibilities* and "The Dream of Knowledge"; Jarrell wrote "Dreams," "The Dream," and "The Dream of Waking"; Berryman wrote *The Dream Songs*; Lowell wrote "Dream of Fair Ladies," "Orestes' Dream," "Harriet's Dream," and many others.

To the Middle Generation poets—who perhaps tended at times to simplify Freud—dreams represent two things. First, it is in dreams that one's true feelings about waking life come closest to the surface. Ideally, if one understands one's dreams completely, one understands oneself completely. "To dream and to know," wrote Schwartz, "are one."[19] Thus dreams were an important hunting ground in the Middle Generation poets' quest for knowledge. And since each Middle Generation poet's mind was his own favorite poetic subject, dreams became a very important source of material for them. In fact, some of their late poems—Lowell's "Dream," for instance, or Berryman's "Dream Song 101"—appear to be transcriptions of their dreams, presented with the understanding that the poet need do no more than present them in order to do his job as poet.[20] In a sense, as Berryman says in the last line of "Dream Song 101," "Everything is what it seems"—Berryman's dream, when handed to the reader, has barely been tampered with by the poet. It is unanalyzed, almost uncommented upon, with the exception of the dreamer's answer to the traditional psychoanalyst's question, "How did you feel about the dream?" Except for this answer ("a sense of total loss / afflicted me thereof," etc.), the dream presents itself in the poem as it presented itself to the poet. The poet, for his part, has mined the ore, and delivered it to his customer, but he has left it to the reader to pick out the valuable mineral of truth. This kind of poetry-writing, of course, reflects admirable Freudian enthusiasm, but hardly sound Freudian thinking. The poets, in writing such poems, fail to recognize that their personal dream symbols and associations cannot possibly be fully deciphered by the reader. One certainly gets a sense of the emotional dimensions of what is going on in such poems as these; each poem reflects the dreamer's feeling of alienation, of loss, of persecution. But beyond that, all is hidden behind private symbols, the meaning of which may not be clear even to the poet.

An extreme case of poem-as-psychoanalysis is Lowell's "The Couple," in which the patient-poet's description of his dream is interrupted by questions from the analyst-reader.[21] But this retailing of real dreams is not the most common manner in which the dream motif manifests itself in Middle Generation poetry. Since both dreams and poetry represented to these poets, in Lowell's words, a "form of knowledge," dreaming, in their work, became a natural metaphor for writing poetry. Thus we have Berryman's title *The Dream Songs*, implying that the poems are dreams, and the heading which Jarrell borrowed from Freud for a section of his *Selected Poems*, "Dream-Work." Berryman wrote that his job as poet was to "recompose experience into dreams"; Jarrell refers to writing a poem as giving up life and "dreaming something else to take its place."[22]

The latter quotation points to the second way in which dreams are significant to the Middle Generation. Dreams are wish fulfillments. They present a version of life more pleasant than that which the dreamer encounters during his waking hours. For the Middle Generation poets, to whom life meant primarily pain and alienation, dreams were thus doubly attractive; in dreams they could find not only knowledge, an explanation of the tortures that wracked their minds, but a temporary release from those tortures into another world far more to their liking. "In dreams," writes Suzanne Ferguson, "Jarrell's characters compensate for the pain and loneliness of their waking lives."[23] This is true of all the Middle Generation poets. In their poetry the dream world is often an ideal world, in which the dreamer may achieve the longed-for sense of unity with everything else in the universe, as in Schwartz's "O Child, Do Not Fear the Dark and Sleep's Dark Possession," wherein the child addressed in the poem "become[s] more and other" than he is—a bird, a beast, a tree, a pony, a beaver.[24] "My dreams are more rewarding than my actuality," wrote Lowell; and the other Middle Generation poets would have concurred in the sentiment. Sometimes the rare moments of joy in their waking lives are described as dreams. Berryman, in one of his *Dream Songs*, describes a few moments of happiness with a child as "a small dream of the Golden World" which intrudes upon the unpleasantness of the real world; and in another Dream Song an interlude spent in the pages of an "old French story" is a dream from which Henry, Berryman's alter ego, awakens to face "the wicked ordinary day." Thus the word "dream" came to refer to any experience that constituted an exception to the alienation and unhappiness of their waking lives.[25]

At times, the Middle Generation poets, especially Jarrell, reverse their imagery. Instead of seeing themselves as desiring escape from the hard reality of waking life into the fairy-tale world of dreams, they choose to depict waking life itself as a dream from which they wish to awaken into a more coherent, happy world. Both Schwartz and Berryman, in their poetry, refer to the conscious hours of their days as a "waking dream"; Jarrell writes of the "dream of life"; Lowell uses Arnold's lines about "the world, which seems / to lie before us like a land of dreams" as an epigraph to *The Mills of the Kavanaughs*. Waking life is, to the Middle Generation poets, an emphatically bad dream, a "sick dream," as Jarrell puts it, and the sooner it is awakened from, the better. One of Berryman's *Dream Songs* begins with a memory of a friend "covered with blood"; the speaker reports that his thought, on seeing this grisly sight, was that this was the dream's end: "now I'll wake up." Schwartz, in one of his extended works mixing prose and poetry, presents a translation of "an anthem by Calderón"—in actuality, a selection from *La vida es sueño*, including the statement that man dreams his life "Until life's dream is undone." And Jarrell, in "Absent without Official Leave," describes a soldier going to bed and "compos[ing] his body" into life, drifting away from the war into a world where people die natural deaths.[26] The poem is insistent: the soldier's life consists of the hours during which he dreams. His waking hours are not life, but an interlude of pain.

To regard life as meaningless, and dreams as the only reality, is close to a death wish. And indeed, a number of Middle Generation poems see death as desirable, as something that is awakened to from the nightmare of life. *"In the end we wake from everything,"* runs a line in a Jarrell poem. A Schwartz poem written on the death of Frost, who "sleeps and wakes forever more," ends with lines suggesting that *"the first day and night of death"* must be *"a metaphysical victory."* And another Schwartz poem ends by asserting that darkness always precedes delight, the *"the long night is always the beginning of the vivid blossom of day."* Of course, many poets, at one time or another, seem half in love with easeful death. But the enthusiasm of the Middle Generation poets, manifested in the above quotations by their use of italics, is well-nigh unparalleled. *"I wish I could die,"* writes Lowell straightforwardly in a *Day by Day* poem. Berryman once identified Mr. Bones of *The Dream Songs* as *"Death,* Henry's friend—who at the end takes him offstage."[27]

But if at times death was a friend, more often the poets saw it as an enemy. Their poetry is full of the awareness that the lonely, wasted years of the past will never return. Schwartz, for example, asks himself what he will do with his "lonely life" before the knife of death "provides the answer ultimate and appropriate." And Jarrell asks the "Little Women" and "Little Men" of the world what beaches they have trodden and slept upon in their "medium-sized lives."[28] Alongside these contemplations of the wasted past are intimations of a dreadful future. Browsing through a volume of Middle Generation poetry, one can generally count on being reminded, on almost every page, of the fact that death will come to us all:

> how do I know I can keep any of us alive?
>
> I must surely die.
>
> Man is born in chains, and everywhere we see
> him dead.
>
> . . . we must die forever. . . .
>
> Each moment is dying.
>
> We are dying: Time is farewell![29]

The first two quotations are from Lowell; the next two from Jarrell and Berryman respectively; the last two from Schwartz. Besides indicating that the theme, "Death comes to us all," is a favorite of the Middle Generation, these lines also demonstrate that death was not simply a reality. To the Middle Generation poets, every moment of life was suffused with death.

Clearly, facing death was as much a problem to the Middle Generation poets as facing life. Lowell once mentioned an interesting theory: "They say fear of death is a child's remembrance of the first desertion." Whether their respective boyhood losses were responsible for their inordinate preoccupation with mortality, we cannot say. But we can state with relative certainty that their quests for knowledge, which represent an attempt to cope with life, were equally designed to help them cope with death. In an early poem, presented as a father-son dialogue, Schwartz offered a way to stop time. The father in the poem tells his son to come face to face with death, to "be guilty of [him]self" in a full-length mirror, to recognize that he is dying because "time is in you," and to "act in that shadow, as if death were now."[30] This is, of course, simply another way of saying "Into the Destructive Element . . . that it is the way." As the solution to life's anguish necessitates intensifying one's awareness of that anguish, so the solution to the fear of death is to face death head-on. It is obvious from their poetry that all of the Middle Generation poets shared this philosophy. Their obsessive writing about death is, in part, clearly the result of their dedication to the notion that the answer to it all lay in the ability, as Schwartz put it, "knit / Time with apperception."[31]

But of course, the ultimate answer, for the Middle Generation poets, was poetry. Beyond religion and philosophy, even beyond Freudian psychoanalysis, and including them all within its wide embrace, poetry was the Middle Generation's reply to life and death. It was, as Lowell said, the ultimate form of knowledge. I have used the word obsession several times in this study and will use it again, but in no place is it more appropriate than here. No obsession came close to equaling the obsession to write poetry. When Lowell wrote that "We asked to be obsessed with writing / and we were,"[32] he was speaking for all four of them. Perhaps this, more than anything else, is what separates the Middle Generation poets from their poetry-writing contemporaries. Elizabeth Bishop, for example, could not understand why Lowell was willing to publish *The Dolphin*. The book included material, particularly excerpts from personal letters, which would deeply hurt his ex-wife, Elizabeth Hardwick, and their daughter Harriet. Argued Bishop: *"art just isn't worth that much."*[33] No Middle Generation poet would have agreed with her.

Again and again one is reminded of the vital importance of poetry to the Middle Generation. Eileen Simpson remembers Berryman's joy at meeting Lowell because "Not since Delmore had John found a contemporary who was as obsessed with poetry as he was." Writing poems, Simpson recalls, was to these men "the greatest joy of all," and second to it was "the joy of discussing them."[34] Jarrell too, remembered Ransom, "was an insistent and almost overbearing talker" about literature, and his obsession with it is attested to by Schwartz, in a review of Jarrell's *Poetry and the Age:*

Behind the witty, passionate intensity of Jarrell's style there is always a huge, half-rhetorical, half-shocked question: How can any human being in his right mind disregard the power and the glory of poetry? . . . Jarrell always speaks to the reader as a dedicated, possessed poet.[35]

However esteemed and successful they were as editors, novelists, critics, or teachers, the members of the Middle Generation always thought of themselves as poets, and wanted the world to think of them that way too. Schwartz was enraged when the newspaper reports of the famous party at which Norman Mailer stabbed his wife identified Schwartz, who was a guest, as a critic, "when, after all, he was a poet."[36] This self-image is mainly what separates Schwartz from the New York intellectuals among whom he moved during his years on the *Partisan Review* staff. According to William Barrett, Philip Rahv, one of the main figures in that circle, "had his own *pietas*, his own religion—and it centered in his Marxist faith."[37] In this, Rahv, although admittedly more fervent a believer than most of his associates, was typical of the New York intellectuals. After the late thirties many of them were no longer Marxists, but if they had any *pietas* at all it was their left-wing politics. This is what set Schwartz and the other Middle Generation poets apart. Although they were fascinated by politics, their *pietas* was poetry. Poetry was not just a beloved vocation, it was a deeply respected form of inquiry. It was the clearing at the end of the long trail upon which they had set forth in childhood. The four boys, deprived of fathers and oppressed by powerful mothers, had grown into insecure men who found life nearly unbearable. They hoped, through knowledge, to overcome their profound sense of alienation. Their poetry is the record of their devotion to that purpose.

PART TWO
The Early Poetry

4

The Eliotic Sensibility

> *My words echo*
> *Thus, in your mind*
> T. S. Eliot

The early poetry of the Middle Generation appeared in fourteen volumes, published between 1938 and 1951.[1] They are:

Schwartz, *In Dreams Begin Responsibilities*	(1938)
Berryman, Jarrell, *Five Young American Poets*	(1940)
Berryman, *Poems*	(1942)
Jarrell, *Blood for a Stranger*	(1942)
Schwartz, *Genesis: Book One*	(1943)
Lowell, *Land of Unlikeness*	(1944)
Jarrell, *Little Friend, Little Friend*	(1945)
Lowell, *Lord Weary's Castle*	(1946)
Berryman, *Berryman's Sonnets*	(1947)
Berryman, *The Dispossessed*	(1948)
Jarrell, *Losses*	(1948)
Schwartz, *Vandeville for a Princess*	(1950)
Lowell, *The Mills of the Kavanaughs*	(1951)
Jarrell, *The Seven-League Crutches*	(1951)

This poetry is characterized primarily by a sensibility which may be traced directly to T. S. Eliot. The best way to understand this sensibility is to turn to three of Eliot's most important essays, which seem to occupy the most nearly central position in the background of the early poetry of the Middle Generation. These essays are "Tradition and the Individual Talent" (1919), "Hamlet and His Problems" (1919), and "The Metaphysical Poets" (1921).

"Tradition and the Individual Talent" sets forth the notion that "the poet must develop or procure the consciousness of the past and . . . he should continue to develop this consciousness throughout his career. . . . The progress of an artist is a continual self-sacrifice, a continual extinction of personality." Eliot compares the poet to "a bit of finely filiated platinum" which "is introduced into a chamber containing oxygen and sulphur dioxide." As the sliver of platinum acts as a catalyst, making possible the reaction of the two gases to form sulphurous acid, so the mind of the poet is "a receptacle for seizing and storing up numberless feelings, phrases, images, which remain there until all the particles which can unite to form a new compound are present together."

Thus the personality, the feelings of the poet himself have no necessary role in the poetry he writes. Poetic knowledge is found not in the self, but in the world beyond the self. "Impressions and experiences which are important for the man may take no place in the poetry, and those which become important in the poetry may play quite a negligible part in the man, the personality." It is not his personal emotions, "the emotions provoked by particular events in his life," that make a poet "remarkable or interesting."

> His particular emotions may be simple, or crude, or flat. The emotion in his poetry will be a very complex thing, but not with the complexity of the emotions of people who have very complex or unusual emotions in life. . . . The business of the poet is not to find new emotions, but to use the ordinary ones and, in working them up into poetry, to express feelings which are not in actual emotions at all. And emotions which he has never experienced will serve his turn as well as those familiar to him.

Poetry is, then, the furthest possible thing from "the spontaneous overflow of powerful emotion." In fact, Eliot writes, "There is a great deal, in the writing of poetry, which must be conscious and deliberate." One mark of a bad poet is that he "is unusually unconscious where he ought to be conscious, and conscious where he ought to be unconscious. Both errors tend to make him 'personal.' Poetry is not a turning loose of emotion, but an escape from emotion; it is not the expression of personality, but an escape from personality."[2]

"Hamlet and His Problems" is a very brief essay which is noted primarily for introducing the concept of the objective correlative. "The only way of expressing emotion in the form of art," writes Eliot, "is by finding an 'objective correlative'; in other words, a set of objects, a situation, a chain of events which shall be the formula of that particular emotion; such that when the external facts, which must terminate in sensory experience, are given, the emotion is immediately evoked."[3]

Perhaps that essay of Eliot's which is most important in understanding the early poetry of the Middle Generation is "The Metaphysical Poets." In this essay, originally a review of H. C. Grierson's
anthology of the same name, Eliot compares a poem by Donne to one
by Tennyson and comments that the difference between them "is not
a simple difference of degree between poets"; it is instead "the
difference between the intellectual poet and the reflective poet." Eliot
makes clear which type of poet he considers better. Reflective poets
like Tennyson, he maintains,

> are poets, and they think; but they do not feel their thought as immedi-
> ately as the odor of a rose. A thought to Donne was an experience; it
> modified his sensibility. When a poet's mind is perfectly equipped for its
> work, it is constantly amalgamating disparate experience; the ordinary
> man's experience is chaotic, irregular, fragmentary. The latter falls in
> love, or reads Spinoza, and these two experiences have nothing to do
> with each other, or with the noise of the typewriter or the smell of
> cooking; in the mind of the poet these experiences are always forming
> new wholes.

According to Eliot, however, this type of poet has not existed since
the seventeenth century, when English poets, like the English drama-
tists of the sixteenth century, "possessed a mechanism of sensibility
which could devour any kind of experience." After Donne, according
to Eliot, "a dissociation of sensibility set in, from which we have
never recovered." A period ensued in which, while the language of
poetry grew increasingly refined, its "feeling" became cruder. "The
poets revolted against the ratiocinative, the descriptive; they thought
and felt by fits, unbalanced; they reflected." Thus, says Eliot, has the
situation remained.

What is needed, he implies, is a new generation of poets who,
like the Metaphysical poets, let intelligence reign in their poetry and
seek to use that intelligence to recognize and convey the unity of all
experience. Eliot says of his ideal poet, "the more intelligent he is, the
better." Since the modern world is complicated, poetry must be
comparably complicated; or, as Eliot puts it,

> poets in our civilization, as it exists at present, must be *difficult*. Our
> civilization comprehends great variety and complexity, and this variety
> and complexity, playing upon a refined sensibility, must produce varied
> and complex results. The poet must become more and more comprehen-
> sive, more allusive, more indirect, in order to force, to dislocate if
> necessary, language into his meaning.

Next, Eliot makes a connection which was to have interesting implications for the Middle Generation poets. Laforgue, Corbière, Racine, and Baudelaire, Eliot suggests, "are nearer to the 'school of Donne' than any modern English poet," for "they have the same essential quality of transmuting ideas into sensations, of transforming an observation into a state of mind." They are comprehensive "explorers of the soul," unlike such neoclassical poets as Milton and Dryden, on the one hand, or, on the other hand, the Romantics, who merely "look into [their] hearts." The ideal poet, says Eliot, must look not only into his heart but "into the cerebral cortex, the nervous system, and the digestive tracts." It is worth noting that in identifying the Symbolist poets with the Metaphysical poets, rather than aligning them with the Romantics, Eliot was dissenting from the usual view of things. He was also bestowing upon those French poets his personal imprimatur, declaring that it was acceptable for the ideal Modern poet to like them and learn from them.[4]

These three essays by Eliot come together to define and to prescribe a type of poetry which, at least when he wrote them, was Eliot's ideal. The concepts of the impersonality of the poet, the objective correlative, and the dissociation of sensibility which these essays introduced shaped the kind of poetry the Middle Generation poets wrote in their early period. Of course, there are few twentieth century poets who have not been influenced by Eliot, but the Middle Generation poets are a special case. Virtually every line of poetry that they wrote during their early years was brought into being by a poetic faculty that had been shaped by Eliot's doctrines. Reading through their early poetry one can clearly see the results of an attempt to catalyze the reaction of the disparate particles of contemporary experience; to be aware of history and its relation to the present; to be impersonal, intelligent, and difficult. Reading a typical early Middle Generation poem, one senses that it originated not from an attempt to capture a state of emotion but to convey an intellectual experience. The details of such a poem do not reflect the stimuli which impelled its writing, but strike one as effects contrived to create an objective correlative for the theme, the idea, with which the poem originated.

What this means is that during their early period, the Middle Generation considered knowledge the province of the mind, not of the heart. Later they would be students of Freud, and knowledge would mean primarily self-knowledge of the type that psychoanalysis aims to achieve. This is a sort of knowledge to which the intellect is irrelevant and over which the reason is powerless. But during this early period, knowledge was completely a matter of the mind. The point in the early poetry of the Middle Generation was not to examine private anxieties but to go beyond them, to surmount the self and thus vanquish its sense of alienation.

Recognizing this, one can hardly resist the conclusion that the Middle Generation poets read Eliot's essays collectively as a manifesto of sorts. As Whitman had answered Emerson's call in "The Poet" for a bard to express the spirit of the new America, so the Middle Generation poets seem in their early poetry to be answering what they appear to have perceived as a call from Eliot.

Why Eliot? Perhaps because everything the Middle Generation poets wanted, consciously or unconsciously, at this stage of their lives, Eliot seemed to be. If they were fatherless young men who intensely needed someone to revere and to mimic, and even to resent, despise, and eventually rebel against, Eliot provided the ideal paternal image. Distant and dictatorial, his pronouncements on poetry had changed the course of English letters. If they felt like outsiders in their own country, Eliot was living proof that someone like themselves could metamorphose from an unsuccessful, unknown alien in his own nation into a successful, famous insider in Europe. Finally, if they were philosophers, seekers of knowledge, desperate to understand the relationships between things, to perceive the principle of order underlying the seeming chaos of the world, Eliot was Kant and Aquinas rolled into one.

That Eliot had transformed himself into a European is significant here. For in their early period, Europe was to the Middle Generation poets a mythical place, a *locus amenis*. American culture did not interest them as much as European culture, and none of them wanted American poets as models. To Schwartz, who never got there, that continent across the Atlantic contained, in Barrett's words, "the sacred places of the imagination." Jarrell, according to Rosenthal, "tried to make a European of himself," and one might say that Berryman, who deliberately used British spellings throughout his adult life, tried to make a Briton of himself. There was, said Richard Eberhart, "nothing American about Robert Lowell." All of them, as Sidney Hook has written of Schwartz, "tended to denigrate American culture and literature" while they "glorified European life and letters." During the first years of their poetic apprenticeships, they all came to feel, as Haffenden says of Berryman, "that America lacked a real verse tradition; and that its sensibilities were raw." This devotion to Europe was, in part, a form of rebellion. The Freudian subconscious identifies all symbols of authority—God, parents, country—with one another; and so a rejection of their country's literary heritage was a way of rejecting their parents, of protesting the pain of childhood. Of all the critics who have written on the Middle Generation, M. L. Rosenthal perhaps comes closest to recognizing this when he observes that Jarrell's interest in European culture "seems in part an effort to repossess for himself a nourishment denied him in childhood."[5] Thus one can understand why Eliot's having transformed himself from an American into a European greatly enhanced his value to the Middle Generation poets as a model.

Most important, however, was Eliot's view of poetry as a form of intellectual inquiry. Far more than any other poet or critic of the day, Eliot represented poetry as a form of knowledge, "at least as valid as scientific knowledge," as Lowell wrote, "and in certain ways more so."[6] Indeed, poetry, as Eliot had recreated it, *was* a science; why else had he chosen to compare writing poetry to performing a chemistry experiment? Poetry, Eliot made the Middle Generation poets believe, was a discipline which could stand beside, and perhaps ahead of, all other forms of inquiry in its ability to help man attain an understanding of himself and his world. To put it simply, poetry, like mathematics and physics, could solve things. Wordsworth, in his declining years, had written of his own youthful enthusiasm for the French Revolution: "Bliss was it in that dawn to be alive, / But to be young was very Heaven!" So might the Middle Generation have described their early devotion to Eliot. For like the ideals of the French Revolution, Eliot's concept of poetry seemed to be the dawn of a new order.

Thus when other American poets tried to tell the young Middle Generation poets that poetry was meant to entertain, they replied that they had outgrown any such notion. If anyone protested, as legions of critics have done since, that "To start with an ideal of 'complexity,' in poetry as in philosophy, runs counter to the real requirements of things," they did not pay attention. Eliot had them.[7]

Such American poets and critics as Allen Tate and John Crowe Ransom, who were close to the Middle Generation poets and in sympathy with the ideas of Eliot, could thus be teachers, high priests in the religion of Eliot; but their poems could never serve as models for the Middle Generation's early efforts. For the best poems of Tate and Ransom simply do not follow Eliot's dicta as faithfully as early

Middle Generation poetics demanded. Ransom's "Bells for John Whiteside's Daughter" and Tate's "Ode to the Confederate Dead," to choose their most well-known and highly rated works, are by the standards of early Middle Generation poetry riddled with flaws. Although both poems are about the Middle Generation's major themes, mortality and the mystery of time, they treat those themes quite differently than an early Middle Generation poem would. They are contemplative where they should be vigorous, exquisite where they should be dazzling, sensitive where they should be learned. Rather than seeking, in Eliot's words, to "amalgamate disparate experience," Ransom and Tate seek to capture a single straightforward experience. Furthermore, although Ransom and Tate control emotions in these poems, they do not escape it; reading the poems, one suspects them to be based on the poets' own thoughts and feelings about genuine personal experiences, and not to be descriptions of imagery events contrived for effect. The poems, although beautifully intelligent, are not intellectual experiences in the way that the early poems of the Middle Generation are. For in Ransom and Tate's poems, the mind of man seems unimportant; death comes to us in spite of our intellectual capabilities. In early Middle Generation poetry, such a sentiment would be very much out of place.

For in their early period, the Middle Generation poets considered the writing of poetry a veritable act of the ordering will, by which the various dissonances of real life were brought into harmony. Poetry existed to amalgamate the disparate, to render the disunity of the world into unity; and among the things which the Middle Generation poets most actively sought to bring together were past and present. A sense of helplessness in the face of time is not completely absent from early Middle Generation poetry, but it is invariably accompanied by some suggestion that through an act of will, time can be vanquished, or at least understood and come to terms with. In a dialogue poem by Schwartz, a father says to his son that he, the son, can stop time. How? By not ignoring it; by standing in "mastery" of it, by "keeping time in you, its terrifying mystery."[8]

Mastery is a key word here. For the early poems of the Middle Generation, with their continual yet unemotional references to time, cannot be understood except as the work of men who felt that by subverting their personal fear of death and writing about time with dispassion and acceptance, they could in some way transcend it. Not for them, in these early years, the hysterical outcries of the helpless

Romantic poet unhinged by and unable to acquiesce in his mortality; rather, the self-possessed musings of a poet-philosopher who, by the very fact that he is considering time not on an emotional but on an intellectual plane, feels that he has accomplished some sort of victory.

A good example of such an early Middle Generation poem is Schwartz's "Sonnet: The Ghosts of James and Peirce in Harvard Yard." Ransom and Tate's contemplation of a still, serene death is nowhere in evidence here. Death hops nervously from line to line, from time frame to time frame, in an ingenious Metaphysical conceit by which Schwartz suggests the universality of death in this complex, mysterious world. Death, the poem tells us, takes not only James and Peirce, who died in the past, but "the poor . . . across the sea" who are dying at present. As for the future, death will eventually come to the speaker, who walks "between heaven and hell." The clanging chapel bell, as a symbol of death, recalls a line from Donne, the master of the Metaphysical conceit: "never send to know for whom the bell tolls; it tolls for thee." Donne's theme is Schwartz's too; and like Donne he does not attempt to communicate through the feelings but through the intellect. Like many early Middle Generation poems, "Sonnet" contains ghosts of the dead which represent the speaker's intense consciousness of the past, and shadows of the living, which suggest their mortality. As in many early Middle Generation poems, the theme is stated bluntly at the end: "Ignorant, you walk between heaven and hell."[9]

Jarrell's poem "On the Railway Platform" also attempts to communicate an intellectual apprehension of the universality of death. We are all, the poem tells us, moving helplessly in time ("journeys are journeys").[10] Like Schwartz's poem, "On the Railway Platform" does not attempt to convey this theme to the reader through the feelings but through the intellect; it does not aim to make the reader feel the anguish, the helplessness of being trapped in time, but rather to make his mind comprehend the experience by being forced to keep up with the developing conceit.

Another early Middle Generation poem in which time and mortality are examined with Metaphysical ingeniousness and dispassion is Berryman's "The Statue." Here, as in the previously mentioned poems by Schwartz and Jarrell, the poet speaks as if from a metaphysical mountaintop from which, independent of time, he can survey past, present, and future simultaneously. In "The Statue," the figure from the past is present not, like James and Peirce, as a ghost, but as a statue. As James and Peirce haunt Harvard Yard, reminders of mortality, so Humboldt haunts the park.[11] Joel Conarroe has complained that in this poem Berryman requires "that a particular image carry too heavy a metaphysical weight." Whether or not we feel that this is true of this particular poem, it is clear that such a danger hangs over any poet who writes poems like these. The bestowal of too heavy a metaphysical weight upon a single image is the natural consequence of a conscious search for objective correlatives, of an insistence upon beginning with the theme and then trying to work up the perfect details to convey it. Conarroe also complains of "The Statue" that to a reader "the mood of wise resignation and world-weariness is difficult to share."[12] But it is a mistake to think that the principal point of this poem is to communicate through the feelings. All three of these poems are, among other things, intellectual exercises. Like a pianist's étude, they are intended, in large part, to demonstrate skill and versatility; they are meant to show that the poet fulfills Eliot's premier qualification for the ideal poet, that he be very intelligent. Rather than feelings, these poems are meant to convey intellectual perspectives, the whole mind's view of the whole world.

Placing these Middle Generation poems alongside the poems of such American contemporaries as Ransom and Tate clarifies the distinction between what the latter achieved and what the former were aiming at. These Middle Generation poems avoid, at every turn, the opportunity to be simple or straightforward; they seek out disparate experiences to amalgamate; they attempt to exclude the poet and his personal life and feelings as fully as possible. Though other poets may have made use of the ideas and terminology of Eliot's essays to explain their practices, to the Middle Generation poets such expressions as impersonality, the objective correlative, and the dissociation of sensibility were not merely useful locutions but dogma, even revelation. They were the rules by which the Middle Generation poets, in their early period, conducted their careers. Eliot advocated difficult poetry, so they wrote difficult poetry; he said a poet had to be intelligent, so they tried to sound intelligent; he said the concern of poetry should not be the poet's present feelings and personal history, but Western culture and the history of man, so they aimed for complete impersonality. And when, in his essay on "The Metaphysical Poets," Eliot offered up the following lines from Donne's "A Valediction: Of Weeping" as an example of first-rate poetry, they responded.

> On a round ball
> A workman that hath copies by, can lay
> An Europe, Afrique, and an Asia,
> And quickly make that, which was nothing, *All*,
> So doth each teare,
> Which thee doth weare,
> A globe, yea, world by that impression grow,
> till thy tears mixt with mine doe overflow
> This world, by waters sent from thee, my heaven
> dissolvèd so.

Eliot's admiration for these lines is founded on his conviction that in them, we find not only "the elaboration (contrasted with the condensation) of a figure of speech to the furthest stage to which ingenuity can carry it," but "a development by rapid association of thought which requires considerable agility on the part of the reader." Such a conceit, Eliot comments, is an example of "material compelled into unity by the operation of the poet's mind." Such a vision of unity was, of course, the ultimate goal of the Middle Generation poets in their early phase. Thus it is not surprising that in their poems of this period we find nearly plagiaristic examples of imitation of this very Donne conceit. Schwartz's "The Ballad of the Children of the Czar," for example, is clearly intended as an exercise in the elaboration of a figure of speech to the farthest stage to which ingenuity can carry it. The poem is concerned with amalgamating the disparate, with drawing connections between this place and that, between past and present. Schwartz once characterized Eliot's chief theme as "the fate of western culture and the historical sense"; this, plainly, is the subject of "The Ballad of the Children of the Czar." It is the poem of an ardent disciple of Eliot. What makes this poem particularly notable, however, is that Schwartz amplifies Eliot's theme by means of a conceit based on one which Eliot had praised. As Donne, in "A Valediction: Of Weeping," connects three round objects, a ball, a tear, and the earth, Schwartz connects six: a ball, a baked potato, a barrel, the earth, the moon, and the sun.[13] Schwartz's aim here is clearly, in Eliot's words, "the elaboration . . . of a figure of speech to the farthest stage to which ingenuity can carry it." Quantity, in other words, is quality. If connecting three round objects is brilliant, then connecting six is doubly brilliant. Jarrell does essentially the same thing in "Eine Kleine Nachtmusik." It may not be clear, on a first reading of this poem, that meandering through it is an extended metaphor along the same lines as the ones in "A Valediction: Of Weeping" and "The Ballad of the Children of the Czar." Again we have a series of round objects subtly connected to one another: the earth ("that sick dream the waking call a world"); tears; eyes; an egg; a "sleep-swollen face."[14] Berryman does the same thing a bit more blatantly in "The Ball Poem." The round objects literally present here are a ball, a dime, and a boy's "desperate eyes"; those whose presence is suggested include the sun ("light returns to the street") and the male gonads ("there are other balls," suggesting that one day the boy will reach puberty and his interests will change).[15] Finally, Lowell develops the same sort of conceit in "The Ferris Wheel." Nearly every object in its two stanzas is round: the ferris wheel, the "townsman's humorous and bulging eye," the world (and the circular course on which it is "racing"), the circus hoops, the curled tail, and the hangman's noose.[16]

All four of these poems owe their existence to Eliot's conspicuous praise for Donne's lines from "A Valediction: Of Weeping." What is important about this imitation is that these poets are doing more than simply adopting from another poet a figure of speech which they find arresting. That would not be at all remarkable; that is how poets work up their own bags of tricks, by dipping into the bags of other poets. The Middle Generation poets are doing something far more telling here; they are adhering, as closely as they can, to the instructions in writing modern poetry set forth by yet another poet, Eliot. His notions of what poetry is, of what it is for, and of what the poet should write about, formed theirs. Indeed, it might well be argued that their early poetry reflects those notions far more faithfully than Eliot's own verse does. This is remarkable; and it is the chief identifying mark of all four Middle Generation poets in their early period.

5

Schwartz, the Paradigm

A good place to begin the close study of the influence of Eliot upon early Middle Generation poetry is Delmore Schwartz's *In Dreams Begin Responsibilities*. This book, the first to be published by a member of the Middle Generation, is something of a paradigm, a keynote volume. When it came out in 1938, none of the other poets had yet published a single poem. Schwartz's success with the book drew their attention, and they followed his example. A fine distinction should be made here. Jarrell, Berryman, and Lowell did not become Schwartz's followers; but it may be said that he showed them whom to follow, and how, if they didn't already know.

In Dreams begins with the famous title story which had first brought Schwartz to the attention of the literary community, and it ends with a play, *Doctor Bergen's Belief*. But the reviewers, for the most part, chose to concentrate on the poetry that filled the pages between. And they came not to bury it, but to praise it. Allen Tate called Schwartz's poems "the first real innovation that we've had since Eliot and Pound," a particularly interesting comment when viewed from nearly half a century's distance, since today the poems in the volume seem more than anything else a testament to the influence of Eliot. Other critics, among them such important names as R. P. Blackmur, F. W. Dupee, Mark Van Doren, and Louise Bogan, added similar encomia. The cumulative effect was to establish Schwartz as the poet-to-watch of his generation. Examining these reviews, one is struck again and again by the curious nature of the praise which the critics accord to Schwartz; their excitement seems, in large measure, to be founded not upon the fact that Schwartz writes good poetry, but upon the fact that he writes the correct type of poetry—impersonal, allusive, concerned with Western civilization. That his poetry is indeed good seems to be important to these critics primarily because it serves to validate, in a way, that type of poetry. "What is in this book," Van Doren writes in the *Kenyon Review*, "is more important than anything personal could be." Bogan, in the *Nation*, concurs, calling Schwartz "a brilliant young man. He has touched all the influences." George Marion O'Donnell, in *Poetry*, begins his review this way: "Delmore Schwartz's *In Dreams Begin Responsibilities* is one of those rare first books that oblige an immediate recognition of their genuineness as poetry. Indeed, no first book of this decade in American poetry has been more authoritative or more significant than this one."

And why is it significant? Because, like Eliot's poetry, it is perfect raw material for what, two years later, Cleanth Brooks would call the New Criticism. And as quickly as possible—indeed, in his second paragraph—O'Donnell starts performing a New Critical analysis of Schwartz's work:

> Both in the longer works and in the lyrics, Mr. Schwartz's strategy depends upon a particular kind of poetic tension which is central to it and which seems to me characteristic of the 1930s. To show the nature of this strategy, it will be necessary to look directly at one of Mr. Schwartz's poems. Consider, for example, the one beginning: [He quotes the first four lines of "In the Naked Bed"] In the first line. . . .[1]

And so on. Schwartz is a great poet, O'Donnell is telling us, because his "strategy" depends upon something that requires a critic "to look directly" at one of his poems.

Thus, to a large degree, the success of *In Dreams* was a matter of luck; it was the right thing at the right time. The New Critics were waiting for a member of Schwartz's generation to produce a good volume of Eliotic poetry. For if the literary community could be convinced that the generation's first innovation in poetry had been brought about by a disciple of Eliot, and that the poems constituting that innovation could only be appreciated by applying the New Criticism to them, it would be a great leap forward for Tate and Ransom's cause. Conversely, for Tate and Ransom to give Schwartz's first book bad reviews would have done them no good. If they panned *In Dreams*, they would be fueling the fires for those few critics who disparaged *In Dreams* for exactly those qualities that its admirers commended—its allusiveness, ambiguity, indirection, intelligence, impersonality, and audacious taking on of imposing themes. I am not suggesting that these critics' opinions about the book played no part in their decision to give it the importance they did; certainly they would not have determined to gather together and sing hosannas to a third-rate work. But it seems likely that, for their own reasons, these critics chose to focus attention upon a book to which, under other circumstances, they would have paid somewhat less attention.

I do not mean by this to disparage the poems of *In Dreams*, but merely to put their phenomenal critical success in perspective. For the critics' magnification of Schwartz's accomplishment in his first book, and his admirers' agreement as to the nature of that accomplishment, are jointly responsible for the common conception that Schwartz's later work represents a falling-off from the promise of *In Dreams*.

Most of the poems in *In Dreams* concern Eliot's chief poetic theme, which Schwartz described as "the fate of western culture and the historical sense." "Coriolanus and His Mother," which at sixty-odd pages occupies more than a third of the book, is dominated by a dialogue between Freud and Marx, Schwartz's two major nonliterary touchstones of the modern sensibility. The poem announces its theme almost too brazenly in the opening lines, which establish the setting as a theater in which five ghosts, Freud and Marx among them, are awaiting the beginning of a show. Then the curtain ascends, revealing "the heart of man," and on a backdrop we see the war-torn arena of history, "world without end of hatred." In a few lines the author has made his poetic mission clear. He means to write about intellectual matters; he means to be impersonal and difficult; he means to say something, not about his own personal experience, but about modern life and Western civilization.

Granted, the poem does reflect Schwartz's personal concerns. The relationship between Coriolanus and his mother Volumnia in Schwartz's poem is clearly based on that between Delmore and Rose Schwartz. In a prose section of the work, Volumnia tells Coriolanus, "You cannot depart from me. You are nothing apart from me, you do not exist without me."[2] Obviously this is not Volumnia of Rome speaking, it is Rose Schwartz of Brooklyn. Yet what is remarkable in this long work is not Schwartz's interest in his private problems, but his compulsion to conceal the personal relevance of his theme. Here is a poet, clearly, who is moved to write poetry by a desire to express his feelings about personal matters; but he has committed himself, for reasons that seem to him good ones, to a type of poetry which requires that he keep himself, for the most part, out of his verse.

"Coriolanus and His Mother" derives, of course, from Shake-

speare, and Schwartz could hardly have picked a model more congenial to Eliot. The Elizabethan is mentioned approvingly in both
"Tradition and the Individual Talent" and "The Metaphysical Poets"
as an example of a poet who does things the way Eliot likes them
done. From the entire canon of Shakespeare, no play could have
served Schwartz, or any Eliotic poet, better than the relatively obscure *Coriolanus*, which Eliot rated higher, in relation to Shakespeare's
other plays, than perhaps any other critic in history. One of the
things that "Hamlet and His Problems" is notable for is Eliot's
audacious statement that *"Coriolanus* may not be as 'interesting' as
Hamlet, but it is, with *Antony and Cleopatra,* Shakespeare's most
assured artistic success."[3] Does Schwartz's appropriation of *Coriolanus* require any further explanation?

The other poems of *In Dreams* are comparatively short, most of
them no more than a page long. Even the seemingly most personal
poems are, when one examines them closely, not really personal at
all. Perhaps the best known such poem is "In the Naked Bed, in
Plato's Cave," one of Schwartz's two or three most anthologized
works in verse. The speaker in this poem is not so much a real man in
a real room as he is an archetypal man facing a philosophical dilemma
common to all mankind. As Ellmann observes, the first line of
Schwartz's poem—which is identical to the title—"forces us to consider each detail of this early-morning meditation in the light of
Plato's great allegory of the dualism of appearance and reality." Thus,
although the poem may owe its existence to Schwartz's insomnia and
the sense of alienation which that condition aggravated, his concern
in this poem is to depict the speaker not as an isolated sufferer but as
a representative man whose experience has universal significance.
"In the Naked Bed," then, is not about one man's insomnia but about
"the mystery of beginning / Again and again," the speaker's awareness of which is heightened by his sleeplessness.[4] This mystery is, of
course, an equally important concern in *The Waste Land,* from which
Schwartz takes the phrase "son of man." The phrase is originally
from the second chapter of Ezekiel, in which God commands Ezekiel
to present himself to the children of Israel, who "shall know that
there hath been a prophet among them." In Ezekiel 37, in the valley of
the dry bones, God asks Ezekiel, "Son of man, can these bones live?"
Ezekiel replies, "O Lord God, thou knowest." In both contexts, the
words "son of man" are associated with the knowledge of the
mystery of life and death which God may choose to bestow upon

man. The phrase is thus particularly useful to Eliot in *The Waste Land* ("Son of man, / You cannot say or guess . . ."), where it serves to emphasize ironically the inability of the would-be prophet in a godless modern world to explain the mystery of life and death.[5] In "In the Naked Bed," Schwartz uses the phrase in exactly the same way: "O son of man, the ignorant night . . . / . . . the mystery of beginning / Again and again." Thus, in three words, Schwartz manages to suggest his thematic affinity to Eliot. It is a method which he learned from Eliot himself. But this is not the only echo of Eliot in "In the Naked Bed." For the last words of Schwartz's poem, "History is unforgiven," refer obliquely to these lines of "Gerontion":

> After such knowledge, what forgiveness?
> Think now
> History has many cunning passages . . .[6]

This parallel between Eliot and Schwartz, besides illustrating both poets' preoccupation with history, demonstrates that the theme of forgiveness is one that the Middle Generation poets share with Eliot. Finally, "In the Naked Bed" may derive directly from the third of Eliot's "Preludes." Like "In the Naked Bed," this poem concerns a sleepless night in a grubby room overlooking a city street; its sixth line ("They flickered against the ceiling") is echoed directly in the seventh line of Schwartz's poem ("The ceiling lightened again"). Like the Schwartz poem, it presents us not with a real individual but with an Everyman, and aims to achieve a timeless, universal vision of human life.[7]

Schwartz's lifelong preoccupation with Eliot began in his teen years. By age seventeen Schwartz was collecting first editions of Eliot, and at George Washington High School was so tiresome, apparently, on the subject of the artistic supremacy of Eliot that the editors of the yearbook inscribed under Schwartz's picture the sentence, "T. S. Eliot is God, and Delmore Schwartz is his prophet." In his early years as a writer, Schwartz referred to Eliot as "the greatest living literary critic" and brought a story, "Screeno," to a climax by having the protagonist read from "Gerontion," a work by "the best of modern poets." Schwartz, who, as Atlas says, was "always shy in the company of those he most respected," admired Eliot so much that he could not bring himself to meet the famous expatriate. He was able to converse casually with Auden and Stevens, and carried on a lively, unrestrained correspondence with Pound, in which he offered blunt, unselfconscious criticism. But Eliot awed him. A letter from Eliot praising *In Dreams* was his most prized possession. Even Eliot's brother, Henry Ware Eliot, was too closely related to Schwartz's god to be dealt with comfortably and, according to Atlas, "terrified him almost as much as Eliot himself." Combined with this profound regard for Eliot, however, was an equally profound resentment and jealousy. Schwartz seems to have made an avocation of collecting, inventing, and disseminating malicious gossip about the poet-critic.[8]

This seemingly paradoxical attitude is reflected in two of Schwartz's three published essays about Eliot, "T. S. Eliot as the International Hero" (1945) and "The Literary Dictatorship of T. S. Eliot" (1949). As the titles indicate, Schwartz takes two very different positions in these essays. The "Hero" essay extols Eliot, claiming that

> The width and the height and the depth of modern life are exhibited in his poetry. . . . Eliot cannot help but be concerned with the whole world and all history. . . . The true causes of many of the things in our lives are world-wide, and we are able to understand the character of our lives only when we are aware of all history, of the philosophy of history, of primitive peoples and the Russian Revolution, of ancient Egypt and the unconscious mind.[9]

The essay, in short, is something of a rewrite of "Tradition and the Individual Talent."

Schwartz defends Eliot's deliberate integration of characters and situations from the past with those of the present, saying that, for example, describing "the seduction of a typist in a London flat from the point of view of Tiresias" in *The Waste Land* "illuminates the seduction of the typist just as much as a description of her room." Likewise, "the plight of Prufrock is illuminated by means of a rich, passing reference to Michelangelo, the sculptor of the strong and heroic man. Only when the poet is the heir of all the ages can he make significant use of so many different and distant kinds of experience." This apologia for Eliot, of course, can also be read as a defense of Schwartz's own poetic practice of the time; for the integration of characters and situations from the past with those of the present was a favorite device of the Middle Generation poets during their early period.

The "Dictatorship" essay, published a mere four years later, takes a substantially different tack. First of all, one must keep in mind that in 1949 no sensitive American writer would use the word dictatorship lightly or admiringly or even ironically; Hitler and Mussolini were still fresh in the memory, and Stalin still very much alive. In this essay, Schwartz accuses his erstwhile hero of inconsistency; Eliot, he charges, had by 1934 "contradicted, modified, or qualified" almost everything he had written in "The Metaphysical Poets." This inexcusable tergiversation leads Schwartz, apparently, to question whether someone like Eliot has the right to mold critical opinion in the first place; "it might be desirable," Schwartz suggests, "to have no literary dictators."[10] Why, Schwartz asks, should this man's changeable prejudices determine ours?

It is a fascinating essay which tells us a lot about Eliot but even more about Schwartz. How revealing it is to see Schwartz denouncing Eliot for being unfaithful to Eliot; and to see Schwartz, Eliot's number one disciple, chiding everybody for being an Eliot disciple. Coming as it does in 1949, the essay may indicate that Schwartz was already beginning to soften toward the Romantic conception of poetry that characterized his later period, and to harden toward the Eliotic principles that guided him in his early period. But reading the essay one perceives that Schwartz's upcoming poetic metamorphosis does not really explain what is going on here. For in this essay Schwartz is not rejecting Eliot's ideas about poetry; on the contrary, he is defending them—from Eliot himself. It is not so much that Schwartz is approaching the end of his apostolate, but that he is in the thick of his obsession, an obsession that involves the most contradictory, seemingly paradoxical emotions toward the great critic. To Schwartz, Eliot was simultaneously hero and nemesis. As he at once harbored feelings of intense love and deep resentment toward his late father, so he had the same confusing mixture of feelings about Eliot.

Some of Schwartz's most obviously Eliot-inspired poems from the *In Dreams* period are unpublished. For example, among Schwartz's papers are the following lines which date from the 1930s. I have indicated the poet's own emendations:

>   grey
> O   ~~vague~~ morning is
> ~~My~~ dark uneasy one, how ~~uncertain~~ is morning
> Its oyster-grey sky pink but dabbed,
> Come, I have shut the motor off, come,
> On the cold white table of the cafeteria
> We will drink coffee and look at each other.[11]

In the margin of this poem, in Schwartz's own hand, adjacent to the lines containing the references to "the motor" and "the cafeteria," is the comment: "striving for modern particulars." But we do not need a gloss to recognize the poet's attempt, in these lines, to sound like a younger T. S. Eliot. The move from "uncertain" to "vague" to "grey" represents his desire to be less direct in communicating the idea that the morning is uncertain—that is, to be ambiguous about ambiguity. The colors—grey, pink, white—are a device Eliot and the Symbolist poets favored. Of course, the opening lines of this poem call to mind Eliot's "Love Song of J. Alfred Prufrock."[12] The imitation takes almost everything from the original. In both poems, the speaker addresses someone, perhaps an unidentified companion, perhaps the reader, whom he beckons repeatedly in a sedate, mysterious, somehow hypnotic imperative ("Let us go . . . Let us go"; "Come . . . come"). Tension is created by juxtaposing the sky, a traditional poetic staple and a reminder of the eternal things, and contemporary, unpoetic imagistic details. In both poems the main point seems to be the speaker's alienation in the modern world, his inability to communicate with anyone successfully. Even the diction is deliberately, and gratuitously, imitative; why, except to point up the imitation, would Schwartz find it necessary to use the word oyster? And why write a line like "We will drink coffee and look at each other" if not to echo the line from *The Waste Land*, "And drank coffee, and talked for an hour"? Even the rhythm in the first two lines is similar.

One's first inclination, upon coming across such lines, is to suppose that they were not meant to be taken as actual original poetry; perhaps, one guesses, they were simply a mechanical exercise in imitation, never meant to be read by anyone—part of an apprentice poet's self-education, like Benjamin Franklin's copying out lines from Addison and Steele. Or perhaps they were a parody. But a comprehensive examination of Schwartz's early work quickly disabuses one of such notions; for similar passages fill Schwartz's early manuscripts. On virtually every page one finds lines, phrases, and passages which evoke some poem or poems by Eliot. Who can read

> And when will I begin again?
> And when will I begin again?

without thinking of the line from "Prufrock,"

> And how should I begin?

or, from "Ash Wednesday,"

> Because I do not hope to turn again
> Because I do not hope
> Because I do not hope to turn[13]

Most of the imitation of Eliot in Schwartz's early poetry is more subtle than this. It is, in fact, more a matter of substance than of sound. Schwartz's introduction to his autobiographical poem *Genesis* (1943) is enlightening in this regard. Nowhere in the three pages of these prefatory remarks does he so much as mention Eliot's name. But that poet's presence hangs over these pages, and, for that matter, over the poem that follows, like a scorching white sun over a stretch of the Sahara. Schwartz's introduction begins with a few words in the terse, authoritative, self-consciously modest style of Eliot's major criticism: "This is the first part of a work which is finished. I think that it can be read as a part which is interesting in itself. I would like to try to remove some of the preconceptions and 'habitual expectations' which would condemn the formal character of the whole work." Schwartz goes on to say that "the use of prose and verse in the same work is nothing new or strange if one remembers the Bible and the Elizabethan play"; "the use of a chorus of commentators ought to be seen as the same kind of thing as the chorus in a Greek drama." And so forth. He pretends to be apologizing, while he is actually congratulating himself for having such a wide field of reference. This introduction, clearly, is his substitute for the notes at the end of *The Waste Land*. And jumping from one form to another, as Schwartz does in *Genesis*, is of course something that Eliot does in *The Waste Land*.

Indeed, Eliot's great poem of 1922 is the only poem Schwartz mentions by name in this introduction. "No author of modern times," he writes,

> can assume a community of ideas and values between himself and his audience. Hence he must bring in his ideas and values openly and clearly. This necessity has shown itself many times in modern literature, but I cite one example because it is the inspiration of the form of much that I have written, the seduction scene in *The Waste Land*, which occurs in modern London, but in which the poet finds it necessary to bring in Tiresias from ancient Greece, to comment and to judge.

This is the second time we have seen Schwartz cite the Tiresias episode as an important influence on his poetry. The importance of this episode to Schwartz is manifestly due to the fact that here the doctrines of "Tradition and the Individual Talent" are most memorably, most succinctly, and most effectively put into practice. Tiresias, in *The Waste Land*, is Eliot's own best example of how a comprehensive historical sense can benefit the poet and enrich his poetry.

Schwartz's apologia for his formal predilections in *Genesis*, which like *The Waste Land* is about the modern urban alien, might have been written by Eliot himself.

> I do not understand the extreme aversion expressed for this use of chorus and commentary. What is this hatred of the effort to paint the struggles of the understanding, to show the intelligence striving to understand and evaluate experience? Such is the compulsion, so much is this need a part of modern life, that I cannot but think and hope that many other literary works will seek forms and modifications of old forms which will strive to go further and do better what is done here and has been done often before.

This modus operandi, in which the words intelligence and experience figure so prominently, is clearly straight out of "The Metaphysical Poets." Given this fact, it is not surprising that in the next paragraph Schwartz declares his attempt, in the present work, to imitate certain aspects of Donne and Webster and the French Symbolists, all of whom receive Eliot's approbation in that critical essay. Nor, after all this, is it surprising that Schwartz ends his introduction to *Genesis*, "I hope that there is in this work some truth about all human beings: *Hypocrite lecteur!—mon semblable!—mon frère!*"[14] The French quotation is from Baudelaire's *Fleurs du mal*, but it is more familiar to most English-speaking readers from its appearance in *The Waste Land*, where it closes the first section, "The Burial of the Dead." That Schwartz uses it as an envoi to this first portion of *Genesis* may be a last subtle suggestion on his part that this work is intended to be Schwartz's *Waste Land*, his attempt to render not merely his own experiences and emotions but the "truth about all human beings."

There are other obvious similarities between *Genesis* and *The Waste Land*. Both poems evolved over a long period of time; both represented, to some extent, a bringing-together of fragments of various uncompleted antecedent works. Moreover, Schwartz seems to have written *Genesis* with the hope that it, like *The Waste Land*, would be the definitive poetic work of its day, and was crushed when it failed to fulfill this dream. Indeed, it may well have been that with the failure of *Genesis*, Schwartz began to recognize that he would not succeed in the way that Eliot had; further, that such success was a foolish goal anyway; further yet, that trying to write like anyone else was foolish; and finally, that to try to write like Eliot might be particularly foolish for him, because his strongest poetic gifts and inclinations were perhaps of a different sort than Eliot's.

If any single work of the Middle Generation's early period may be said to demonstrate these facts, it is *Genesis*. Like "Coriolanus and His Mother," it attempts to deal with Schwartz's real and powerful emotions about his childhood; but, as with "Coriolanus and His Mother," one comes away with very little in the way of an emotional reaction. *Genesis* is, indeed, not an emotional but an intellectual experience. Schwartz, his tone half Bible and half *Waste Land*, his form a learned hybrid of blank verse and "poetic prose," sets forth the simple, genuinely pathetic story of his childhood like a fragile brocade stretched out to dry in the gentle breeze; then he proceeds to pile the biggest names in history upon it. Cervantes, Euripides, and Socrates climb on; they are joined in short order by Freud, Blake, Dante, Dumas, Shakespeare, and many others. It is as if Schwartz is trying to cover up the delicate, distinctive designs on his brocade, to take the Romantic sting off his material with the balm of classical names. Rather than concentrate on bringing to life the pathos of his childhood experiences, Schwartz mythologizes his childhood self. He describes every event of his childhood as if it were not merely personally painful but profoundly tragic and universally significant. His Hershey Green is not a real child but a representative boy, a waif amid forces, an "Atlantic Jew" through whose life move "the divinities"—America, Europe, capitalism. Clearly Schwartz is trying, in *Genesis*, to reconcile the notion of writing a poem about his personal life and feelings with the tenets of Eliot, which demand that the poem be an intellectual contemplation of the variety and complexity of modern civilization. What Schwartz ends up with is a pastiche that accomplishes very little poetically, one way or the other. What might have been a lyrical evocation of childhood becomes a pretentious grab-bag of allusions; for example, the narrator, at one point, brings in Rousseau in connection with the concept of childhood innocence, and says of Rousseau and other "Captains of the modern age" that they are now in the company of Buddha, Lao-Tsze, and Augustine. "I hardly understand your irony," says Hershey Green, who is all of six years old. Granted, the poem is obviously not supposed to be realistic; but then, it is sometimes difficult to tell what it is supposed to be. Schwartz is, it seems, such an unregenerate Eliotic poet at this point that, although he wanted nothing more than to write a poem that would express his feelings about childhood, he managed to write one which has very little feeling in it at all. Everything has been intellectualized; one man's childhood experience has been twisted beyond recognition into a gigantic objective correlative for a comprehensive, if jumbled, set of ideas about life and death in the modern world; the boy's feelings of pain and alienation have been subsumed by the adult's, the poet's, conscious attempt to amalgamate disparate experience, to form new wholes. The ultimate aim of *Genesis*, in fact, seems to be to express the unity of all experience. Thus, on the last of the poem's 208 pages, Schwartz writes that all things take place "in the mind of God."[15] The problem with writing a poem like *Genesis* according to the dicta set forth in Eliot's essays is, of course, that the material of *Genesis* is not the kind best suited to the methods of an intellectual poet. Memories from childhood have very little to do with the intellect. To introduce such concepts as are associated with the names that Schwartz pours into *Genesis* is to falsify the experience of childhood.

But of course, Schwartz could hardly do any differently in these early years. He was an intellectual poet, an Eliotic poet, and to such a man poetry is more than just feelings laid bare. Eliot had said of his ideal poet, "the more intelligent he is, the better." Writing in his journal, Schwartz agreed: "the secret of success is genius." He was a man obsessed with his private agonies, but dedicated to a doctrine of poetry which forbade their expression. It was an interesting situation, but hardly unique. For Jarrell, Berryman, and Lowell followed the same pattern.[16]

Jarrell and the Influence of Auden

Randall Jarrell's early poetry is perhaps more impersonal, in one sense, than that of Schwartz, Berryman, or Lowell. Hardly a single poem in Jarrell's early volumes, the predominant subject of which is a war in which he did not participate, can conceivably be based upon the poet's feelings about his own experiences. Wherever, in these volumes, there are discernible characters and clearly defined situations and settings, they are, for the most part, far removed from Jarrell's real life. His contribution to *Five Young American Poets* (1940) includes poems in which he imagines a train full of refugees ("The Refugees"), a forest full of dead soldiers ("The Automaton"), and a Spanish road where Loyalist gunners have died ("For the Madrid Road"). *Blood for a Stranger* (1942) reprints many of these poems and adds one ("London") about a city Jarrell had never seen, and another ("For an Emigrant") which is a virtual travelogue of places Jarrell had never visited. In *Little Friend, Little Friend* (1945) are poems set in a German port city ("Angels at Hamburg") and a Russian port city ("Protocols"); in *Losses* (1948), poems set in a prisoner of war camp ("Stalag Luft") and in Melanesia ("The Dead in Melanesia"). And the list goes on. The speakers in these poems range from a dead American soldier ("New Georgia") to a live German soldier who escorts prisoners of war ("A Camp in the Prussian Forest"); from the wife of an American pilot ("Burning the Letters") to a European Jew arriving in Palestine after the Holocaust ("Jews at Haifa").

Indeed, sometimes it seems that nearly everyone is here except Jarrell himself. An average reader would hardly believe that all this poetry about bombed cities and battlefields, concentration camps and refugee trains, was written by a man whose only trip outside North America during the 1940s was to a literary conference in Salzburg in

1948. Clearly Jarrell heeded the dictum of Eliot's "Tradition and the Individual Talent": "Impressions and experiences which are important for the man may take no place in the poetry, and those which become important in the poetry may play quite a negligible part in the man, the personality."

The early poems of Jarrell adhere with equal fidelity to the tenets of "The Metaphysical Poets." Jarrell's early poetry often seems designed, above all else, to reveal the underlying connections that belie the seeming chaos of the world. So intent is he on the universal perspective, as opposed to the personal, that one often senses that Jarrell considers the individual emotional experience to be misleading and even unreal; that real truth, to his mind, can be glimpsed only by going beyond the individual and seeing the large picture. One of Jarrell's early poems, "When You and I Were All," more or less says this directly. The poem's speaker refers to a time when he was caught up in a romantic relationship which made time appear to stand still. But Jarrell introduces this pretty romantic formula only to negate it. For the speaker goes on to say that this sense of stopped time was an illusion, and once that illusion faded, he and his lover recognized that they were involved with the world. The bells, they realized, tolled for them, and their acts "were sodden with acts' common end." In Eliot's words, Jarrell is here compelling material into unity. Our way, his speaker is saying, is the way of all flesh; our end is the common end. We are merely part of a greater whole, and it is self-delusion to think otherwise. Such Eliotic recognition of the connections between seemingly disconnected persons, places, and events takes place in many other early Jarrell poems. "The Soldier" ends with lines that suggest a cause-and-effect relation between the deaths of soldiers and financial events in Germany and Manchester. And "Because of Me, Because of You . . ." begins by saying that various events—cosmic, human, cellular—took place "because of me, because of you."[1]

Jarrell also seems to make an effort in his early poetry to demonstrate that he has that necessary asset of the Eliotic poet, a highly developed historical sense. In "Port of Embarkation," a poem about soldiers departing for war, the speaker remarks that "The foolish ages haunt their unaccepting eyes" and calls the soldiers' bones "The coral of the histories." If one happens to detect an echo of Shakespeare in the latter phrase, it is, of course, from an Eliotic perspective, all to the better. "A Lullaby," a poem about a soldier whose life Jarrell describes as being "smothered like a grave, with dirt" by the barracks conditions and the rudeness of officers, ends with a reference to "The lying amber of the histories." Like Berryman's "The Statue," Jarrell's "The Head of Wisdom" invokes the past by describing a sculpture of a great historical figure—here, Beethoven. Finally, "Sears Roebuck" ends with lines that incorporate John Doe and Don Juan into Saint John the Divine, thus amalgamating three highly disparate figures representing the prosaic, the profane, and the pious aspects of man's nature.[2] But why, one may ask, does Jarrell have St. John the Divine order items from Sears? Because he learned from Eliot that this is the perfect way to introduce historical perspective, to force the reader to recognize our materialistic age, symbolized by Sears Roebuck, as the twilight of an era which dawned when John dwelled on Pátmos. These two lines from Jarrell are the direct descendants of that scene in *The Waste Land* in which Tiresias observes the typist's seduction. This scene, the influence of which upon his own work Schwartz makes a point of publicizing, is an equally strong influence upon Jarrell's early poetry.

Such learned allusions as these to St. John the Divine and Beethoven are as much a part of Jarrell's early poetry as they are of Schwartz's. As they sometimes seem ludicrously out of place in Schwartz, so they often seem out of place in Jarrell. Schwartz has a child, in *Genesis,* involved in a discussion of Swedenborg and Rimbaud; Jarrell, in "The See-er of Cities," has children musing about Goethe: " 'Great Goethe was a child,' the children think."[3]

If critics have anything to say about Jarrell's early poetry, it is usually that the influence of W. H. Auden is very noticeable. Indeed, all four Middle Generation poets have been described as having begun their careers as disciples of Auden. Conrad Aiken called Berryman and Jarrell's poems in *Five Young American Poets* "vin Audenaire"; James Laughlin called Schwartz "the American Auden"; and Jarrell was faulted by M. L. Rosenthal for having filled his early poetry with "Auden-static."[4] In certain specific ways, such characterizations of early Middle Generation poetry are valid. But in terms of their conception of poetry, and their thematic preoccupations, the Middle Generation poets were during their early period strict disciples of Eliot, to whom Auden's view of poetry was anathema.

Since critics generally fail to recognize the distinction between the early poetry of the Middle Generation, particularly of Jarrell, and the early poetry of Auden which is said to have influenced them, it is necessary to examine those distinctions at some length. Both early

Middle Generation poetry and early Auden poetry are impersonal, intellectual, and concerned with the current state of Western civilization. But while the Middle Generation poets viewed the world through a philosophical prism, Auden viewed it through a political prism. If a poem was to them a locus for metaphysical ideas, it was to Auden a locus for socioeconomic ideas. To Auden knowledge meant not metaphysical but moral awareness; and his morality, during his early years, had a decidedly Marxist orientation. Although no mere propagandist, he nevertheless clearly saw poetry as having, above all else, a social function. "Poetry," he wrote in *The Poet's Tongue*, "is not concerned with telling people what to do, but with extending our knowledge of good and evil, perhaps making the necessity for action more urgent and its nature more clear, but only leading us to the point where it is possible for us to make a rational and moral choice."[5] Such a concept of poetry was foreign to the Middle Generation poets. Poetry, to their minds, did not exist to clarify moral issues or to incite political action. Yes, they admired Marx, but as Atlas says of Schwartz, they prized the founder of socialism "less as a radical than as a determinist who had fashioned one of the great intellectual systems."[6] Auden was also an admirer of intellectual systems, but to his mind the intellectual system existed primarily for the practical benefit of the economic system. As he wrote once, recalling his ideological interests of the thirties: "we were interested in Marx in the same way that we were interested in Freud, as a technique of unmasking middle class ideologies, not with the intention of repudiating our class, but with the hope of becoming better bourgeois."[7] These thinkers were valuable, in other words, in exact proportion as they helped Auden to develop himself as a socioeconomic organism.

In their early poetry, the Middle Generation poets reveal an intense consciousness of the past, and make a point of bringing characters, settings, and situations from the past into conjunction with those of the present. Auden, as a poet, is interested in the relationship of the past and present, but in his thirties poems he consistently rejects anything tending toward an absorption in the past, and asserts the need of political revolutionaries to live in the present. In "Another Time," for example, he says: "It is to-day in which we live."[8] The second stanza of this poem might almost have been written about the Middle Generation poets during their early period. Many people attempt to say "Not Now": is this not an apt description of their obsessive incorporation of people and events from the past into their poems of the present? Many cannot remember "how / To say I Am": does this not reflect their readiness to write poetry according to someone else's narrow doctrines? Auden's poem ends with the line: "Another time has other lives to live." One cannot imagine Eliot, or any of the Middle Generation poets during their early period, writing such a line. They simply could not have assented to the notion that "It is to-day in which we live," with its implication that there is no way of comprehending the gap between now and then. And Auden, for his part, simply could not have shared their intense interest in the past, in the nature of time. Such metaphysical musings occupied a minor position in Auden's pantheon of concerns.

These distinctions between early Middle Generation poetry and Auden's early verse are reflected in the differences between Jarrell's and Auden's war poems. It is perhaps because of their mutual interest in this theme that Jarrell and Auden have been so often linked. But more enlightening than their common concern with war is the difference between their perspectives on this theme. Auden writes about World War II and its human victims because he wants to express his obsession with the present moment, his solidarity with the common man, and his conviction that evil inheres in the political status quo. Jarrell, in his war poetry, has different motives and concerns. He uses the war setting to make not timely political points, but statements about the human condition which transcend immediate political concerns. A brief examination of Auden's "Refugee Blues" and Jarrell's "The Refugees" demonstrates this contrast vividly. Written in March 1939, "Refugee Blues" announces to the world the poet's conviction that it is today in which we live.[9] Far from being deliberately difficult or trying to make a universal, timeless statement, the poem is about Hitler, Europe, the German Jews; it is as straightforward, as direct, as confined in its range of reference as possible. The poem may well have something to say about all wars throughout history, but this universal dimension does not serve to distract the reader's attention from the immediate public events that occasioned the poem. Rather, the poem is very firmly and vividly focused on those events, and on the unambiguous political theme which the poet extrapolates from them. Compare Jarrell's "The Refugees." That he chose to write a poem about refugees may well have a good deal to do with the influence of Auden. But the type of poem which Jarrell has written about refugees bears little resemblance to

Auden's work. The poet is clearly not interested in the particular political circumstances that occasioned the flight of these refugees from their homeland. They are archetypal refugees, the ultimate lesson of whose story, for Jarrell, is not a political, social, or economic one, but a metaphysical one. The main reason for Jarrell's interest in their plight is that it is reducible to an epistemological observation: "What else are their lives but a journey to the vacant / Satisfaction of death?"[10] Their situation, in other words, is a consciously contrived objective correlative for a universal philosophical conception. Far from wanting to make a political comment, the author of this poem wants to make a timeless statement about the nature of life.[11]

Thus the Middle Generation poets' conception of poetry during their early period was very different from Auden's. In what way, then, is their early poetry Audenesque? The influence is mainly stylistic. What the Middle Generation poets prized in Auden, and imitated in their early verse, was his language. Schwartz, in an early essay, cites Auden's "immense gift for language" as the saving grace from what Schwartz considered the elder poet's misguided ideas. And Jarrell, while caring that Auden, even in his best poems, was "bad at organization, neglectful of logic," commented that those same poems were "full of astonishing or magical language." This, by the way, from a poet-critic who in 1950 sneered that Auden's work of the past twenty years represented "a couple of decades of moralizing us to the top of our bent."[12]

It is, then, in their use of language during their early period that we find the most striking examples of Auden's influence upon the Middle Generation. Justin Replogle devotes a good portion of his book, _Auden's Poetry_, to discussing half a dozen or so of the most prominent characteristics of Auden's verse style. Each of these characteristics is also a hallmark of early Middle Generation poetry.

The first of these hallmarks is the tendency to animate concepts and objects—to personify. Personification is, of course, a common figure of speech, but it is uncommonly prominent in Auden. Replogle explains that Auden uses personification because his poetry deals so often with concepts, and personification gives "a 'charge' to a bare sentence filled with conceptual words." It bestows upon intellectual notions "a life and feelings lacking in their essential selves."[13]

The usefulness of personification to the Middle Generation poets during their early period is obvious. Although they did not deal in Auden's kind of ideas, they were nonetheless intellectual poets, generally concerned with the physical world only insofar as they could shape descriptions of it into objective correlatives that reflected a state of mind. It is not surprising, then, that Auden's heavy use of personification has a strong effect on them. In Schwartz's poetry, the heart is a medieval nobleman: "I am to my own heart merely a serf." Or it is a runner: "love exhausts itself and falls and time goes round." In Jarrell's poetry, "darkness / Sucks from the traveler his crazy kiss," "Love . . . gropes for the stranger," and "Time held his trembling hand." Berryman observes that "Time . . . cannot love old men" and that "Stillness locks a hundred rooms." Lowell's poetry contains a bell that grumbles, a cathedral that "lifts its eye," a heart that "race[s] and stagger[s] and demand[s]," and guns which, "cradled on the tide," choke out a "hoarse salute."[14]

Then there is Auden's habit of making short declarative statements which Replogle calls "descriptions." He refers to brief generalizations which "do not trace the qualitative aspects of an object, getting the feel of its sensory surfaces. Instead they discover its logical essence, the verbal classification that sets it apart from alien data and determines its place in the chain of being." Replogle offers these examples: "Wisdom is a beautiful bird"; "For time is inches"; "Touching is shaking hands." Replogle remarks that "these rhetorical practices are partly forced on Auden by his almost entirely conceptual diction." They also result partly from his desire to sound "Very Important."[15]

Again, this is something the Middle Generation poets copy for obvious reasons. Like Auden, they felt that poetry was a failure if it did not yield some truth, some knowledge. The "descriptions" which Replogle identifies in Auden's poetry are, quite often, poetic truths expressed as succinctly as possible. They are the poems' topic sentences, as it were. We find the same sort of thing in early Middle Generation poetry, used to the same purposes. Schwartz writes:

> The heart of man . . . is a cactus bloom.
>
> Love is inexhaustible, and full of fear.
>
> Love is the tact of every good. . . .

Note that this last one is also an example of personification. Jarrell's "descriptions" include the following:

> Tomorrow is death.
>
> . . . wisdom is more than knowing
> what we knew. . . .

Berryman's are often briefer: "Money is external"; "Disfigurement is general"; "Images are the mind's life, and they change."[16] Lowell, who in his early poetry almost never writes short declarative sentences at all, is the only Middle Generation poet whose early work is free of these short declarative "descriptions."

Replogle also points out Auden's "oratorical" syntax, particularly his habit of confounding the usual word order. "Here on the cropped grass of the narrow ridge I stand" is Replogle's example. We see such inversions in Jarrell's "The Bad Music"—"how many know or love at all / You, Anna?"—and in Berryman's "Caravan": "The lady . . . / / . . . prepares, / / Of son and daughter the careers."[17] Eliot had said, in "The Metaphysical Poets," that the modern poet must "force, . . . dislocate if necessary, language into his meaning." Such very noticeable locutions, clearly derived from Auden, equally clearly serve an Eliotic purpose. Linguistic disjunction, moreover, effectively suggests other types of disjunction—psychological, social, spiritual—all of which are relevant to the picture the Middle Generation poets paint of the contemporary world.

Auden's poetry contains disruptions not only of syntax but of sound. Auden, Replogle writes, "prefers collections of unlike sounds. . . . Pronouncing these, the mouth keeps changing shape." Replogle's examples are the following lines:

> In Breughel's *Icarus*, for instance: how everything turns away.
>
> For this and for all enclosures like it the archetype.[18]

Such writing, says Replogle, results from an "antipathy for the verbal music of assonance." Auden, according to Replogle, seemed to consider particularly harmonious sound patterns frivolous and found them useful only in humorous verse; the repetition of sounds to achieve "emotional intensity," particularly an intensity "that has little or nothing to do with the meaning of the repeated words," was apparently alien to him. Since in their early period the Middle Generation poets shared Auden's hostility toward the idea of poetry as mere meaningless music, it is not surprising that they followed his example, producing dissonant collocations of vocables which, if they are music, are closer to Wagner than to Mendelssohn.[19]

The antimusical tone, however, is only one of Auden's characteristic voices. Replogle, in his discussion of Auden's deliberately dissonant style, neglects to account for such Auden ballads as "O What is That Sound," the effect of which depends largely upon the counterpoint between the chilling theme and the lulling music of the verse.

Obviously, such Auden poems as this one suggested to the Middle Generation poets the usefulness of the ballad form in the hands of a modern, ironic poet, and are responsible for the form of such Middle Generation "ballads" as Berryman's "Communist," whose first line gives a good idea of the style and theme of the poem: "O tell me of the Russians, Communist, my son!"[20]

One stylistic habit which the Middle Generation borrowed from Auden is the repeated use of the word "O." In Auden's poems of the thirties, the device turns up constantly.[21] Replogle, commenting that Auden uses this device "to elevate the poet," finds it sometimes successful, sometimes not. "If some of these pass as decorative and unobtrusive, others seem arbitrary and rather unsuccessful attempts to raise the level of emotion and solemnity by simply sticking in that familiar symbol for emotional intensity, 'O.'" In other words, Auden sometimes forces the word "O" upon "nonoratorical sentences" to make them oratorical.[22] We find the same to be true in the work of the Middle Generation, whose early poems betray a wholesale appropriation of the "O" device. In some cases, it is used to good effect—for instance, in Schwartz's "The Ballad of the Children of the Czar" ("O Nicholas! Alas! Alas!"), Jarrell's "London" ("London, London, O where are you gone?"), Berryman's "Fare Well" ("O easy the phoenix in the tree of the heart . . ."), and Lowell's "The Drunken Fisherman" ("O wind blow cold, O wind blow hot . . .").[23] In other cases, it stands out and looks quite distracting and odd—for instance, in Schwartz's "Coriolanus and His Mother" ("O as / The leaning doctor listens"), Jarrell's "Song: Not There" ("To find it, O, I will look anywhere"), Berryman's "Boston Common: A Meditation Upon the Hero" ("Watching who labour O that all may see"), and Lowell's "New Year's Day" ("The Child is born in blood, O child of blood.").[24] To the Middle Generation poets, one suspects, the borrowing of Auden's invocational interjection was a convenient, one-syllable way of enriching a poem's sense of tradition while at the same time harmlessly indulging their repressed desire to be, not impersonal makers in conformance with the dicta of Eliot, but Romantic balladeers. Note too that the use of "O" before the name of a place, thing, or concept effectively personifies it, which is a rhetorical aim all four poets shared in their early period. "O little Charles," Schwartz writes, addressing the river in Boston.[25] Moreover, prefixing "O" to the name of a person from history, as in Schwartz's "O Nicholas! Alas! Alas!," is an easy means of enhancing the sense of past and present being

These are the respective beginnings of three of Eliot's essays: "The Metaphysical Poets," "The Music of Poetry," and "Dante."

Reading "A Note on Poetry," one recognizes further debts to Eliot. Like Schwartz, in the *Genesis* introduction, Berryman alludes to Donne and to Greek mythology. In the course of analyzing his own poem, "On the London Train," Berryman praises his own use of "strain, torsion" in arrangement of words, saying that this strain "is useful to the subject." This of course recalls Eliot's remarks in "The Metaphysical Poets" to the effect that the modern poet must "force, dislocated if necessary, language into his meaning." Berryman sounds like Eliot too when he says that "Poetry provides its readers . . . with what we may call a language of experience. . . . The language is not the language of prose. It requires a different kind of reading and a different process of sensibility." Like Schwartz, Berryman is at pains here to demonstrate that he fulfills Eliot's criteria for the modern poet; in Eliot's words, he possesses "a mechanism of sensibility which could devour any kind of experience."

If we can read a late Berryman poem from *Love and Fame* as autobiography, then some lines from "Monkhood" are significant. Berryman writes in this poem that he twice refused to meet Eliot, because he knew that he (Berryman) wasn't yet "with it" and "would not meet my superiors. Screw them."[3] The attitude toward Eliot jibes interestingly with Schwartz's. Like Schwartz, Berryman refused to meet Eliot because he was too much in awe of the man. But the awe, like Schwartz's, was mixed with hostility: "Screw them." Haffenden's account of Berryman's attitude toward Eliot during his early years reminds one of accounts of Schwartz's attitude toward Eliot during the same period: "Berryman regarded Eliot as an *eminence grise* that he had to surmount. He felt envious of Eliot's fame." The hostility suggested by the above lines from *Love and Fame* is attested to as well by an anecdote from Haffenden. "When Macmillan . . . turned down a manuscript by Mark Van Doren, Berryman took the occasion to suggest that he should bear a copy to Eliot and beat him into publishing it: 'the beating idea occurred to me because I should like to beat Eliot on my own account.' " Why should Berryman want to pummel the great poet? Haffenden tries to explain but is unable; the best he can offer is that Berryman "had recently discovered that Eliot's line, 'The army of unalterable law,' had been borrowed from Meredith's poem 'Lucifer in Starlight.' He was cross and disillusioned with Eliot for appropriating a line to which he himself was so attached as to allude to it in the line, 'Compulsion and inexorable law,' of his own poem 'Ritual.' "[4] It is amusing that Berryman, who had made use of a line from Eliot in his own poetry, could be miffed at the thought that Eliot had in turn borrowed that line from somebody else. After all, it was Eliot from whom Berryman had learned that game in the first place.

Critics, as it happens, have generally noticed Berryman's borrowings from Yeats and Auden more than they have those from Eliot.[5] This may be because the critics are standing too close to the picture, are too busy noticing the form, style, and tone, to see that the concept of poetry at work in Berryman's early poems is distinctly Eliotic. At least one critic, Winfield Townley Scott, seems to corroborate this; what you notice about Berryman's poetry, wrote Scott of *Twenty Poems*, is "the method."[6] As with the early poetry of the other Middle Generation poets, the method of Berryman's early poems—the form, the style, the tone—is largely Yeatsian and Audenesque. The influence of Eliot is primarily upon the poems' themes, and upon the notions of poetry that guide their composition. Perhaps the best way to demonstrate the nature of these various influences in Berryman's early poetry is to examine a typical poem, "The Disciple."[7] In this poem, the speaker and his fellow townspeople are called from their homes and offices to hear a man sing, do magic tricks, raise the dead, and tell the crippled and poor of children and birds. This man, full of love, becomes notorious, incurs the wrath of "The State," is betrayed with a kiss by a disciple, and ends up executed alongside thieves. The names of Jesus and Jerusalem, Peter and Pilate, are never mentioned.

When we read this poem, we can understand the oversights of the critics. For if we are seeking instances of imitation, a dozen little things in this poem strike our eyes immediately, enough to keep us busy for quite a while, and none of them has a thing to do with Eliot. There is some Audenesque diction, such as the reference to "The State," one of Auden's favorite expressions, and in turn one of the Middle Generation poets' favorite expressions.[8] But the poem is mostly a compendium of Yeatsian figures and effects. The form, to begin with, is Yeatsian, virtually identical to the eight-line stranzas of loose iambic pentameter that we find in "A Prayer for My Daughter," "Sailing to Byzantium," "The Tower," and "Meditations in Time of Civil War." The style too is Yeatsian. Richard Ellmann has produced perhaps the most useful disquisition upon the subject of Yeats's style, and most of the characteristics that he singles out for notice may be found in "The Disciple." Ellmann observes that, in order to prevent slowing his pace, "Yeats habitually used 'had' to mean 'would have' . . . [and] 'for' rather than 'in spite of' or 'notwithstanding.'" And so on. In keeping with this principle, Berryman says "most" instead of "most of all" in this line: "But most he would astonish us with talk." Ellmann further notes that "Yeats has a predilection for the word 'all,' which encompasses everything in what purports to be a familiar world." Berryman uses "all" in this poem to exactly this effect: "Calling them his, all men's, anonymous." Furthermore, "To give his verse a ring of immediacy and colloquialism," Yeats "is fond of clauses beginning with 'now.'" So is Berryman: "now that I'm / Old I behold it as a young man yet." Moreover, says Ellmann, Yeats "is addicted to affirming by repudiating the contrary position." For example, in "The Dolls," instead of writing "This is a good place," Yeats writes, "There's not a man can report / Evil of this place."[9] Likewise, Berryman ends his poem by saying not "We remember" but "We do not forget."

Of course, we do not have to read Ellmann to recognize the style of "The Disciple" as Yeatsian. The very first line has a Yeatsian ring: "Summoned from offices and homes, we came." Nonetheless, Ellmann's discussion of Yeats's stylistic principles helps clarify what it is that we recognize as Yeatsian in such a line. For instance, Ellmann writes that Yeats prized "activity in his verbs," changing a phrase like "curd-pale moon" to "climbing moon" to get in some sense of action, or altering another poet's "The dawn stands suddenly beside my bed" to "The Dawn runs suddenly up to my bed." Moreover, the words of Berryman's first line are simple, in keeping with Yeats's mature interest in the "disinfection of his diction" from the excesses of his early extreme poeticism. Furthermore, the syntax is not perfectly normal; like Yeats's, Berryman's word order here is a bit "stylized." In Yeats, as Ellmann notes, "The language of a love lyric can even bear a legalistic conjunction."[10] "The Disciple" is no love lyric, but does not the word "summon" inject a hint of the courtroom into the poem?

"Summon," of course, is not the only Yeatsian word in the poem. "Compassion," "terror," "song," "indigent," "upland brook," "doom" all sound like Yeats. "Mage" (an obsolete form of the word "magus"), which Berryman uses to refer to Christ, sounds like the kind of archaism Yeats would have used. Indeed, Yeats uses the plural of this word in the title of a poem, "The Magi."[11]

A brief look at "The Magi" may lead a reader to believe that Berryman derived more than the language of "The Disciple" from Yeats. For both poems at least appear to share a theme. Though Berryman's mage is Jesus and Yeats's magi are the temporal monarchs who visited Mary and Joseph at the manger, the fact remains that both poems are concerned with "the uncontrollable mystery" of Christ. But this is where the thematic similarities end. For in "The Magi," the emphasis is not, as in Berryman's poem, on probing that metaphysical mystery, but rather, as John Unterecker observes, on expressing his belief in "the inexorably cyclical movement of history which Yeats would later define in *A Vision*."[12] Thus Yeats's poem about the Nativity does not bear a strong thematic relation to Berryman's poem about the Crucifixion. Though the style of "The Disciple" harkens back to Yeats, the substance does not, except in the most general way. For an explanation of the poem's origin we must turn to Eliot.

For Eliot too has a poem about the magi. Like "The Magi," "The Journey of the Magi" is about the legendary kings who were present at the Nativity. But this superficial resemblance to Yeats's poem is eclipsed by its strong thematic affinity to Berryman's "The Disciple." For although Berryman's poem is about the Crucifixion, it is largely a variation on "The Journey of the Magi."[13] Both poems begin with the speaker being drawn to the holy presence, and the same verb is used. " 'A cold coming we had of it,' " writes Eliot; "Summoned from offices and homes, we came," writes Berryman. The speakers' experiences of Christ, who is never mentioned by name in either poem, are necessarily different in detail, but in result they are strikingly similar. In both cases, a metaphysical revelation too great to comprehend leaves its witnesses uneasy.[14] Note that, at the end of Eliot's poem, the speaker turns from past to present; he informs us that, after the encounter with Christ, his memory remained fresh in the minds of those who had seen him, and that it made them very uneasy, for it upset their former sense of things, it contradicted their old beliefs. Their presumably once-beloved subjects became "an alien people clutching their gods." Berryman's poem ends in much the same way, with the speaker turning from his past acquaintance with Christ to a present in which those witnesses that remain are filled with unease, and are no longer comfortable with their old "loves and disciplines." Both poems, then, amount to examinations of a human mind that comes suddenly into contact with the ultimate metaphysical truth. I say metaphysical and not religious because, although Eliot had become an Anglican by the time he wrote "Journey" and Berryman had periods of devout Christian belief, these are not, strictly speaking, religious poems. Seeing Christ has not transfigured the speakers, it has only disturbed them. This is hardly the scenario of an orthodox Christian poet. Nor does the fact that the savior's name appears nowhere in either poem suggest that the fundamental concern of these poets is to glorify Christ or Christianity. Patently, the intent of these poems is far from a religious one. Granted, the poets may well have been attracted to the Nativity and Crucifixion as subject matter by virtue of their personal religious convictions. But in each of these poems the poet concerns himself not with those convictions but with a more general, impersonal matter, the psychological effect of metaphysical revelation, of which the bodily manifestation of Christ on earth is but a convenient example. In each case the poet's personal religious beliefs, and indeed all aspects of his personality, are ultimately irrelevant.

Here, incidentally, is where Berryman's approach to poetry during their early period differs most radically from that of Yeats. Berryman holds with Eliot that "Poetry . . . is not the expression of personality but an escape from personality." Yeats feels very differently. "A General Introduction for My Work," Yeats's most extensive discourse, apart from *A Vision*, upon his own poetic theories, begins with this statement: "A poet writes always of his personal life."[15]

Another early Berryman poem which contains multitudinous echoes of Auden and Yeats but remains an Eliotic poem is "Rock Study with Wanderer."[16] A critic looking for traces of Yeats would find an abundance of them here. The "beast" (l. 2) brings to mind the "rough beast" of "The Second Coming"; the "ravished doll" (l. 3) recalls Yeats's famous poem "The Dolls." In the second stanza, the words "gay," "faery," "dances," and "unrationed" are all deliberately evocative of Yeats, and the picture they help to conjure up of "the faery cities" reminds one unavoidably of Yeats's Byzantium. And so on.

A critic seeking echoes of Auden would also be satisfied. The fifth stanza, with its references to planes and arms and peace and its heavy-handed irony, is strictly derivative of Auden. The word "State" (l. 21) is an Auden staple, as is "hegemony" (l. 26). The references to Detroit, the scene of a confrontation between striking workers and police in 1932, and to LST ("Landing Ship, Tanks") are reminiscent of Auden as well. Furthermore, many details of the poem, as Linebarger points out, are from Auden's "September 1, 1939."[17]

Yet despite this crazy quilt of allusions to Yeats and Auden, the

vision that binds "Rock Study with Wanderer" together is not Yeatsian or Audenesque, but Eliotic. The easiest way to understand this
poem, in fact, is as a version of *The Waste Land*. The pattern of
allusions to other writers itself is reminiscent of that poem. Moreover,
like *The Waste Land*, Berryman's poem centers on a wanderer who
meanders through a landscape symbolic of contemporary death-in-
life. "A paralysis," Berryman writes, "Is busy with society and souls."
This statement, which we may well see as the theme of "Rock Study,"
expresses the theme of *The Waste Land* as well. Linebarger calls "Rock
Study" a sociopolitical work, implying that it derives mainly from
Auden, but it is sociopolitical only in the sense that *The Waste Land* or
"The Hollow Men" is sociopolitical. For the poet here is not concerned primarily with the politics of the day but with, in the words of
the poem, "the western mind, an entity that has existed through
many centuries and in many different political climes." Berryman is
concerned not merely with one war but with all wars. "All wars are
civil," he writes, and we cannot but be reminded of Eliot's neat
connection of the First World War with the Punic Wars: " 'Stetson! /
'You who were were with me in the ships at Mylae!' " The perspective
in "Rock Study," then, is clearly not the relatively narrow contemporary perspective of Auden, but the deliberately broad, comprehensive, centuries-embracing perspective of *The Waste Land*.

A close look at the specific echoes of Eliot in the poem adds
dimension to our sense of it as a version of *The Waste Land*. The echoes
begin in the title. The word "rock," of course, figures significantly in
the work of Eliot. There is, among other things, Eliot's *The Rock*. But
probably more important from the point of view of a Middle Generation poet, and for this poem in particular, are the rocks in *The Waste
Land*. The "shadow of this red rock," in Eliot's poem, represents some
form of escape from the desolation, sterility, and other horrors of the
waste land, but more often, in Eliot's poem, rocks are an integral part
of that desolation.[18] The word "wanderer" likewise recalls Eliot. Not
only *The Waste Land* but "Prufrock," the "Preludes," "Rhapsody of a
Windy Night," and many other Eliot poems are, as Cleanth Brooks
notes, about "a wanderer moving through deserted city streets long
past midnight," through "a genuine nightmare . . . a fantastic world"
of meaninglessness and purposelessness.[19]

The opening line of "Rock Study" comes neither from Eliot nor
Yeats nor Auden, but from Pirandello: "Cold cold of a special night."[20]
Yet it reminds us not of Pirandello but of Eliot, of those poems about

nocturnal wanderers which contain similar lines. It is significant that Berryman places this borrowed line in quotation marks. By doing so he helps to suggest his dependence in this poem upon the words of others. This, of course, is tantamount to confessing his intention to write another *Waste Land*, the great anthology poem of English literature. It may well be that Berryman took this device directly from Eliot, for the opening lines of "Journey of the Magi" are also in quotation marks.

As if to dispel all doubt about the close affinity between "Rock Study" and *The Waste Land*, the word "waste" itself appears conspicuously in Berryman's poem. It comes at the end of the third line, and forms a slant rhyme with the Yeats-echoing word "beast." The placement of this allusion to Yeats's "The Second Coming" is perfect, for Yeats's poem is nothing more or less than a depiction of a twentieth-century wasteland.[21] Berryman's echo of "The Second Coming" in "Rock Study" is exactly the kind of echo which Eliot himself would have incorporated into such a poem.

Eliot also would have been quite comfortable with Berryman's phrase "ravished doll," an allusion to Yeats's "The Dolls"; for that poem's brief, vivid contrast between, on the one hand, the wet and living and, on the other, the dry and lifeless, is a contrast that is also central to *The Waste Land*. And ravishment constitutes the motif of "A Game of Chess," the second section of *The Waste Land*.

Many of the Eliotic references in "Rock Study" allude to poems other than *The Waste Land*. Who can read the line "Waiting for the beginning of the end" (l. 9), for example, without thinking of the *Four Quartets*? "In my beginning is my end." And the reference to "waiting" is equally evocative, and the evocation equally relevant, recalling the opening of "Gerontion," wherein the old man is "waiting for rain" in a dry period. A dry period, a need for rain—this describes the situation not only of "Gerontion" but of *The Waste Land* and "Rock Study." "Gerontion" is also alluded to, perhaps, in line 33 of "Rock Study," in which we find a "tired and old man resting on the grass."

The broken glass (l. 14) recalls "The Hollow Men," which is probably also the model for the poem's lack of punctuation and the intraline spaces which were to become a trademark of the later Berryman.[22] This may, in fact, be the place where Berryman picked up his "Alas" (l. 6). "The Hollow Men" may also be the source of his "twilight birds" (l. 29), which remind us of "death's twilight kingdom" the rough equivalent, in "The Hollow Men," for death.

There is more, but this should suffice to make the point that "Rock Study" avoids the fundamentally sociopolitical perspective of Auden, or the subjective one of Yeats. Like *The Waste Land*, the poem is about things that go too far beyond the individual for a rigorous Yeatsian, and too far beyond the moment for a strict disciple of the thirties Auden. If Auden writes primarily about societies, and Yeats about the soul, Berryman is concerned in this poem with a condition which, as he reminds us, involves both: "A paralysis / Is busy with societies *and* souls" (my emphasis). The impersonal, comprehensive, allusive poem which is "Rock Study with Wanderer" can only be seen as the product of a young poet who is trying his best to do for his time the kind of thing that Eliot did for his time in *The Waste Land.*

A somewhat less ambitious but equally Eliotic poem is "Letter to His Brother."[23] Linebarger sees this as a sociopolitical poem in the Auden mode. Arpin, however, is closer to the truth. "The stanza is Yeatsian, the tone of despair Audenesque," he acknowledges, but "the ideas in the poem" derive from neither of these poets. Although the poem is, on the surface, about "the Nazi threat," Arpin explains that "Hitler is only 'the latest guise of fate.' The blows at Dachau are essentially the same as those that 'Becket's brains upon the pavement spread'—both forbid the poet's 'hopeful prophecy.' "[24] This connection between Hitler's crimes and the murder of Becket is exactly the sort of linkage between past and present which Eliot forges in his poetry. The nexus reminds us, among other things, of the connection drawn in *The Waste Land* between the ravishment of Philomel and the violation of the London typist; or between twentieth-century flirts and Queen Elizabeth I. Berryman, in choosing Becket's murder as the representative crime from history for this poem, may also have had Eliot's play *Murder in the Cathedral* in mind.

Conarroe makes errors of judgment similar to Linebarger's. Writing of Berryman's *Poems* (1942), he observes that these verses contain no "unique presence," and attributes this failing to the fact that "the poet, dealing with ideas and politics, almost wholly ignores his feelings."[25] It is, of course, true that Berryman ignores his feelings in these poems; but this has more to do with Eliot's "Tradition and the Individual Talent" than with Berryman's politics. In truth, apart from "Communist," there is virtually no genuine political content in this early volume of poems, at least not in the strictest sense of the word. For when Conarroe speaks of politics, he seems to be referring to such things as the Nazi invasion of Poland ("1 September 1939"), the labor disturbances in Detroit ("River Rouge, 1932" and "Thanksgiving: Detroit"), and the Japanese incursion into Manchuria ("The Dangerous Year"). But these public tragedies are omnipresent in Berryman's early poetry not because he, like Auden, saw poetry as a vehicle for political statement but because he, like Eliot, saw the large-scale human tragedies of his time as clues to that paramount Eliotic concern, the fate of Western culture. Whereas Auden's poetry of the thirties presents these contemporary tragedies as failures of the political status quo, which can be rectified by a change of political systems, Berryman, following Eliot, sees them as clues to a larger truth that goes beyond the politics of the moment, and beyond the subjective perspective, to embrace all of human history.[26]

Perhaps the clearest example of this is provided by the contrast between Berryman's and Auden's poems about the Nazi invasion of Poland. Auden's is called "September 1, 1939," and Berryman's "1 September 1939." The first inclination of many a critic confronted with Berryman's poem would be to remind us breathlessly that Auden has a poem with a strikingly similar title and to classify the Berryman poem posthaste as species sociological, variety Audenesque. Yet an unbiased examination of the two poems demonstrates that they are very different animals indeed. Auden's is a deliberately personal poem, or at least begins with a fair bid to be taken as one. The first word, in fact, is "I." The speaker is sitting in a Fifty-second Street dive, "uncertain and afraid" at the end of a miserable decade in a world full of fear and anger, and the night is "offend[ed]" by the "odour of death."[27] The speaker goes on to draw the lessons of this night. Some of them are moral: do evil to someone, and he will return the favor; we must choose between loving each other and dying. Some are political, having to do with "Democracy," "Collective Man," "Imperialism's face / And the international wrong." The speaker's thoughts are full of the other people in the world who share culpability for the tragedy of the day, and who must act to make things better: the "dense commuters," the "helpless governors," the "man-in-the-street." But the speaker returns in the end to himself, in the club on Fifty-second Street, and to a personal resolve: that he, made like his fellow human begins of love and dust, and filled like them with despair, will nonetheless "Show an affirming flame."

The poem is, then, in Auden's words, concerned "with extending our knowledge of good and evil," with "making the necessity for action more urgent and its nature more clear." In Berryman's poem there is no such concluding resolution, let alone a clearly defined personality, an "I" composed of Eros and dust, to make such a resolution. Indeed, whereas Auden labors to make it clear that his poem's concern is with people and their "private lives," Berryman seems, with equal deliberateness, to make his poem almost devoid of people.[28] Where Auden's poem begins with an "I," this poem begins by eliminating the human dimension of the events of 1 September. Here we find not people dropping bombs on people but "The first, scattering rain on Polish cities." Those people whom we do find here—the children, the man with the cellophane—are obviously symbols, like the Bear and the Eagle; we are not meant to see them as actual human beings. Furthermore, in the Bear and Eagle we find Berryman reducing the millions of people of two countries into two nonhuman symbols. Thus, where Auden is concerned with drawing straightforward connections between the invasion and real people in the real world, Berryman's poem is concerned with making ingenious connections in the manner of Donne and Eliot, representing bombs as rain, a continent as a piece of cellophane. Indeed, in his use of rain as a metaphor, Berryman again seems to be parroting *The Waste Land*, and certain lines and phrases in "1 September 1939" sound all too familiar; "His shadow / Lay on the sand before him," for example, recalls Eliot's "Your shadow in morning striding before you."

The eight-line-per-stanza form of "1 September 1939" is, of course, characteristically Yeatsian. It is a form that we find reproduced in many early Middle Generation poems, among them Schwartz's "Prothalamion," Jarrell's "The Dead Wingman," and Lowell's "The Drunken Fisherman." Of course, this is only one of several common Yeatsian forms that we find throughout early Middle Generation poetry. One of these common forms is the rhymed trimeter of Yeats's "Death."[29] Many early Middle Generation poems not only copy the form of this type of Yeats poem, but attempt to achieve the same austere, understated power. Like Yeats's "Death," these poems are often rich in action verbs and concrete nouns, many of which are personified abstractions, and poor in modifiers. Schwartz's "O Love, Sweet Animal" is one such poem.[30] Among the many obvious Yeatsian characteristics of this poem is the continual use of negatives; like Yeats, Schwartz is, in Ellmann's words, "affirming by repudiating the contrary position." We find Berryman doing the same thing in a line of "On the London Train": "He'll swear no man has lied."[31] Aside from the loose trimeter and the affirming negative, Berryman's poem contains at least one strong echo of a line

from Yeats; "Summon an old lover's ghost" recalls the opening line of
"A Prayer for My Son," "Bid a strong ghost stand." Also, the
substitution of "who" for "those who" in the last line is characteristically Yeatsian. The same form appears in Jarrell's "When You and I
Were All."[32] Lowell, the only Middle Generation poet who in his early
work does not pick up Auden's stylistic habit of punctuating his
thematic points with short declarative statements, likewise fails to
adopt a short Yeatsian line in any of his early poems. He does,
however, join the other Middle Generation poets in borrowing Yeatsian forms that involve longer lines. Among the early Middle Generation poems that follow a distinctively Yeatsian form are Schwartz's
"For the One Who Would Take Man's Life in His Hands," "Dogs are
Shakespearean, Children are Strangers," and "Saint, Revolutionist";
Jarrell's "The Bad Music," "The Soldier," "Mother, Said the Child,"
and "The Dead in Melanesia"; Berryman's "A Point of Age," "Meditation," "At Chinese Checkers," "The Apparition," and "Boston
Common"; and Lowell's "The First Sunday in Lent," "The Quaker
Graveyard at Nantucket," and "In Memory of Arthur Winslow."

Thus, while the major influence upon the language of early
Middle Generation poetry was Auden, the major influence upon the
form of that poetry was Yeats. But, as is true of their borrowing from
Auden, they took nothing from Yeats which did not belong in a poem
written according to Eliot's tenets. Even Berryman, who said that his
youthful ambition was to be Yeats, and who of all the Middle
Generation poets is most often linked to Yeats, remained a devoted
disciple of Eliot throughout his early period.

Perhaps the closest thing to an exception to this rule is *Berryman's
Sonnets*. These poems cannot be identified with Berryman's other
early poetry without qualification. Berryman wrote them in 1947 for a
woman, identified in the poems and biography only as "Lise," with
whom he was in love, and they were, to him, utterly separate from
his "work"—that is, the other poetry he wrote. He did not publish
them till 1967. Simply by virtue of being love sonnets, they are less
impersonal than the bulk of Berryman's early work. The "I" in these
poems, unlike the "I" in most of Berryman's other early poems, is
recognizably the poet.[33] More than any other Berryman poems of the
forties, these sonnets clearly foreshadow Berryman's late poetry.
Ironically, it is only in these relatively non-Eliotic poems, these
ostensible love sonnets, that Berryman was able, in his early work, to
write about the experience of meeting Eliot, as in sonnet 5.[34]

Even in the sonnets, however, one often finds Berryman backing off from his personal material, retreating from his passions even while in the heat of recording them, and, as his biographer notes, "uncannily assuming objectivity or some quality of emotional distance." During this period, Berryman seems ultimately unable to avoid an Eliotic perspective even when writing about his own love affair. There is often, for example, a deliberately contrived historical sense in these poems, however ludicrously inappropriate it may seem to the situation. As Haffenden notes, Berryman

> constantly surveyed famous precursors of his role as adulterer or sonneteer. He saw his own adultery as continuous with an immortal series. In Sonnet 75, he compared himself to Petrarch, in 29 to Balzac, in 21 to David in relation with Bathsheba; Sonnet 16 was suggested by Sidney's second sonnet to Stella. Sonnet 38 alludes to the frescoes executed by Pinturicchio relating the life of the poet Aeneas Sylvius Piccolimini, who was elected to the papacy as Pius II in 1458: "A vanished poet crowned by the Duke for song."[35]

As if this were not enough to satisfy the small voice of T. S. Eliot within him, sonnet 44 is an imitation of Donne's "Canonization."[36]

Haffenden concludes these observations, unfortunately, with a sentiment that I find completely wrongheaded. Having established Berryman's propensity to compare himself with the lovers and poets of history, the biographer writes:

> At worst, then, Berryman's sonnets seem enormously self-engrossed. They reveal just how little Berryman could respond—from want of contact and knowledge, not desire—to Lise herself. More and more he drew on his own imaginative invention and on literary analogues. Much of the obscurity and inscrutability of the sonnets may be attributed, not only to the necessity of subterfuge and deliberate obscurantism, but to the fact that their content and thematic linkage were self-generated, the efflux of a personality working often in a vacuum.

On the contrary, such sonnets as the ones Haffenden is speaking of reveal a poet no more engrossed in himself than in his lady love. Berryman's avoidance of Lise in these poems results not, as Haffenden would have it, from the poet's absorption in himself, but from his desire to be objective and inclusive, to write not merely about himself and Lise, but about all lovers throughout history. Not to do this in at least some of these one hundred and fifteen sonnets would be too extreme a violation of Eliot's tenets for Berryman to countenance in himself during these early years. Haffenden is, I feel, much closer to the truth when he says that "In another aspect, it was salutary that

Berryman should seek detachment from his passion. To formulate and structure sonnets, individually and sequentially, was to compose his feelings." Indeed it was not just to compose his feelings, but to erect above them a construct of words and ideas and allusions so extensive and intricate that, as in the sonnets of Donne, the personal romantic attachment that had inspired the poem was barely visible or recognizable. In fact, when Berryman reworked his sonnets into final drafts, according to Haffenden, he did so largely with an eye to making them more "impersonal and representative, general rather than local."[37] Impersonality and generality are, indeed, the rule in all of Berryman's early poetry. Although, like his fellow Middle Generation poets, he was an admirer and imitator of Yeats and Auden, the early Berryman was above all a follower of Eliot, and borrowed nothing which did not further his purposes as an Eliotic poet.

8

Lowell and the Symbolists

Robert Lowell became a Catholic in 1941, and remained one for about five years. During that period he wrote poems that are full of allusions to Biblical figures and Catholic doctrines. In spite of this fact, however, they are not strictly religious poems, in the way that is usually indicated by that phrase. Like the poems that Eliot wrote after his own conversion to Anglicanism in 1927, Lowell's poems are not about one man's faith; rather, they are the product of a highly conscious impersonal artist who has combed through the motley grains of Roman Catholic teachings and picked out whatever metaphysical perceptions, and literary material, he could find. It is, as Leslie Fiedler has written, a poetry of "deliberate detachment," and all the more striking on that account.[1] More than one critic, however, has been led astray by the heavy religious content in *Land of Unlikeness* (1944) and *Lord Weary's Castle* (1946) into mistakenly believing that the Lowell of these volumes is writing in the grand tradition of religious poets, a successor to George Herbert and Gerard Manley Hopkins. Nothing could be further from the truth. The simple fact is that, Christian symbolism or no, Lowell is doing essentially the same thing in his early poetry that the other Middle Generation poets are doing in theirs. Like Eliot's conversion to Anglicanism, Lowell's temporary membership in the Roman Catholic church during the forties was part of a larger psychological pattern. Eliot's conversion was merely a stage in his continuing metamorphosis from an American into an Englishman, "classicist in literature, royalist in politics, and anglo-catholic in religion."[2] Likewise, Lowell's conversion to Catholicism was an integral part of his rejection of home, family, and country, a rebellion for which Eliot provided something of a model for all four Middle Generation poets. All four strove in their early period to be, to some extent, non-American poets. For Lowell, scion of the Lowell and Winslow clans and heir to the New England Protestant tradition, being an American poet meant being a Protestant poet; so in order to be a non-American poet, he had to change his religion. This is not to say that his faith in his adopted religion was not sincere, but simply that, like Eliot's, it did not arise in a vacuum. His Catholicism was an additional piece of psychological luggage which, due to his famous name and heritage, he, unlike the other Middle Generation poets, needed for the sojourn through Eliotic modernism which the early period of all four poets represented. As Ehrenpreis has written, "Whether Lowell espouses Southern agrarianism or Roman Catholicism, his principles attract him less as ideals of aspiration than as possibilities disdained by his ancestors."[3] When Catholicism had, as Lowell put it, "served its purpose," his need for the church came to an end, and he renounced his faith.[4]

Thus we should not see Catholicism as being at the center of the early poems of Robert Lowell. The Lowell of this era is not primarily a Catholic poet; he is primarily an Eliotic poet, one of whose psychological and literary accoutrements is Catholicism. The Catholic references in his poem serve the same purpose as the various allusions in the early poems of the other Middle Generation poets. Like those poets, Lowell, during this period, takes as his subject the same theme Eliot tackled in _The Waste Land:_ "the fate of western civilization and the historical sense." In Lowell's early poems, as Jarrell has written, Jesus Christ represents "pure liberation from the incestuous, complacent, inveterate evil of established society."[5] Jehovah holds out hope to Lowell because he alone has the power "to break up this inertia" of modern Western civilization. Clearly the landscape of these early Lowell poems is exactly that of _The Waste Land._ The main difference is that whereas Eliot's landscape is populated by the pagan gods described in _From Ritual to Romance_ and _The Golden Bough,_ Lowell's landscape is inhabited by Christ. In a modern world of chaos, confusion, sin, and sterility, Lowell's Christ serves the same symbolic purpose as Eliot's figures of sacrifice and resurrection. Both represent the poet's hope for some type of spiritual regeneration, for the resurrection of a mythical past in which the world had some virtue, some vigor, some vitality. Herbert Leibowitz, writing of Lowell's _Land of Unlikeness,_ remarks that

> Resurrection, a central tenet of the Catholicism he has adopted, is a
> vague symbol of his will to transcend chaos—but he mistrusts it as a

dogma. . . . The effect of this volume therefore is one of willfulness, of a gesture toward belief, a set of elaborate misfitting metaphors for the poet's real concerns. . . . There is, despite the profuse religious nomen- clature, little of Hopkins's awe of Jesus and tenderness toward Mary; there is none of the grave sweetness and piety of Herbert; there is not even the humbleness and reticence of an Edward Taylor. Instead we have a series of willed literary effects.[6]

"Willed" is exactly the right word. During their early period, not only Lowell, but all the Middle Generation poets, looked upon poetry as an act of the will, an attempt to overcome, through the order imposed upon the materials of the poem, the poet's sense of disorder in the world. However, he can endorse Leibowitz's objective descrip- tion of the function of willful Catholic references in Lowell's poetry without agreeing to his judgment of their appropriateness. Leibo- witz's opinion that Lowell's Catholic references are "misfitting" is clearly related to his recognition that the poems are not really reli- gious poems, like those of Hopkins or Herbert or Taylor. Such allusions don't belong to Lowell's early poems, Leibowitz seems to feel, because the poet's central motivation is not Christian faith, and it is ultimately Eliotic concerns, not Catholic ones, that shape the poem and govern the use of its figures of speech. That is, while the god of Lowell the man may be Jehovah, the god of Lowell the poet is Eliot; thus, Leibowitz reasons, Catholic references are out of place in Lowell's poetry.

But are they? Just as a poem containing historical references need not be about history, so a poem with religious references need not be a religious poem. Indeed, in an Eliotic poem, the idea is to be inclusive. A critic concurring in Leibowitz's judgment that Lowell's Catholic references are "misfitting" would be forced to condemn *The Waste Land* as well; for although Eliot's poem does not have any more of "the grave sweetness and piety of Herbert" than does *Land of Unlikeness,* Christ is nevertheless a very important presence in it.[7]

Indeed, as Christ is present in *The Waste Land* alongside the gods of Frazer and Weston, so Jehovah and Jesus, in Lowell's early poems, are not alone either. "A Suicidal Nightmare" contains a figure called "the maimed man" of which Stephen Yenser comments: "If 'the maimed man' is a likely symbol of Christ, he is also a possible symbol of fallen man and even of the cloven-hoofed devil."[8] More than either of these, however, it seems to me that to any reader familiar with *The Waste Land,* Lowell's "maimed man" recalls Eliot's "Hanged Man";

and thus it invokes not only Christ but all the Christ-like figures of Weston's and Frazer's books whose deaths and resurrections symbolize nature's fundamental rhythms.

The first poem in _Lord Weary's Castle_, "The Exile's Return," illustrates Eliot's influence upon Lowell's early poetry as well as any.[9] The poem looks like something by Eliot, difficult, compressed, enjambed, many of its lines approximating iambic pentameter but many of them shorter. Like "Prufrock," the poem presents a character crossing an inhospitable urban landscape; like _The Waste Land_, it contains the names of landmarks in a German city. The Hostenwall and Rathaus are Lowell's counterparts of Eliot's Starnbergersee and Hofgarten.[10] Like _The Waste Land_, "The Exile's Return" invokes the seasons, "Fall/And winter, spring and summer." And Lowell's quotation from Dante, "Voi ch'entrate," which refers to the entrance into hell, recalls similar borrowings from Dante in _The Waste Land_. In both poems, the echo of Dante serves to compare the world described in the poem to hell. The hotel's "braced pig-iron dragons" at the beginning of Lowell's poem reinforce this comparison, for, as Yenser observes, they "guard the entrance like a pair of infernal beasts."[11] What makes a hell of the landscapes of these poems? The answer is the lack of order, of continuity, of a sense of tradition. "The Exile's Return," like _The Waste Land_, is obsessed with history. And what, in Lowell's poem, in history? History is Europe; history is, in a couple of images borrowed from Yeats, the "ancestral house" and the "walnut tree." And Americans are the barbaric conquerors who blast the tree with dynamite. That Lowell, in 1946, can cast the American army of occupation in such a role only demonstrates the degree to which an unreasoned hostility toward his own country and culture and an empathy toward European life and art is a force in his early work.

Catholicism, by comparison, is not a thematic force in this poem so much as it is a supplier of symbols. It provides the conception of hell which Lowell uses imagistically in essentially the same way that Eliot, no Catholic, uses it in _The Waste Land_. There are, of course, early Lowell poems in which the Catholic allusions are more numerous than they are in "The Exile's Return," but the nature of those allusions is the same; however significant a given Catholic allusion may be in a particular poem, it is, in the words of Burton Raffel, substantially "a borrowed symbol," brought into the poem in order to make it thematically richer, weightier, more comprehensive.[12]

Being comprehensive, in fact, is a major aim of Lowell's in his early poetry. Like Eliot, he seeks to amalgamate the disparate, to find unity among the seemingly most disconnected things. Yenser has written that Lowell's early poetry is "preoccupied with paradoxical unity."[13] Of all the critics who have written about Lowell, though, Raffel alone has recognized the significance of this fact and accorded it the proper emphasis. Raffel quotes Eliot's passage from "The Metaphysical Poets" about "amalgamating disparate experience" and "forming new wholes," and then says, "Lowell tried to be the poet T. S. Eliot had described. . . . His impressionability was close to disastrous."[14] The latter is an opinion, but the former is fact; with Lowell, as with the other Middle Generation poets, an attempt to be the poet Eliot had described was the main motivation behind the early poetry. And Raffel is correct in focusing on the amalgamation aspect; for perhaps even more than any of the other Middle Generation poets in this early period, Lowell was concerned with finding unities, with drawing connections. As Alan Williamson notes in discussing "On the Eve of the Feast of the Immaculate Conception," "the Virgin Mary is addressed as a military conqueror ('another Nimrod') and a Hollywood star ('Celestial Hoyden')." Williamson explains the poet's rationale here as follows: "To a degree, this is simply satire in the manner of Donne: Lowell points up the blasphemous opposition between the world and God by expressing each in the other's terms."[15] The device is indeed very much like Donne, Eliot's touchstone of poetic greatness, but I believe the satirical element is secondary, and that Williamson's notion that Lowell is primarily concerned here with oppositions is completely misguided. Rather, by describing the Virgin as another Nimrod, or as a hoyden, Lowell is emphasizing the essential unities between even the most different things. It is something that we find him doing in many early poems. In "New Year's Day," for example, Lowell draws a connection between the crucifixion of Christ and the death of a kitten; in "In Memory of Arthur Winslow," he links Christ to Charon, ferry-master of the dead; and in "At the Indian Killer's Grave," he parallels the rape of a Puritan settler by Indians and the Annunciation of the Virgin Mary.[16] More than likely, Lowell was thinking here of the second section of *The Waste Land*, "A Game of Chess," in which Philomel's ravishment is paralleled to the rape of a Cockney woman in London.

Often, Lowell uses the favorite modernist device of ambiguity to draw his Eliotic connections. In "On the Eve of the Feast of the Immaculate Conception," the words Hun and Roman are ambiguous, and as Yenser notes, this ambiguity "introduces a historical perspective."[17] Indeed, to a reader in 1946, "Hun" could mean Attila or Hitler. In this poem, it clearly means both, and helps to create a sense of the cyclicality of history of a sort that cannot but remind us of *The Waste Land*.

In fact, the historical content of these early poems of Lowell's is at least as prominent as the religious content. As Ehrenpreis notes, Eliot's cherished sense of history is a key element in Lowell's early poetry.[18] A good example of Lowell's linking of past and present is provided by "Salem," in which the thought of a napping sailor of the present puts the speaker in mind of the seamen of an earlier day, who "Once hung their numble fleets on the Great Banks."[19] Like Eliot in *The Waste Land*, Lowell is here remembering a time in the past which, for its valor and vigor, makes the present look near-dead by comparison.

As the personal poet who wrote *Life Studies* and *Notebook* includes in his poems passages from personal letters, the Eliotic author of *Lord Weary's Castle* incorporates pieces of historical documents into his poems. "Our Lady of Walsingham," the sixth section of "The Quaker Graveyard at Nantucket," is, for example, based on part of E. I. Watkin's *Catholic Art and Culture*, and "Mr. Edwards and the Spider" contains lines from Jonathan Edwards.[20]

There is yet another significant ingredient in the recipe for early Lowell poetry, and for the early poetry of all four Middle Generation poets. As critics have called the early poetry of Jarrell Audenesque, and labeled the young Berryman a pale copy of Yeats, so Lowell has often been pigeonholed as a post-Symbolist. In truth, as Auden and Yeats exerted certain influences upon all four poets during their early years, so did a handful of nineteenth-century continental poets, each of whom is usually described as a Symbolist or widely recognized as having been strongly influenced by the Symbolists. The most important of these poets, in terms of their influence upon the Middle Generation, are Baudelaire, Rimbaud, and Rilke. While Berryman, at Cambridge University, was having hallucinations of Yeats, Schwartz, at the University of Wisconsin, was having hallucinations of Rimbaud. And Lowell singled out Rimbaud and Rilke as poets for whom he had "felt some sort of closeness" in his youth.[21] Unlike the influences of Auden and Yeats, that of these continental poets did not diminish with the years. The Symbolists would remain as important during the Middle Generation's later years as during their early period.

What initially attracted the Middle Generation to the Symbolists?

For one thing, the poetry of the Symbolists was rooted in experiences of childhood and youth similar to those that had scarred the early years of the Middle Generation poets. Baudelaire's father, like Berryman's, died when the poet was a child; Rimbaud was six when his father, like Schwartz's, abandoned the family; and Rilke, like Lowell, had a very difficult relationship with his father, and got through the university, as did Jarrell, with the help not of his father but of an uncle.[22]

Though rebels against the respectability that their mothers represented, Baudelaire, Rimbaud, and Rilke seem nonetheless to have been tied to their mothers quite strongly. Baudelaire adored his mother, and Rimbaud returned to live with his mother after his rebellious years were over, and wrote *Une saison en enfer* under her roof. (Interestingly, a good deal of Schwartz's translation of that book was written under Rose Schwartz's roof.) The anger, the energy, the rootlessness, the rebelliousness, the alienation, the suicidal tendencies of these three continental poets' lives were duplicated in the lives of Schwartz, Jarrell, Berryman, and Lowell. When Engelberg speaks of the Symbolists' acute "sense of distance" from the world they lived in, and of their obsession with the "inner reality—vision, dream, drugs, hallucination, nightmare," one might think he were talking about Schwartz and Berryman, not Rimbaud and Baudelaire. When Louis Simpson observes that Lowell shares Baudelaire's desire "to transcend lust and decay through his art and Rimbaud's "view of childhood as a time of primitive innocence," one is tempted to add that the same might be said of Schwartz, Jarrell, and Berryman. And when Marjorie Perloff speaks of Rimbaud's "attitudes toward childhood and corrupted innocence that remind one at once of *Life Studies*," one may think that were she writing a study of Schwartz she might well be reminded of *Genesis;* if writing of Jarrell, of many of the poems in *The Lost World.* "Mme. Rimbaud as 'Mother' inexorably recalls Mrs. Lowell," Perloff remarks; but the overbearing, possessive Mme. Rimbaud, whose son's poetry is concerned largely with the "traumatic effect of a mother's neurotic behavior on her sensitive child," equally recalls the mothers of Schwartz and Berryman.

Finally, when Geoffrey Brereton speaks of Baudelaire's notion that "physical debauch . . . would broaden experience of evil as good, and would lead to spiritual lucidity," at least three of the Middle Generation poets come to mind; and the parallels become stronger the further one reads. Baudelaire, Brereton writes, has no patience with the prospect of maturing slowly. He must snatch at everything—experience, knowledge, understanding—and get it at once in its integrity. The only way to do this is by the short cut which is also the direct route: through sensation, which is instantaneous and within his immediate grasp. Afterwards, it will not matter if he has destroyed himself. At least he will have *been there* and others can go on (he believes) from the point which he has reached.[23]

Decades after Baudelaire's death, all four Middle Generation poets would express strikingly similar sentiments. "Into the Destructive Element," Schwartz would write, "that is the way." The poet, Berryman would assert, "has got to know pain."

There was, then, a strong natural affinity between the Middle Generation poets and the Symbolists. Another factor is that the Symbolists had Eliot's blessing. That Eliot, in "The Metaphysical Poets," characterized these seemingly Romantic poets as modern-day Metaphysical poets, and thus suitable models for young modern poets, must have seemed to the Middle Generation poets quite wonderful. For here were poets who had had the same instinctive approach to poetry as they did, who conceived of themselves as seers, but who at the same time were lauded by Eliot as supremely gifted makers. No wonder then that the Middle Generation poets, in their formative years, identified strongly with Baudelaire, Rimbaud, and Rilke.

What exactly makes a poem Symbolist? Brereton expresses the Symbolist credo in this fashion: "The first study of a man who wished to be a poet is knowledge of himself—entire knowledge. He searches for his soul, inspects it, tries it out, learns it." Ehrenpreis defines Symbolism as "the movement that defined the creative mind as the supreme object of poetic contemplation." Brereton writes, "The poetry of the Symbolist school does not usually refer back directly to phases of lived experience. It aims rather at reaching an entirely new plane of experience (as in Rimbaud) or at constructing a new technique of apperception (Mallarmé)."[24] To put it simply, Symbolist poems describe situations that could not take place and objects that could not exist in the physical world as we know it; the setting of the events of a Symbolist poem is the landscape of the mind. Coleridge's "Kubla Khan" and Shelley's "Ozymandias" are two English Romantic poems that can be seen as precursors to the Symbolist movement. Such poems, as Engelberg says, use language.

to evoke and to suggest, rather than to describe or to declare. . . . The poet's language begins to respond to the world he sees, hears, and feels, not according to some general laws of poetic decorum, but according to the poet's subjective feelings stimulated by what his senses perceive. If a poet hears a nightingale or a maiden singing in a valley, he will not be content to describe the beauties of bird or human song; he will give expression to the emotions that he finds correspondent to whatever has stimulated his senses.[25]

Like the typical Romantic poet, then, the Symbolist poet aims to "give expression to the emotions." Unlike the typical Romantic poet, the Symbolist poet does this not by telling us directly what he is feeling but by presenting us with what we may call a vision—a picture of the world, or a narration of a series of events, that exists only in his mind. Although this vision is completely informed and controlled by the poet's highly subjective emotions, it is nevertheless the product of a poet who, simply by virtue of avoiding the directly personal method of such poems as Keats's "When I Have Fears" and Coleridge's "This Lime-Tree Bower My Prison," can justly be called a maker. Thus we can see how both classical and Romantic poets may understandably claim a Symbolist poet as their own.

Likewise, we can see how the Middle Generation poets, during their early years, managed to reconcile the seeming solipsism implied in the Symbolists' dedication to exploring the creative mind with Eliot's dictate that the young poet should escape his own personality. The way out of the seeming paradox is simply that, during their early years, the Middle Generation poets read the Symbolist credo the way Eliot did. Eliot had said that "One must look into the cerebral cortex, the nervous system, and the digestive tracts." This was different from looking into the heart. Feelings untempered by the intellect sprang from the heart; Romantic poetry sprang from the heart. Poetry with true vision, a vision that was only given to the very intelligent, was utterly different from the type of poetry produced by the typical Romantic poet. Symbolist poetry had true vision; *The Waste Land* had true vision; the Middle Generation poets, during their early years, aimed to write poetry with true vision. Thus, while they were disciples of Eliot, the Middle Generation poets laid more stress upon the Symbolists as makers and paid less attention to the more pronounced Romantic aspects of the Symbolists. Nowhere in early Middle Generation poetry, however strongly it may be influenced by Baudelaire, Rimbaud, or Rilke, do we find a self-expression quite so unhesitant, so eager, as that which characterizes some of the most memorable works of the Symbolist poets. Baudelaire, Rimbaud, and

Rilke were not afraid to identify the visions that they brought to life in their poetry as the products of a Romantic sensibility. "Paris may change," writes Baudelaire; "my melancholy is fixed." "Dreaming, I feel the dampness at my feet," writes Rimbaud. "Appear to me, take form, / God, witness eternal!" writes Laforgue.[26] There is little of this type of thing in early Middle Generation poetry. The vision is there, but the poet prefers that we take it as a much-labored over tour de force conceived by the intellect, rather than as a spark thrown out by his subconscious, a hallucination produced by an extreme emotional state. It is worth noting that Schwartz, in his early period, characterized Laforgue as one who put too much personality into his poems. Clearly Schwartz, in making this accusation, was trying to be a good Eliotic critic.

Many early Middle Generation poems have obvious Symbolist characteristics; there are a few, however, in which the influence of the Symbolist sensibility is particularly prominent. One such poem is Schwartz's "Out of the Watercolored Window, When You Look."[27] This is not only a Symbolist poem, but a poem about the Symbolist view of poetry. What Schwartz sees through his watercolored window is the poet's vision; a vision, in this case, of a world in which life can be seen as night and death as day, rather than the other way around. Death is, then, in this vision, something not to be dreaded but to be welcomed. The windowpane is a key image in Symbolist poetry. Mallarmé uses it, for example, in his poem "Les Fenêtres," which, in Engelberg's words, presents a dying hospital patient who looks out a window at

> visions of swans and galleys, a profusion of colors, a dream. . . .
> Mallarmé identifies himself with the dying patient: he, the poet, like the patient, stands at the window dreaming of himself as an angel, prepared somehow to transcend the pane. But he cannot. . . . Alas! the here and now, the world of reality on *this side* of the windowpane, is master.

Engelberg goes on to explain Symbolism in terms of the windowpane metaphor, saying that Mallarmé's poem

> most nearly bares the dilemma facing the Symbolist poet: he seems forever alienated from an ideal world and also forever conscious not only of this separation but also of the sordid reality from whose perspective he is obliged to seek the azure of the ideal world. In short, the poet is trapped between his impulse to recover the transcendent world and his awareness of the utter impossibility of ever doing so, except by resorting to the illusion of the windowpane.[28]

Like the reality that is experienced by Mallarmé's dying patient, the reality of Schwartz's speaker in "Out of the Watercolored Window" is "as complex as disease." His vision is the opposite of complex: clear, neat, simple, still. That it is watercolored as well, and the sky an illimitable blue, is to be expected; for the visions of Symbolist poets are notable for being full of color. "The apple which has sewed the sunlight up" is a typical Symbolist figure, a tight little complex of impossibilities and incongruities, each element of which is charged with symbolic energy. We find many such striking, and strikingly Symbolist, images in early Middle Generation poetry. Berryman's "A Poem for Bhain," for instance, imagines the speaker and his friend conversing "as over a lake of fire" where two white birds play, "Certain of the nature and station of their mission." The white birds flying over a lake of fire form a characteristic Symbolist image. Similarly, in Jarrell's "Moving," the child-speaker, who is about to be taken away from the only home and friends he knows and installed in a new house which he has never seen, muses that he is going to reside in a pumpkin "Under a gold star."[29] It is interesting that in both of these poems, a strong Symbolist influence accompanies subject matter which is unusually personal for an early Middle Generation poem. Bhain Campbell was a close friend of Berryman's, and the book containing "A Poem for Bhain" is dedicated to him; while "Moving" has much in common with Jarrell's later poems about his own childhood.

Engelberg only includes two Middle Generation poems in his anthology of Symbolist poetry. Both poems are by Lowell, and are from Lord Weary's Castle. The first is "In the Cage," with its image of screaming canaries shaking the bars of their cages. The poem derives from Lowell's incarceration during World War II as a conscientious objector, yet, as Hugh Staples observes, "this rather intimate aspect of his personal career is dealt with in an atmosphere of calm objectivity, from which any suspicion of self-pity or sentimentality is rigidly excluded." The poem, he suggests, makes it look as if "Lowell regards his imprisonment not as a personal catastrophe but as a kind of footnote to the human condition."[30]

In "A Poem for Bhain," "Moving," and "In the Cage," the Middle Generation move furthest, in their early period, from the impersonal ideal. The poets seem driven to involve themselves with personal memories, and to transform their feelings about those memories into poetry. Tied to their Eliotic principles, the Middle Generation had no acceptable model for a type of poetry based on one's feelings about one's own experiences, except for those Symbolist poets whom Eliot had praised in "The Metaphysical Poets." Whitman, Wordsworth, and Tennyson all "thought and felt by fits, unbalanced"; Baudelaire, Laforgue, Rimbaud, and Corbière, however, were great "psychologists . . . explorers of the soul."[31] Thus it is not surprising that when, during their early years, the Middle Generation poets faced powerful memories of painful personal experiences, which absolutely demanded to be made into poetry, they attempted, at least in part, to treat these themes in Symbolist fashion. The things that they feel strongly about are there, but the feelings, as such, are not; they have entered the poems in good Symbolist fashion, in the form of fantastic images: lakes of fire, pumpkins under gold stars, screaming canaries beating their heads against cage bars. With few exceptions, this Symbolistic objectification of intensely personal material is the closest the Middle Generation poets are able to come, in their early poetry, to dealing directly with their own lives and feelings.

Considering the intensity of the personal anguish which the Middle Generation poets must have longed to express, their continued restraint in their early poetry, their steadfast loyalty to Eliot's critical doctrines, sometimes seems incredible; how, one cannot help but wonder, could they have gone on for so long yearning for personal expression and yet stifling it at every turn? Yet one must always keep in mind that, to their minds at least, their aim was higher than this; their ultimate desire was to bring together in their poetry all the apparently disordered pieces of contemporary life in such a way as to demonstrate the unseen principle of unity that held them together. They wanted, in short, to express not their own personal feelings, but the spirit of an age. To write beautifully and with heartfelt emotion of a particular experience, or of a certain individual, was too limited an aim for them. They wanted not particular but comprehensive truths.

PART THREE
The Later Poetry

9

A Break with Eliot

The Middle Generation poets' later poetry appears in the following volumes:[1]

Berryman, *His Thought Made Pockets and the Plane Buckt*	(1958)
Schwartz, *Summer Knowledge*	(1959)
Lowell, *Life Studies*	(1959)
Jarrell, *The Woman at the Washington Zoo*	(1960)
Berryman, *77 Dream Songs*	(1964)
Lowell, *For the Union Dead*	(1964)
Jarrell, *The Lost World*	(1965)
Lowell, *Near the Ocean*	(1967)
Berryman, *His Toy, His Dream, His Rest*	(1968)
Lowell, *Notebook 1967–68*	(1969)
Berryman, *Love and Fame*	(1970)
Lowell, *Notebook*	(1970)
Berryman, *Delusions, Etc.*	(1972)
Lowell, *For Lizzie and Harriet*	(1973)
Lowell, *History*	(1973)
Lowell, *The Dolphin*	(1973)
Lowell, *Day By Day*	(1977)
Berryman, *Henry's Fate and Other Poems* (posthumous)	(1977)
Schwartz, *Last and Lost Poems of Delmore Schwartz*	(1979)

The poetry in these volumes represents a clear break with the tenets that governed the composition of the early poetry. The Middle Generation poets came to feel that a strict adherence to Eliot's doctrines of poetry made it impossible for them to do in their poetry what they really wanted to do, and hindered their natural development as artists. Eliot, to their minds, forced them to rise above their intense anguish and to be impersonal catalysts; he demanded that they ignore their troubled impressions of a world in chaos and aim instead to convey some sense of an underlying universal unity in their poetry. As time passed, writing according to the dictates of Eliot began to seem, in their view, less a heroic intellectual endeavor and more an act of dishonesty, of self-betrayal. Thus, over the course of several years, the Middle Generation poets moved away from Eliot and gradually became the type of poets that Eliot's tenets had kept them from being.

As Eliot had meant many things to them, so their rejection of him took place on many levels. If they had, as young men, turned to Eliot as a father figure to revere and learn from, they eventually came to the point at which they had had enough of worship; it was, they felt, time to reject the father and to assert themselves, time to speak in their own voices. If, feeling intensely alienated in America, they had seen in Eliot a self-made European whose life and art were graced by order and tradition, the time came when they began to be preoccupied with the fact that they were Americans, and to recognize their American literary heritage. If in their early poetry they saw knowledge as something objective, universal, and eternal, in their late poetry they came to conceive of it as something subjective, personal, and ephemeral. To them, "to know" no longer meant to be aware of enduring universal truths, but rather to be completely in touch with one's experience of the moment. All one could really know, they felt, was oneself. Having in their early poetry assumed the posture of metaphysicians of a strict anti-existentialist breed, the Middle Generation in their later period came to sound like existentialists.

Eliot would not have found much to admire in their later work. Nearly everything that he had told them to be, they ceased to be. Precepts that had once been gospel to them were cast aside one by one. "Poetry," Eliot had written, "is not a turning loose of emotion . . . it is not the expression of personality." But for the Middle Generation poets in their late period, it became both. Eliot had warned against becoming the type of romantic poet who "thought and felt by fits, unbalanced." But that was what the Middle Generation poets became; for if one was unbalanced, that unbalance was the reality of the moment, and one could not achieve truth in poetry by feigning a sense of unity which one did not genuinely feel. Modern poetry, Eliot instructed, must be difficult. But to the Middle Generation poets in their later period, poetry did not have to be anything except emotionally honest. Deliberate difficulty, once indispensable, was now indefensible. The way they saw it now, they had begun as very conscious craftsmen, apprentices to a harsh, exacting master, and were now masters themselves, whose only rule was to follow their own sense of what was the correct way to write a poem. Being intelligent meant little or nothing under these new circumstances; what mattered was being acutely sensitive. Eliot had disparaged writers who "had no guidance except the Inner Light, the most untrustworthy and deceitful guide that ever offered itself to wandering humanity."[2] But in their later period, the Middle Generation poets followed that light fervently. Eliot was no longer their beacon.

The onset of the Middle Generation poets' late period may be perceived in either of two very different ways. On the one hand, it may be seen as a triumph of their long-suppressed desire to express themselves over the Eliotic concept of the poem as an impersonal object. On the other hand, it may be seen as a failure of the will. For in the early poetry, the poet's will creates in the poem an object of order, in defiance of the poet's own anguished sense of the world's disorder; in the later poetry, the ordering will fails, and we find the poet able to do little more than react, with undisguised emotions, to that disorder. Whereas in the early poetry the idea was that the poet catalyzes a chemical-type reaction among fragments of disparate experience, in the later poetry the roles are reversed. Experience becomes the catalyst, and the poet's feelings the reactants. Thus, that which in their early poetry the Middle Generation poets aim not to do, in their late poetry they aim *to* do. And so even the seemingly most personal early poems, such as "In the Naked Bed, in Plato's Cave," look utterly impersonal alongside the typical later efforts. The allusions in "In the Naked Bed" are impersonal, and its method is an homage to the poetic masters of Schwartz's youth. It is a poem which unarguably arises out of the poet's bouts with insomnia, his angst, his struggle to survive his numerous personal torments; but the poem is not about these things. It is, rather, about something that men have, as the poem suggests, known throughout history: "the travail / of early morning, the mystery of beginning / Again and again." Instead of reproducing the hysteria of a sleepless prepsychotic poet, "In the Naked Bed" is highly controlled in tone; far from constituting the outpourings of a heart sickened by the pain of life, the poem is the product of a mind which believes that it can achieve something important by setting one heart's anguish into the constraining contexts of history, religion, philosophy, and literary tradition. The references in the poem are thus not to Schwartz's personal life but to Plato and Eliot and Ezekiel. The poem does not look as if it might have poured from the poet's pen one night during such an experience as the poet describes, but, like *The Waste Land*, gives the impression of having been painstakingly constructed. It aims for an ideal of order, of everything-in-its-proper-place; Plato's cave is exactly the "right" allusion here, and would have been equally right had the poet been not Schwartz but Berryman, Jarrell, Lowell, or, for that matter, Eliot. This is the way early Middle Generation poetry works.

Not so their late poetry. In his late period, if Schwartz cared to write about a sleepless night, it turned out very differently. Like the speaker of "In the Naked Bed," the insomnia-ridden speaker in Schwartz's "Poem" goes to his window, looks out upon his world, and is troubled by thoughts of mortality.[3] The difference between the poems is implicit in the last line of each of the two poems. "In the Naked Bed" ends with a reference to history, the racial past, the past we all share. "Poem" ends with a reference to memory ("the inescapable mockery of memory," to be exact)—the personal past, the unique version of history which the speaker alone carries in his mind. Thus, if in the earlier poem Schwartz aims to subordinate a subjective experience to the ordering power of his intellect, in the later poem he is attempting to subdue the intellect and let his subjective impressions flow unchecked onto the paper. The allusions and metaphors in "Poem," rather than sounding like secondhand Eliot, are wildly eccentric—the comparison of pears to bagpipes, for example. One might well say that "In the Naked Bed" is written to be thought about, and "Poem" is written to be felt.

And what are we supposed to feel? The poet's sense of futility at being a victim of life, his frustration at his inability to make, in the words of his poem "Disorder Overtakes Us All Day Long," a "lucid picture" of the world. The world, as Schwartz sees it in "Poem," is not lucid and cannot be made to seem lucid. For Schwartz, as "Poem" tells us, finds bedlam in his dreams, reminders of mortality outside his window, and insuperable pain in his memories of the past. He can no longer pretend to be able to impose order upon and eke meaning out of such horror; he can only record his raw, unadulterated experience of life's senselessness, his vivid awareness of the world's disorder. This awareness, coupled with the consciousness of his mortality and the conviction that all the cogitation in the world is not going to do anything to save him from the pain of life and the fate of death, is all he can offer by way of knowledge.

Like Ezra Pound, then, the Middle Generation poets in their late period admit: "I cannot make it cohere."[4] Indeed, as Eliot is a touchstone of their early poetry, Pound is something of a touchstone for their later poetry. Their interest in Pound during this period is particularly interesting in light of the Middle Generation poets' relative indifference to his work during their early years. Although the author of the *Cantos* stood beside Eliot at the forefront of modernism, the Middle Generation poets in their early years found little in his work that was of practical use to them. He was, indeed, just the opposite of what they wanted in an idol. If they felt the need for a father figure who was authoritative and decisive, serious and solid, the bumptious, bohemian Pound was not it; experimental, tentative, and colloquial in his poetry and a vulgar crackpot in his personal life, always shuttling from one movement to another, he never seemed to be sure for very long exactly what was the right way to compose poetry. He was certainly no competition for Eliot, who seemed to hand down his commanding pronouncements upon the subject of poetry from some lofty, unshakable Olympus. If Pound contradicted himself, very well, he contradicted himself; he was a human being. T. S. Eliot, in his poems and essays, aimed for consistency, coherence; wishing, as Eliot the critic and poet, to rise above the frailties of Eliot the man.

Nor could Pound ever represent to the Middle Generation, as Eliot did, the glory of Europe, of tradition, of order. Eliot had gone to England and had become English. By an act of will he had transformed himself, an alienated American, into an English poet; and no man on earth, it seemed, could be more beautifully integrated into his society. As Harry Levin writes, "Eliot had put down roots in England, and had acquired a British accent along with a furled umbrella and bowler hat." This was the model the Middle Generation poets, desperately alienated in their own society, longed for. Pound would only show them how to deepen their sense of detachment. "The longer Pound stayed away from the United States," writes Levin, "the more American he considered himself."[5]

Finally, if they wanted a poem to yield some sort of objective knowledge, Pound was not the idol for them. So far was he from their early ideal of the philosopher-poet that sometimes they even patronized him as if he were some incompetent youngster and they were the knowing authorities. Schwartz, for example, writes in an early essay that the *Cantos* "are never more than a book of souvenirs of a tour of the world and a tour of culture."[6] What Schwartz is excoriating Pound for here is the fact that in the *Cantos* there is little attempt at objectivity or amalgamation. The Thomas Jefferson of the *Cantos,* for example, is Pound's Thomas Jefferson, and in Pound's mind need not bear any resemblance to anyone else's Jefferson in order to be a legitimate part of the poem. Harry Levin says much the same thing as Schwartz when he writes that Pound placed "delight in the subject above mere knowledge." This, to the knowledge-hungry Middle Generation poets, was a failing, at least as long as they conceived of knowledge as something objective and unchanging; during their later period, when knowledge was to them something subjective and ephemeral, they came much more into line with Pound's point of view.

This should not be construed as signifying that the poets abandoned Eliot's directives for Pound's. For their day of cutting their poetry to fit someone else's precepts was over. Rather, Pound, along with a few other poets, provided a useful model for them. They picked and chose as they wished from among these poets' offerings, leaving behind what would not be useful to them. From this poet they took this piece of fabric, from that poet that type of stitch. But the overall design into which they worked these bits and pieces was very much their own.

The poets who joined Pound in influencing late Middle Generation poetry run the entire gamut of the history of American poetry. The most important of these influences are Walt Whitman, William Carlos Williams, Robert Frost, Allen Ginsberg, Sylvia Plath, Anne Sexton, and W. D. Snodgrass. Other names might be mentioned as well: Emily Dickinson, Edgar Allan Poe, Stephen Crane, and Anne Bradstreet. It is significant that all of these names are American. Indeed, the only non-American names that demand mention alongside these are Baudelaire, Rimbaud, Rilke, and Dylan Thomas.

It may be difficult to realize how little interest, relatively speaking, the Middle Generation poets had in the American poetry scene during their early years. In 1940 Robert Penn Warren had surveyed that scene in the *Kenyon Review.*[7] The poets he discussed were Frost, Millay, MacLeish, Williams, Van Doren, and Moore. (Eliot was included in the British survey.) None of these poets figures as a major influence upon the Middle Generation poets' early poetry; and rarely were they the topics of the Middle Generation poets' early criticism. Eliot, Auden, and Yeats reigned supreme. The American poets to whom the Middle Generation, in their early years, paid the most attention were those who were themselves disciples of Eliot's critical doctrines: Ransom and Tate. In the later period all this changed. Of course, certain European influences, notably those of the Symbolist poets, would remain strong, but one of the most striking aspects of later Middle Generation poetry was the surprising new echoes of a host of American poets whom the Middle Generation poets had taken half a lifetime to recognize as their own.

The most important of these names, apart from Pound, are Whitman and Williams. Both of these poets consciously aim to be American poets, to be anti-intellectual, and in this they provided helpful models for the Middle Generation poets during their later period. But the influences even of these poets on the Middle Generation is not nearly as comprehensive as, and is far less easily categorized than, that of Eliot, Yeats, and Auden on the early poetry. For what we have here is not simply two periods characterized by two different types of poetry. During the former period, a poem may take its theme from Eliot, be written in Auden's voice, and occupy a form made popular by Yeats. In the Middle Generation's later period, such clearcut divisions are rare. The influences are filtered through and transformed by the poet's consciousness.

Since the concept of the American poet was important to the Middle Generation poets during their later period, it is important to understand what distinguishes an American poet from a British poet. "English writers," Louis Simpson has observed, "use poetry as a means of discourse; they are conscious of the weight of the past and of their place in a literary tradition. Americans believe, as Wallace Stevens put it, that 'poetry is not a literary activity; it is a vital activity.'"[8] This generalization is extremely helpful in understanding the later poetry of the Middle Generation. In writing poetry, they became less concerned with filling their poems with literature and more concerned with filling them with life. Growing less conscious of themselves as members of a literary tradition, they began to feel their primary responsibility as being not to the main currents of literature but to the rapids and eddies of their own souls. Coleridge had once described George Herbert as "a poet *sui generis,* the merits of whose poems will never be felt without a sympathy with the mind and character of the man."[9] This might justifiably be said of the later poems of the Middle Generation. In writing their later poems they put themselves on paper; one's reaction to the poems has a great deal to do with one's feelings about the poets.

What, we may ask, spurred the onset of the Middle Generation's later period? Even if it was only a matter of time before they turned against Eliot, what made it happen when it did? The answer is that a combination of psychological, literary, and historical factors is responsible. Perhaps the most important goad was the work of some of the poets' contemporaries.

First there were the Beats. In 1957, shortly before Lowell began writing the poems of *Life Studies,* he went to the West Coast on a reading tour which, as Hamilton notes, "he was later to describe . . . as an important influence on his quest for a 'new style.'" In California, Lowell gave numerous readings to young audiences to whom poetry meant the work of Allen Ginsberg and his associates. Aware of the expectations and limitations of these audiences and eager to communicate with them, Lowell found himself changing the language of his early poems as he read them aloud, making his style simpler, more direct, less allusive. He added syllables to make the poems clearer and more colloquial, and translated Latin quotations and the like into English. "I'd make little changes just impromptu," Lowell said later. "I began to have a certain disrespect for the tight forms. If you could make it easier by just adding syllables, then why not?"[10] Lowell seems to make no great fuss over "just adding syllables," but in fact what we see here is a poet undergoing a complete alteration of his ideas about poetry. Once he had aimed for difficulty in his verse; now he believed in simplifying. Eliot would have had a very firm and clear answer to his "why not?" The changes in Lowell's poetry which grew out of his California trip spread in turn to the poetry of the other Middle Generation poets.

Perhaps as important as the influence of the Beats is that of the so-called confessional poets. Both Lowell and Berryman have often been classified as members of the confessional school, along with Sylvia Plath, W. D. Snodgrass, and others.[11] These poets were all students of Lowell's during the late fifties, and there seems to be considerable disagreement among critics as to who influenced whom the most. It is clear, though, that several poems later published in Snodgrass's *Heart's Needle* appeared before Lowell began writing *Life Studies,* and they apparently had a profound effect on him. Snodgrass, he wrote in 1957 to Jarrell, "is incomparably the best poet we've had since you started. The _Heart's Needle_ series, written to his little daughter after his divorce, are heart-breaking and dazzling technically."[12] Again, here is a poet changing his values; that it is necessarily an excellent thing for poetry to be heartbreaking is a notion that Eliot would not have been comfortable with. And that a poem of the type Snodgrass writes can be technically admirable in spite of its failure to achieve, or even to aim for, the type of difficulty that Eliot found necessary to modern poetry, is also a new way of thinking for Lowell.

Later Middle Generation poetry has much in common with confessional poetry. Rosenthal calls confessional poetry "a poetry of suffering. The suffering is generally 'unbearable' because the poetry so often projects breakdown and paranoia." The same might well be said of many later Middle Generation poems. Robert Phillips notes that confessional poets conceive of poetry as a form of purgation, perceive madness as the contemporary norm, and write mainly about the self, "the Self treated with the utmost frankness and lack of restraint." This is equally true of the Middle Generation poets during their later years. Phillips's definition of confessional poetry might serve equally well as a description of later Middle Generation poetry. Confessional poetry, he writes, is

> that writing which is highly subjective, which is in direct opposition to that other school of which Auden and Eliot are modern members— writers who consciously strove to obliterate their own concrete personalities in their poems. It is poetry written in opposition to, or reaction from, the Eliotic aesthetic which influenced several generations of poets, and which can be summarized in Old Possum's statement, "Poetry is not a turning loose of emotion, but an escape from emotion; it is not the expression of personality, but an escape from personality."

Confessional poetry, writes Rosenthal, "puts the speaker himself at the center of the poem in such a way as to make his psychological vulnerability and shame an embodiment of his civilization."[13] The same is true of later Middle Generation poetry.

That the confessional poets and the Middle Generation influenced one another extensively seems incontestable. Yet some very clear distinctions may be made between the two schools.

One difference is that unlike confessional poetry, later Middle Generation poetry does not rebel against form. While the confessional poets rarely wrote anything except unrhymed free verse, the Middle Generation poets, in their later poetry, either remained faithful to traditional forms or invented new ones. Schwartz's _Last and Lost_

Poems, for example, contains several sonnets. In Jarrell's later volumes one may find poems that go on for pages in rigorous iambic pentameter. The great majority of Berryman's *Dream Songs* adhere strictly to the form he invented for them. And the poems of Lowell's *Notebook*, *History*, *For Lizzie and Harriet*, and *The Dolphin* are almost all unrhymed sonnets.

There are other differences. "A true confessional poet," writes Robert Phillips, "places few barriers, if any, between himself and direct expression of that self."[14] Later Middle Generation poetry offers very few examples of genuine barriers of the type Phillips refers to, but often in later Middle Generation poetry one finds the poet making an effort to erect such barriers, or at least going through the motions, the way an ex-smoker, unable to shake off the last vestiges of a discarded habit, finds it necessary to draw on an unlit cigarette or to clamp an empty pipe between his teeth. Such devices as Berryman's speaker Henry in *The Dream Songs* and Jarrell's female speakers in several late poems seem, more than anything else, to be testimony to both poets' early devotion to impersonality, relics of an earlier way of thinking that stayed with them like a tan in winter. Almost always in such cases, the mask is in reality no mask at all; although Berryman may insist that Henry is not him, one cannot help noticing that Henry has friends named Delmore, Randall, and Cal, and that the details of his life match those of Berryman's. Ineffective as they are at hiding the poems' essential subjectivity, the point is that these devices are present in a great many later Middle Generation poems, and are virtually absent in confessional poetry.

"The language of the confessional poem is that of ordinary speech," writes Phillips. The Middle Generation poets, in their later poetry, eschew the formality, the allusiveness, and the convolution of the early poetry, but their language is quite often nowhere near that of ordinary speech. In "For Sale," for example, Lowell describes his father's cottage at Beverly Farms as a "Poor sheepish plaything, / organized with prodigal animosity." And Schwartz writes such deliberately unconversational lines as "This is the surrender to the splendor of being's becoming and being!"[15] This is not ordinary speech.

"Openness of language," writes Phillips, "leads to openness of emotion." This is true of both the Middle Generation poets and the confessional poets. But there is a world of difference between what they present to the reader when they open up. The Middle Generation poets name names—of their friends, of the schools they went to, and so forth. Plath and Sexton and Snodgrass rarely do this. More-over, the Middle Generation, for the most part, manage to avoid writing the hate poems, as Sexton calls them, which form so large a part of the confessional oeuvre. There are some exceptions to this, notably a couple of very angry *Dream Songs* by Berryman about the death of his father. But even in these poems, hate soon gives way to despair. The enmity of the line, "I spit upon this dreadful banker's grave," becomes despondency: "O ho alas alas . . . When will indifference come." There is very little of Plath's seemingly simon-pure hostility: "Daddy, you bastard, I'm through."[16] However bitter the resentment of one's parents in Middle Generation poetry, that resentment is virtually always tempered by enduring love and acute guilt. The dominant emotion in such poems by the Middle Genera-tion is more likely to be profound anguish than intense hostility.

"The most successful confessional poetry," writes Phillips, "is usually the immediately personal, rather than the familial or histori-cal." This is undeniably true of Plath, Sexton, and Snodgrass. But some of the best later Middle Generation poetry is the familial, the family poems in *Life Studies*, for example, and Jarrell's poems about his grandparents in *The Lost World*.

Finally there is the matter of range. M. L. Rosenthal observes that "Sylvia Plath's range of technical resources was narrower than Robert Lowell's."[17] I believe this comparison may be extended, for to my mind, the Middle Generation poets are far more versatile than the confessional poets. In theme, in style, in form, their later poetry is richer, more inventive, more varied than that of the confessional poets. For one thing, while remaining essentially subjective the Middle Generation are able to write about or translate the works of other people who have some personal significance to them. Schwartz writes about Vivaldi and Marilyn Monroe, Lowell writes about Marx and Beethoven; Jarrell translates Rilke, Lowell translates Baudelaire. There is little of this sort of diversity in the work of the confessional poets.

Before examining the later poems of the Middle Generation, let us look briefly at two earlier books, both of which contain characteristics of the later poetry. Berryman's *Homage to Mistress Bradstreet* (1953) is a transitional volume, falling between the early and later periods. This poem, which Edmund Wilson called "the most distinguished long poem by an American since *The Waste Land*," is really two poems at once.[18] One of the poems, for which Berryman did a great deal of research, is about Anne Bradstreet, the early American poet; this poem is concerned with colonial life and times, with the themes of history and literature. Partly hidden in the shadows of this poem is a poem about Berryman himself; it is concerned with Berryman's feelings about his personal experiences, with the sense of alienation and rebelliousness that he shares with Bradstreet. The former poem is a typical early Middle Generation work; the latter is typical of the poets' later period. That the two poems are one and the same makes *Homage* a true transitional work, a stopping place on the road from objectivity to subjectivity.

Or perhaps one should say, on the voyage. For in *Homage*, Bradstreet has sailed from Europe to America. She has left England for a continent cold and forbidding, where "the English heart quails, stunned."[19] The voyage is a symbolic one, for while writing *Homage*, Berryman was crossing the ocean between the impersonal, objective poetry of order, which was represented for him by the civilized comfort of England, and a more dangerous, more American type of poetry which would indeed stun the English heart.

Homage is, then, as Linebarger notes, concerned with "the poet and America, early and late."[20] But it is also about the poet in love. Berryman claimed to have fallen in love with Bradstreet while writing the poem, and in the poem itself, he and Bradstreet, its two speakers, carry on a liaison across time and space. Lines from *Berryman's Sonnets*, which were written to his mistress Lise, reappear in *Homage*, addressed to Bradstreet. As Arpin puts it, "Berryman projected onto history the affair recorded in, but not completely exorcised by, the *Sonnets*. . . . Thus, Mistress Bradstreet repeats Lise's words. . . . It is tempting to say that *Homage to Mistress Bradstreet* is *Berryman's Sonnets* writ large, but this would be a bit misleading."[21] Yes, but enlightening as well; for *Homage* may well be the product of an attempt to render the too-personal material of *Berryman's Sonnets* into the impersonal poetry that he, in his early period, found acceptable and publishable. "The notion of a tryst at an impossible distance in time," writes Haffenden, "suited his need for a form of objectivity: the poem was to be a dramatic subterfuge rather than a personal lyric."[22]

Yet the poem is not completely an objective Eliotic poet's subterfuge; for while managing to hide Lise behind Anne Bradstreet, Berryman was unable to resist putting himself into the poem undisguised, unable to avoid his growing necessity to deal directly in his poetry with raw feeling, unable to overcome the sense of unmitigated despair which is at the center of the poem.

Berryman's style and form in *Homage* are a clear departure from those in his early poems. The eight-line stanzas are very similar to the six-line stanzas he would later invent for *The Dream Songs;* and the inverted syntax one finds all through *Homage* likewise foreshadows the *Songs.* Yet, in style as in thematic approach, Berryman has not yet crossed into the territory of his later period. Helen Vendler feels that in *Homage* Berryman has achieved the colloquial style that characterizes much of his later poetry, but who can call this colloquial?

> Beloved household, I am Simon's wife,
> and the mother of Samuel—whom greedy yet I miss
> out of his kicking place.
> More in some ways I feel at a loss,
> freer. Cantabanks & mummers, nears
> longing for you. Our chopping scores my ears,
> our costume bores my eyes.
> St. George to the good sword, rise!

As Linebarger observes, Berryman's language here is a mixture of the "formal, archaic, biblical, elevated; it is seldom colloquial."[23]

Indeed, though Berryman, in *Homage,* leaves many of the trappings of his early manner behind, he has not yet found the chatty, irreverent, and powerfully original style of his later poetry, which can convey humor in one line, pathos in the next, with what often seems the greatest of ease. Linebarger correctly notes a certain air of artificiality about *Homage;* John Ciardi questions "whether the passion is . . . truly love . . . or more nearly a thing literary and made."[24] Though one may believe in Berryman's genuine love for Lise and his utter fascination with Bradstreet, the passion in *Homage* reminds one more of something one has encountered in other books than of something one has known in real life. Reading the poem, one has little sense of Berryman's devotion to Bradstreet, only of his burning devotion to the act of crafting the well-made poem.

So devoted was Berryman, in fact, that he spent five years on this poem. For better and worse, it shows. The spontaneous quality of the *Songs* and of virtually all of Berryman's later work is in no way present in *Homage;* the Bradstreet poem is a good deal more labored than most of his early work. In truth, there is still a great deal of the Eliotic poet, the impersonal maker, about the Berryman who wrote *Homage.* His reason for admiring Bradstreet and picking her as the subject for his opus is that of an Eliotic poet; "her great effort to create, to exercise her intellect is to be greatly admired."[25] Moreover, like a true Eliotic poet, Berryman worked lines and images from

Bradstreet's own poetry into his poem. Finally, like Eliot, Berryman could not resist the tendency to append a few pages of notes to his magnum opus, to point up its difficulty.

Schwartz's *Vaudeville for a Princess* (1950) is an early work, but it is useful to discuss it here, for it vividly demonstrates the distinctions between early and later Middle Generation poetry. In *Vaudeville* we find the tenets, the commonplaces of early Middle Generation poetry being assaulted vigorously by those which would become dominant in the later poetry. In other words, we do not simply find Schwartz's early poetry melting gently into his later poetry, but instead discover the two periods clashing dramatically, in open conflict. We see Schwartz under siege, his id and his Eliotic superego competing for mastery in his work. The superego wins, for the time being, but the battle is very close, portentous, and instructive.

"On a Sentence by Pascal," the first poem in the book, is about a habit the Middle Generation poets had learned from Eliot, that of making a poem out of quotations from other writers. The poem begins with a quotation from Pascal—"True eloquence mocks eloquence"—and goes on to say that "Eloquence laughs at rhetoric" and that "truth is ridiculous."[26] To Schwartz, the word rhetoric must have meant, more than anything, the writings of Eliot. The air of cultivation, the habit of learned reference, the illusion of authority: classical rhetoric is made of this, and so is Eliot. Schwartz's poem makes jest of Eliot's type of writing. To say that "Eloquence laughs at rhetoric" is to say that the secret of true eloquence lies in capturing in words one's own feelings of the moment; it is to say that divorcing oneself from one's own way of thinking, seeing, feeling, and expressing oneself, and to write according to rules which discount the value of those things, is ludicrous. To say "Truth is ridiculous" is to say much the same thing. Schwartz means, I think, that the notion of achieving objective, universal truth in poetry is fallacious. He is beginning to write like an existentialist.

Yet at the same time he remains fettered to Eliot. He is, indeed, more obsessed with that which he is breaking away from than with that which he is breaking away to. Though he purports to reject Eliot, "On a Sentence by Pascal" is very much the poem of a disciple of Eliot. For Schwartz is still engaged in the pseudo-Eliotic enterprise of making literary allusions, indeed of basing a whole poem upon a literary allusion. By the definition implicit in it, this poem is itself not eloquence but rhetoric. Though Schwartz is laughing at Eliot, "On a

Sentence by Pascal" is less a rebel's cry than a goad to himself to rebel. A poet who had already succeeded in shaking off Eliot would not be drawn into writing such a strange little poem as this. Only the uneasy, restless disciple, who is still a disciple in spite of himself, would write such a thing.

"On a Sentence by Pascal" is, in a sense, _Vaudeville for a Princess_ in miniature. For the book thumbs its nose at Eliot, and makes a point of rejecting, or seeming to reject, everything Eliot has said about tradition. Schwartz models the form of the book not on anyone else's book of poems but on something from an entirely different sphere of aesthetic activity, the vaudeville bill. To Schwartz, the worshipper at the shrine of Eliot, this is obviously a supreme act of heresy, one that would occur only to a devout congregant. If Eliot represents high tradition, vaudeville is vulgar, seedy contemporaneity; if Eliot is order, vaudeville is disorder, one act following another, each completely autonomous. If Eliot's poetry is meant to say something about all men and for all time, vaudeville is of the moment, each skit or song leaving its mark only till the performer goes offstage and the lights come up on the next act. If one does not like music, the song will be over in a moment and there will be an acrobat, a dog act, a comic. Disorder is the order of the day.

Yet the ploy does not really succeed. Schwartz's obsession with order fails to crumble, despite his valiant attempts to make it do so. Ironically, as a result of his choosing the vaudeville show as his organizational model, _Vaudeville_ ends up seeming far more consciously ordered than any other early volume of poetry by the Middle Generation poets. The first part of the book follows a very rigorous organizational scheme. Each poem, except the first, is preceded by a short humorous essay which touches on the same theme. Thus " 'My Mind to Me a Kingdom Is,' " which dissects the "Civil War" between the poet's "mind and self," is preceded by a piece called "Existentialism: The Inside Story," which deals with the same topic.

Schwartz's prose does not lie within the province of this study, but it should be noted that the prose pieces in _Vaudeville_ are far more successful, in terms of achieving genuine personal expression, than are the poems.[27] Yet the obsession of the _Vaudeville_ poems with Eliot carries over into the prose. The essays seem to be written in a style that is deliberately opposed to the style of Eliot's essays. In some cases, in fact, Schwartz chooses topics that Eliot has already covered. He has a _Hamlet_ essay, for example, titled "Hamlet, or There is

Something Wrong with Everyone." But rather than writing in Eliot's impressive, authoritative style, Schwartz adopts a breezy *Reader's Digest*-type manner, characterized by clichés, banalities, bad jokes, and wildly unlikely interpretations. Rather than trying to sound like a highbrow, he tries his best to sound like a lowbrow:

> People have been arguing for hundreds of years about what was really wrong with Hamlet. Some say that he must have been a woman, some say that he was a homosexual, in love with his uncle or with Horatio, and unable to bear the fact that his uncle slept with a woman, and there is one fascinating view which maintains that all the mystery is utterly clarified if we suppose that everyone is roaring drunk from the beginning to the end of the play. This view is very fine except that I don't see how it clarifies anything, for drunk or sober, not everyone behaves the same, and the real question is why Hamlet behaved as he did: certainly just hitting the bottle does not account for all his emotions and opinions, and *in vino veritas*, anyway.

Sometimes the sneer at Eliot is more obvious than at other times; Schwartz has Hamlet saying, "I had not thought life had undone so many."[28] Schwartz does have some points to make, and he makes them entertainingly. But one of his main objects in these prose pieces is simply to play off Eliot's highbrow prose style. Atlas, apparently not recognizing this, is puzzled by and disappointed in the *Vaudeville* essays. He says that the pieces "revealed how little confidence Delmore had in his own authentic voice," describes their tone as self-deprecating, and calls his interpretations of *Hamlet* and *Othello* contrived.[29] But it is obvious to anyone with a sense of humor that in these essays Schwartz does not want to write in an authentic voice; he does not mean to be completely serious in his interpretations; and if he deprecates himself, he deprecates everything else too. The critical analyses are silly because Schwartz is beginning to feel that criticism, as Eliot practices it, is silly. Thus when he calls a piece "Existentialism: The Inside Story," he is, with reason, deliberately using a corny play on words, and deliberately aping the type of clichéd title that one would find in lowbrow magazines such as the *Saturday Evening Post* or *Collier's*.

When one moves from a prose essay in "Vaudeville for a Princess" to its companion poem, one discovers that Schwartz is exploring the same theme but modulating into a completely different voice. The titles alone show what I mean; if "Existentialism: The Inside Story" sounds like something out of the *Saturday Evening Post*, " 'My

Mind to Me a Kingdom Is' " sounds like something out of Elizabethan poetry; and, of course, it is. The title comes not from contemporary lowbrow literature but from centuries-old highbrow literature. If Sir Edward Dyer's poem makes the statement, "Content I live, this is my stay," Schwartz's poem says the very opposite: "The mind to me a North Pole is."[30] Intellectual poetry, in other words, is something he finds cold and inhospitable. As in "On a Sentence by Pascal," Schwartz is here repudiating T. S. Eliot, intellectual poet, while at the same time indulging in the poetic mannerisms which he learned from Eliot. For in the course of " 'My Mind to Me a Kingdom Is' " Schwartz compares himself to "James' governess," alludes to several public figures from the Civil War era, and suggests a parallel between Ulysses S. Grant and the hero of the *Odyssey.* The poem is, indeed, exactly the sort of thing which Schwartz is criticizing; it is poetry which is at least as much about literature as it is about life. Such perseverance in the Eliotic habit of basing a poem upon someone else's poem, even if to ridicule it, confirms that in *Vaudeville* the mind still has the upper hand. Schwartz's desire to express his deepest feelings is hampered as much as ever. As the title of one of his *Vaudeville* essays puts it, "The Ego is Always at the Wheel"; when writing *Vaudeville,* apparently, the possibility that the id might one day move uncontested into the front seat in his poetry seemed remote to Schwartz.

A particularly interesting *Vaudeville* poem, in terms of Schwartz's desire to rebel against Eliot, is "I Did Not Know the Spoils of Joy." The poem, which chronicles Schwartz's poetic development, as he had come to perceive it, begins by telling us of Schwartz's early conversion to Eliot's doctrines of "thought and art."[31] These doctrines caused him, in his early poetry, to turn away from his "heart," to ignore his real personal concerns. He broke faith with his "native" style, themes, and approach, choosing instead to be bewitched by Eliot's conception of poetry as something impersonal and intellectual. As a result, Schwartz's natural voice wilted from neglect.

Yet as time passed, he came to feel that Eliot, the poet of the intellect, was wrong: the mind, he writes, lied in the manner of a waltz "which chants love as a brilliant ball." Poetry of the intellect does not lead to knowledge. The word "ball" can mean not only a sumptuous dance, but a round object. It is, as I have mentioned, an image that appears in several early Middle Generation poems, in imitation of Donne's "A Valediction: Of Weeping." Like all round objects, a ball symbolizes unity, the cyclical rhythms which, in such poems as *The Waste Land*, represent the hope that there is some principle of order beneath the apparent chaos of the world. In these early years of thought and art, Schwartz is saying, his cogitation convinced him that love must be the answer, that in a senseless world love must be the only thing that can provide order and meaning. Yet later, as he says, he came to feel this notion was utterly misguided; and so he ceased allowing his conscious mind to rule in his poetry, and instead learned to follow his dreams, his unconscious mind. However, the pain he found there, unsalved by the cynical intellectualism which had once protected him, forced him to drive "the quickest car to bliss," to be "charmed," rather than terrified, at the thought of mortality. This is, oddly enough, a good way of describing what Schwartz would do in later poems, but which he had not yet done when this poem was written. In those later poems, he writes about the inevitability of death in a tone that does indeed suggest the words "bliss" and "charmed." But the seemingly ecstatic tone which makes so many of Schwartz's later poems sound like "parodies of hope" is in reality the sound of a manic poet's horror. Schwartz may be "glad that I exist," but however pleased he is to be alive, we could hardly call him happy.

Thus the truth to Schwartz, in his later period, is a relatively simple thing. It is the full experiencing of the present moment, for the present moment is all one can know; it is the celebration of even the barest possibility of knowing joy in this life, for even a moment's joy is a miracle in the face of mortality. Truth is not objective but subjective, not eternal but ephemeral. Thus, to this metaphysician, this student of Kant and Hegel, "How strange the truth appears at last!" His knowledge may be almost entirely negative; all he knows is that he has lost the past forever, that the present is fleeting, and that the future will bring death. "And yet this knowledge . . . / Can make me glad that I exist!" Simply the discovery that this, after all his metaphysical flirtations, is the meaning of life, can uplift him. Death amounts to a "ha ha at last." The poem is more thematically consistent with Schwartz's later poems than anything else in *Vaudeville*, with the exception of "Starlight Like Intuition Pierced the Twelve." Significantly, these are two of the three poems, out of the fifty-six in *Vaudeville*, which Schwartz carried over into *Summer Knowledge*, where they are included among his later poems.

What separates "I Did Not Know the Spoils of Joy" from most of Schwartz's later poems is that in this poem he is still clinging to Eliot. The poem is, after all, modeled on a song by Shakespeare, proving that even though Schwartz appears to be rebelling against Eliot, he still knows which writers the proper young modern poet must allude to. Moreover, Schwartz does not so much express his feelings in this poem as give a history and analysis of them. He has begun to metamorphose into a different kind of poet, but has not yet cut himself completely free of Eliot of self-objectification, of thought and art.

The next poem in *Vaudeville* demonstrates this continuing enchantment by Eliot. "True Recognition Often is Refused" is about the poet's vocation.[32] The "strict perception" of the impersonal Eliotic poet, which Schwartz describes in the previous poem as an unadmirable hiding from the heart, he describes here as an admirable purification of the heart. Note the echoes of Eliot. The "girl upon the sofa's ease" sounds like something out of "Prufrock"; "April's underground" is an allusion to *The Waste Land*; the roundness of the girl is an Eliotic symbol of order; the diction, form, even the rhyme are exactly like Eliot's. Thus, in *Vaudeville*, though Schwartz feels tempted to write subjective poetry, he remains in the great poet's thrall. In "The Passionate Shepherd to His Love," the speaker promises his love that they will do all that thought can "Against emotion's Genghis Khan."[33] These are the words of an orthodox Eliotic poet, who affirms the value of thought over emotion, echoes Christopher Marlowe, and is cynical. Yet, as "Most Things at Second Hand We Touch" makes clear, Schwartz is sorely tempted to let his feelings be his guide; he suggests that we all "lay bare our hearts" and "take away the masks."[34]

More than any other poem in *Vaudeville*, "Starlight Like Intuition Pierced the Twelve" is in many ways a typical late Schwartz poem. This is particularly true in terms of its attitude toward time. Although the Middle Generation poets, upon entering their later period, changed their approach to poetry and altered their styles, they did not abandon their major themes. These themes are what give Middle Generation poetry its continuity. Time, the most important theme in the early poetry, is an equally prominent concern in the later poetry. The treatment of it, however, is very different. Whereas the early poems endeavor to deal with time intellectually, to subdue its effect upon the individual sensibility by an act of the ordering will, the later poetry expresses an intense emotional reaction to the fact of time. If in the early poetry the poet is the manipulator of time, in the later poetry time is in control. This is clearly the situation in "Starlight," in which Christ's disciples take turns bemoaning the irrecoverability of the past: "This life will never be what once it was!"[35] This is the last line of "Starlight," and also the last line of *Summer Knowledge.* Schwartz, apparently feeling that the poem made an important summary statement, placed it at the end of his selection of later poetry in that book. The poem indeed has the sound of a later Middle Generation poem; the poet is obsessed with the fact of the passage of time, and deeply disturbed by his inability to do anything about it.

Jarrell's "The Woman at the Washington Zoo," the introductory and title poem of his first volume of later poetry, grows out of much the same feelings. The last line and a half of this poem—"You know what I was, / You see what I am: change me, change me!"[36]—amount to a slight variation on the last line of "Starlight Like Intuition Pierced the Twelve." The speaker, far from imprisoning time in his poem, which is of course the conceit of the Middle Generation poets' early period, is here imprisoned by time. The same is true in Berryman's seventh Dream Song, " 'The Prisoner of Shark Island' with Paul Muni," which begins "Henry is old, old." Like Schwartz's and Jarrell's poems, Berryman's Song is about the irrevocability of the past; here Jarrell's vulture, a symbol of time's passage, is replaced by an equally unwholesome bevy of rats who "have moved in" on his life. "This is for real," says Berryman; the present moment is the only reality. Henry may wish he could return to the days of movies like *Ben-Hur* and *Mr. Deeds Goes to Town,* but those fondly remembered moments from earlier times, when he lost himself in the fantasy of film, cannot be relived.[37] As Schwartz writes, "we shall never be as once we were, / This life will never be what once it was!" Among those later Lowell poems in which he expresses his obsession with what he once was is "For Sheridan," from *Day by Day.*[38] The despair of these poems is not always the rule in later Middle Generation poetry. Often, in their later period, the Middle Generation poets seem to find delirious pleasure in the role of time's victim. Actually, it is more delirium than pleasure. Still, to the Middle Generation poets in these later years, the very fact of feeling is an accomplishment to be celebrated, even if one is feeling pain. To feel is to live; I feel, therefore I am. In this the poets were very close to the Symbolists. Rimbaud wrote *A Season in Hell* during what he called a "very severe" hour, but his tone at the end of that book is almost exultant as he boasts: "I shall be free to *possess truth in one soul and one body*."[39] Perhaps this existential sentiment best sums up the philosophy that guided the composition of the later poetry of the Middle Generation.

$$\overline{\qquad\qquad} \; 10 \; \overline{\qquad\qquad}$$

Summer Knowledge:
Schwartz's Later Poetry

Robert Lowell and John Berryman made a point of saying that whole volumes of their later poetry—*Notebook, The Dream Songs*—were meant to be read as single long poems. Schwartz never made such a statement about his later poems, but he might well have. Perhaps as much as any body of later Middle Generation verse, Schwartz's later poems seem to comprise a single long work, with one major theme, one voice, one style, and one consistent tone. The theme is the individual's experience of, awareness of, and attitude toward life in the face of the inevitability of death. The voice is undeniably that of the poet, unrestrainedly speaking out of his own deepest preoccupations. It is hard to know whether the tone should be characterized as one of intense joy or profound anguish; it is, at least, safe to say that it is anxious and unconstrained. During these years Schwartz was psychotic, and perhaps when one is speaking of the state of mind of such a deeply disturbed person the words joy and anguish are irrelevant.

As these two opposing tonal qualities may appear to come together in Schwartz's later poems, so do two seemingly opposed philosophies of life. For often we find Schwartz lamenting the approach of death in one line and celebrating "the deathless present" in the next. *"Eternity is now!"* he writes in "Hölderlin." His late poems are full of such ostensible contradictions. Even a short occasional poem, such as "Christmas Poem for Nancy," becomes the occasion for epistemological vacillation. We live, the poem says, between heaven and hell, between sky and earth. "And all shall be well," it insists—but in the next line directly contradicts this prognostication, saying that everything will be "unwell."[1] The poem can be read either as bitterly ironic or utterly sincere. The more familiar one becomes with Schwartz's later work, the more one is inclined to suspect that it is intended to be read in both ways simultaneously. Indeed, the very point of the poem is that life is a paradoxical mixture of the joyful and painful and that, therefore, the only proper view to take of the human condition is the dichotomous, self-contradictory one espoused in the poem.

Self-contradiction is, in fact, almost unavoidable when one is writing the type of poetry that Schwartz writes during his later period. Since he is a poet of the moment, his conception of truth is circumscribed completely by whatever sentiments possess him at the time of composition. Moreover, a self-contradictory perspective comes naturally to a man with Schwartz's psychiatric problems. Perhaps the ultimate irony for Schwartz, during his later years, was that, as a manic depressive, he could not even be certain of his uncertainty, secure in his misery. For his manic depressive curve rose and fell unpredictably. Such was his state of mind that it is no wonder he could describe pain and joy as if they were twins, life and death as if they were identical. "Confusion is variety," he writes, equating nature with life as well as death, with winter as well as spring; and "confusion" is the operative word.[2] However much it may seem that the speaker in these poems has reached some comfortable resolution, these linkages which Schwartz is constantly making between utter opposites do not signify that he has reached some transcendent sense of unity, but merely that he is utterly confused by the chaotic signals from an anarchic world which pound his brain. "The only thing," he writes in a late poem called "The Foggy, Foggy Blue," "is to believe in everything": that way, it's more fun, more safe.[3] The lines sound flippant. But they are, in truth, the pathetic cry of a brilliant, diseased mind which is bewildered beyond hope of deliverance by the irresolvable complexity of life.

When Schwartz collected his poems in 1959, he named the book *Summer Knowledge,* and gave the same name to the second part of the book, which contained his later verse. Having reached his mid-forties, Schwartz felt that he had entered the summer of his life, and the purpose of the poems in "Summer Knowledge" was to convey the new understanding of the meaning of knowledge which had come to him after years of playing in T. S. Eliot's intellectual backyard. As Richard McDougall writes, this new type of knowledge is "intuitive rather than analytical" and "is, above all, exemplified by the works of the artists, poets, and musicians, whom Schwartz now celebrates not as 'culture heroes' enduring the martyrdom of isolation, but rather as celebrants and seers endowed with a transcendent and life-transforming vision."[4] It would be closer to the truth, I think, to call the vision "life-escaping"; for the life that Schwartz deals with in these poems is not real life, but a life that is lived by people who do not exist in a world that does not exist. If in his early poetry he escapes from his personality into the real world, in his later poetry he escapes from the real world into his personality, into a fantasy world created by the artist's imagination. As Atlas says, "Delmore turned away from a terrible existence in search of a purer Mallarméan mode."[5] It is indeed in his later period that the Symbolist influence becomes most important for Schwartz. Breaking loose of the chaos of the real world, Schwartz allows himself to withdraw into a finer, if unreal dimension, of whose order and timelessness and beauty he can sing without self-contradiction. In "Seurat's Sunday Afternoon Along the Seine," one of his finest later poems, he escapes into the world of a neo-impressionist painting, a world free of the anxiety and pain of the real world. Schwartz describes the people in the painting. There is "A little girl" who clings to her mother's arm "as if it were a permanent genuine certainty" and there is a bourgeois man whose "dignity is as solid as his *embonpoint.*" This man and his wife, Schwartz observes, act "as if they were unaware or free of time, and the grave." And of course, these people in the painting are free of time and the grave. In the fixed world of the painting the girl's mother's arm is a permanent certainty, the gentleman's dignity is unshakable. It is a world in which, far from the anarchy of the real world, "All things are fixed." Schwartz praises the creator of this oil and canvas world as a poet, painter, alchemist, and architect who preserves this Sunday afternoon for all time. "O happy, happy throng," he writes, echoing Keats's "Ode on a Grecian Urn."[6] Like Keats, he is celebrating an artist who has captured a happy moment forever. Neither poem, however, is a truly happy one. Each springs from its author's obsession with the unpleasantness of the real world. Like Keats, Schwartz is profoundly disturbed by the fact that "old age shall this generation waste," and so involves himself with a created world in which aging does not exist. In "Ode on a Grecian Urn," Keats speaks to the lover on the urn who is pursuing his beloved:

> Bold Lover, never, never, canst thou kiss,
> Though winning near the goal—yet, do not grieve;
> She cannot fade, though thou hast not thy bliss,
> Forever wilt thou love, and she be fair![7]

Reading this, one does not share the speaker's supposed joy over the eternal youth and sensuality of the figures on the vase, but the essential melancholy that lies behind the speaker's absorption in the urn. The same is true of Schwartz's poem. The paean to the frozen moment of time only makes one all the more aware of the speaker's anguish in the real world. Indirectly, the theme of "Seurat's Sunday Afternoon Along the Seine" is the pain of living in a chaotic world afflicted with the curse of time. Whatever joy there is in such a world is fleeting; it is for the artist to capture whatever moments of joy come his way, or to absorb himself in the lovely moments which other artists have frozen in works of art.

Yet one cannot escape the real world forever. Although time does not alter the people in the painting, in the real world time passes, things change, Seurat's painting has moved to a museum in Chicago. The people in that painting "stretch out their hands to me: but they are too far away!" Thus, although the speaker has lost himself in the world of Seurat's painting, he ends by bemoaning the fact that he cannot truly live in that world. Note the way in which Schwartz defines truth in these lines. To be "with the truth" is to have managed to escape from time, from the chaos of the real world, into a dimension where eternity truly is now. Truth is a subjective, momentary phenomenon.

As Schwartz depicts his own escape into a painting in "Seurat's Sunday Afternoon," so in " 'I Am Cherry Alive,' the Little Girl Sang," he depicts a child's escape into a fantasy world of her own devising. This child believes herself to be *dans le vrai* in the same way as are the people in Seurat's painting. Like many imaginative children, she feels herself to have power over time, over the anarchy of the universe, over the "withness of the body." Adults have confessed their helplessness, but she does not feel herself to be helpless; she is convinced that she will always be youthful, always be able to transform herself in her imagination into a fruit, a tree, a witch. She is, indeed, a good deal like a younger Schwartz, who in his early poetry takes much the same stance as the child takes here. Part of what Schwartz is doing in this poem, in fact, is painting a picture of the confidence in the unifying power of the will that characterized his early period. In this poem, Schwartz sees that confidence as pathetic; the notion of the ability of the ordering will to subdue time which once guided his poetry is now, to him, only a child's poignant illusion.

Perhaps the poem which best and most fully expresses the philosophy of Schwartz's later period is "Summer Knowledge." The poem attempts to define the intuitive subjective type of knowledge which Schwartz discovered in his later years.

> Summer knowledge is green knowledge, country
> knowledge, the knowledge of growing and the
> supple recognition of the fullness and the
> fatness and the roundness of ripeness.

Knowledge, in other words, is the very opposite of what we usually mean by the word. It is completely nonintellectual; it is the animal's, or even the plant's, experience of the subjective moment, its unhampered involvement in the biological processes that are the fundamentals of its existence. The bird or tree accepts itself as a mortal creature, and functions according to the dictates of nature; it does not attempt to subdue nature to its will, or endeavor to grasp nature intellectually. Summer knowledge, writes Schwartz, "is the knowledge of death as birth." He does not mean that it is the conscious awareness of death that only humans can have, but rather the intuitive understanding of and acceptance of death that the animals and trees, living without fear or dread, seem to have. We will age, we will die, but we must die in order for others to be born. This cyclical process is suggested by the phrase "the roundness of ripeness."

But, Schwartz is trying to say, this cyclical process is not for us to concern ourselves with. Not for him, in the summer of his life, a once-prized sense of history, a drawing of Eliotic connections between past and present. His devotion to a process of inquiry which aims to discover some unseen principle of unity in the universe is completely a thing of the past. For summer knowledge has nothing to do with "lore and learning."[9] In "T. S. Eliot as the International Hero," Schwartz had written:

> When we speak of nature and of a new range of experience, we may think of a mountain range: some may make the vehicles by means of which a mountain is climbed, some may climb the mountain, and some may apprehend the new view of the surrounding countryside which becomes possible from the heights of the mountain. T. S. Eliot is a culture hero in each of these three ways.[10]

But now he says that summer knowledge "is not the knowledge known from the mountain's height." He no longer looks at things in Eliot's way. He is not, in this poem, bitter toward Eliot as in *Vaudeville for a Princess;* there is, in his tone, not the slightest trace of hostility toward his former philosophy or the man from whom he learned it. He is simply trying to explain the way he now feels, and to distinguish it from his old view. He seems to allude further to Eliot when he writes that summer knowledge "is not the garden's view of the distant mountains or the hidden fountains." For in *Four Quartets* Eliot's speaker entered "the rose-garden" in which a "drained pool . . . was filled with water out of sunlight, / / Then a cloud passed, and the pool was empty."[11]

These late poems of Schwartz's, unlike many of his early poems, could not be easily mistaken for anyone else's. Nevertheless, the influence of Walt Whitman upon Schwartz's later style is obvious. This influence is explained largely by a strong similarity between the two poets' conceptions of poetry. Like Whitman, Schwartz in his later period wants to be a poet of life, of experience; he wants his poems to record, or at least to seem to record, the impressions of the moment as honestly, as fully, as sensuously as possible. As with Whitman, Schwartz's emphasis on the sentiments of the moment, and his acceptance of the possibility that he may well feel very differently tomorrow from the way he feels at present, makes it possible for him to say without discomfort, "Very well, I contradict myself."

But Schwartz's imitation of Whitman is different from his imitation of Eliot, Yeats, and Auden. Schwartz learns from Whitman without being dominated by him, swallowed up by his ideas. Whitman's genuinely joyful, transcendental sense of unity among himself and all mankind is twisted by Schwartz into a madman's apotheosis of the common doom. "Summer Knowledge," for example, ends with an allusion to death, "the consummation and annihilation of the blaze of fall." Similarly, a poem which begins with the Whitmanesque declaration, "I am a poet of the Hudson River and the heights above it, / the lights, the stars, and the bridges," ends with a description of the buildings of New York as "slab-like tombs."[12] Likewise, in the late poem "A Dream of Whitman Paraphrased, Recognized and Made More Vivid by Renoir," Schwartz turns Whitman's celebration of sexual fruitfulness into a bitter comment on the temporality of all things. His poem begins with lines adapted from *Leaves of Grass* in which young women bathe outdoors, swimming with wondrous lack of consciousness "of their youth and beauty." But he ends with an augur of death; the thirty-year-old who is watching the girls sees fallen leaves, "shadowy light."[13] Clearly, Schwartz's intention in quoting Whitman here is to comment upon him, and not merely to mimic. Schwartz, in these later poems, is free of his masters, past and present; that he can, in his later years, write a poem subtly acknowledging his ties to Whitman and yet sharply pointing up the difference between their philosophies is, in light of his early poetry, evidence of a remarkable new independence.

Whitman is not the only poet upon whom Schwartz comments in this manner in his later verse. In a poem called "Now He Knows All There Is to Know: Now He Is Acquainted With the Day and Night," Schwartz pays tribute to the recently deceased Robert Frost. The poem begins with an imitation of the opening lines of "Stopping By Woods on a Snowy Evening."[14] Schwartz seems to congratulate Frost in this poem for being much the same kind of poet Schwartz himself has become in his later period, a poet who sees the holiness of the moment-to-moment experience of life, and who accepts himself as a mortal part of nature. For Schwartz to say that Frost knows all there is to know is simply to say that Frost has experienced every moment of his life fully and sensuously and without intellectual distraction or attempts at self-objectification, and since one's life is all one has, and objective knowledge is impossible, Frost does know all anyone can know.

A more obvious influence upon Schwartz's later poetry is Dylan Thomas, with whom Schwartz shares a love of repeated sounds and of sensuous nature-images almost divorced from meaning. The poem "Darkling Summer, Ominous Dusk, Rumorous Rain" is strongly evocative of Thomas.[15] And the continuing identification of the Middle Generation poets with the Symbolists is demonstrated eloquently by Schwartz's poem "Baudelaire." The somewhat objective approach and controlled style of this poem make it a very rare exception to the rule of Schwartz's later poetry; but Schwartz by no means escapes his own personality to write about Baudelaire's. The details of the poem, taken from Baudelaire's life, touch upon Schwartz's own deepest preoccupations. If the title did not tell us that the subject is Baudelaire, we might well take it as autobiography. The poem is written in the form of a letter from Baudelaire to his much-loved, deeply resented, and painfully uncomprehending mother. He tells her of his sense of alienation, his unhappiness, his intense awareness of his own ignorance, his unsettled emotional state, his drive to create. Reading this poem, one begins to recognize how much the tormented late Schwartz poems that surround it in *Summer Knowledge* owe to the Symbolists. Indeed, one has the sense that it was, to a large extent, the Symbolists who helped all the Middle Generation poets into their later period. Arpin, in his study of Berryman, observes that "Berryman's style evolved . . . in response to . . . the aesthetic of Symbolism, with its insistence on creating a new language that, in Rimbaud's words, 'would be of the soul, for the soul, containing everything, smells, sounds, colors; thought latching onto thought and pulling.'" Likewise, Atlas remarks that Schwartz, in turning away from Eliot, "found more congenial models in those exemplary figures of revolt Rimbaud and Baudelaire."[16] More accurately, Eliot endorsed Rimbaud and Baudelaire as neo-Metaphysical poets and Schwartz admired them as such even in their teens; but Schwartz, in turning away from Eliotic, came to see that in their subjectivity, in their spirit of revolt, in their obsession with love and death, in their understanding of poetry as an attempt to capture in rapturous music the fleeting glimpse of a momentary personal kind of truth, Baudelaire and Rimbaud represented the type of poet he was beginning to recognize in himself.

Schwartz's later work has received as much criticism as *In Dreams Begin Responsibilities* received praise. This is, I believe, due largely to two factors. First, the overreaction to *In Dreams* placed impossible expectations upon Schwartz for a follow-up volume, and virtually guaranteed that his readers would be disappointed by it. Second, Schwartz's turn away from Eliotic poetry to a very different sort of poetry confused and angered his former admirers and propagandists, many of whom no doubt saw his philosophical realignment as something of a betrayal. Atlas calls the late poems "haphazard, euphonious, virtually incomprehensible effusions," and complains that "too many of them are empty symphonies of sound; while not without a peculiar beauty, they verge on being devoid of any sense whatever."[17] Patently, Atlas is judging these poems from the point of view of someone who considers a Romantic poet's effusions a necessarily inferior type of poem to the crafted object of the Metaphysical poet. Sound and beauty are not as important to Atlas as "sense," that is, meaning, ideas, an intellectual purpose, an attempt to understand.

Robert Phillips disagrees with Atlas. He argues that "Darkling Summer, Ominous Dusk, Rumorous Rain," which Atlas singles out for special condemnation, is different from Schwartz's early poetry in that it is clearly not an attempt to mythologize himself, or to dramatize history, or to pay homage to the world of culture. Rather, it often accurately re-creates a sensuous experience and does so in language that is musical, free-associative, and highly communicative. . . . It is an example of his later style of spontaneous effusion, characterized by energy and delight. . . . To dismiss such poems because of their euphony would be to dismiss Gerard Manley Hopkins, Dame Edith Sitwell, and Dylan Thomas, to name three.[18]

Indeed. What Atlas seems unhappy with is that these later poems are not, like Schwartz's early verse, the restrained, controlled, carefully crafted work of an *homme de lettres,* a poet of the intellect. They are, rather, the seemingly spontaneous spoutings of a manic depressive who has determined to allow his fluctuating feelings to reign in his poetry. To say that these late verses represent a clean break with Schwartz's early poetry is valid; to say that they are not poetry at all is wrong. Schwartz's later poems speak as powerfully to our senses as his early poems speak to our minds.

The Book of Death:
Jarrell's Later Poetry

Like Schwartz, Jarrell in his later poetry is obsessed with the passage of time and seems desperately to desire escape from the real world to a place where time does not exist. If the Middle Generation poets, during their later period, had wanted an anthem, Jarrell's "Aging"— with its references to "these quick-passing hours" and such—would have been the perfect choice.[1] The poem is from Jarrell's 1960 volume, *The Woman at the Washington Zoo*, the first of the two collections of poetry published during his later period. The typical early Jarrell poem, it will be remembered, has a speaker who is clearly not Jarrell, and takes place in a setting with which Jarrell was unfamiliar. I have said of these early poems that sometimes it seems nearly everyone is here except Jarrell himself. In these later poems this situation changes, and the poems become subjective. The process of bringing himself into his poems is, however, a gradual one. In *Washington Zoo*, Jarrell writes essentially subjective poems, but in some he gives the speaker a separate identity. In most cases, this amounts to little more than a gratuitous gesture toward an objectivity which he had outgrown. The speaker in such poems, in other words, is clearly Jarrell in disguise.

The volume's title poem, for instance, purports to present the musings of a woman. It is in every way a departure from Jarrell's early poems. In those poems, the settings—Melanesia, Madrid, Hamburg, Haifa—are often places Jarrell knew only from books and films; here, the setting is the National Zoo, only a couple of blocks from Jarrell's home. In Jarrell's early poems, the characters seem to be representative humans moved about by the author in order to demonstrate some universal theme; in "Washington Zoo," the woman comes across as a real person. She does not exist merely to convey the theme; rather, the poem appears to exist to convey the essence of her anguish, and the theme develops naturally out of that anguish. "Washington Zoo" has an honesty and force of feeling that Jarrell's early poems, for all his eagerness to capture the tragedy of war, do not have. Thus the few contrivances in "Washington Zoo" are particularly noticeable. Making the speaker a woman is a contrivance; Jarrell could just as easily have made her a man, in which case it would have been obvious that the speaker is essentially Jarrell. The only thing besides her sex that distinguishes the speaker from Jarrell is that she works for "my chief, / The Deputy Chief Assistant," a touch of secondhand Auden which provides the poem's only strained note. It is interesting that this incongruous, heavy-handed bit of irony, which Jarrell offers by way of distancing the woman from himself, is so typical of the Auden-derived style that characterizes Jarrell's early poetry. Clearly there were some habits which, at this point in his later period, he had not yet completely shaken.

Yet most of the traces of the early poetry are, by the time of "Washington Zoo," long gone. There is no attempt in this poem to compel disparate experience into unity, or to rob a character of his particularity to make a thematic statement, as is the case in Jarrell's most famous poem, "The Death of the Ball Turret Gunner." In Jarrell's early period, as Kazin writes, "It *mattered* what Eliot thought. . . . Jarrell did not feel that *he* could afford to be wrong."[2] In Jarrell's later period, Eliot no longer represented what was right to him; what was right was what one felt. And so in the poems of *Washington Zoo*, rather than presenting human ciphers in mechanical dramas or monologues which serve to illustrate some metaphysical point, Jarrell concerns himself with his own feelings, his own experiences. More often than not, the poems deal with the theme of time, aging, mortality.

"In Those Days," for example, is a short poem which expresses the speaker's longing for a time in the past when life was better. The speaker of "The Elementary Scene" sees "the dead land waking sadly to my life" and speaks sardonically of "the future that mends everything." In "Windows," the speaker imagines his death. He will look up wordlessly, and the image blurs; "there is drawn across my face / As my eyes close, a hand's slow fire-warmed flesh." "Nestus Gurley" is the name of a paper boy who, the speaker imagines, delivers to him the news "Of what I have done and what I have not done," of what is set down in the "Book of Death" on already-yellowed paper.[3] By the end of the poem, Nestus Gurley, ever the reminder of the inexorable passage of time, comes to be directly identified with death.

Trapped in a world cursed by time, the speakers in *The Woman at the Washington Zoo* cry out, like the Symbolist poets, for escape. And the language that Jarrell uses in such instances is often reminiscent of the Symbolists. The speaker of Jarrell's poem "Windows," for example, is unhappy with his life and, as Ferguson observes, "longs to enter the lives of other people that he sees through windows, his own and theirs."[4] As in Mallarmé's poem "Les Fenêtres," the window in Jarrell's "Windows" is, to the speaker, the barrier between the unhappy world he inhabits and a more pleasant world. The difference is that in Jarrell's poem the other world is not an imagined alternate universe, but merely the life lived by the speaker's neighbors and other strangers. Yet Jarrell's poetry has, by this time, become so rigorously subjective that the world inhabited by someone other than the speaker is indeed a different world, as forlornly inaccessible as a Symbolist poet's purely envisioned world.

In "Deutsche Durch Freud," Jarrell begins with the declaration: "I believe my favorite country's German." A finer world is represented to him by another language of which he knows only a few words. In that world, he, like the little girl in Schwartz's poem, " 'I Am Cherry Alive,' the Little Girl Sang," can believe in fantasies, in fairy stories. "—In German I believe in them, in everything."[5] One is reminded of Schwartz's remark: "The only only thing is to believe in everything!"

Schwartz also comes to mind when one reads Jarrell's poem "The Girl Dreams That She is Giselle." Like Schwartz's " 'I Am Cherry Alive,' " this poem is about a girl who escapes into another identity. What both poems have in common is the influence of Rilke. Charlotte Beck writes that Jarrell and Rilke "both discover the child who lives on in the adult's consciousness and is not subject to change."[6] She might have said the same of Schwartz, for we have met this same child in " 'I Am Cherry Alive.' " She is the eternal naïf, the joyful innocent who is unable to conceive of such a thing as death. Rilke is a major influence on Jarrell's late work. Nine of the thirty-one poems in *The Woman at the Washington Zoo* are translations from Rilke; the majority of them are about the theme of time and mortality. Typical titles are "Lament," "Death," "Washing the Corpse." Many of the poems are concerned with children. "Childhood," for example, is about the things a child does to fill out his day, unaware that precious time is slipping from him. While he is blithely engaged in his "waiting-out of time," numerous "images [are] gliding from [him]."[7]

If in *Washington Zoo* Jarrell finally enters the world of his poems, in *The Lost World* (1965) he introduces himself. For in many of the poems in this volume the speaker is unquestionably Jarrell. He mentions the names of friends, relatives, the streets he grew up on. "For the first time," writes Robert Watson of *The Lost World*,

> he wrote extensively about his own life, a subject that had seldom entered his poems directly. In this book he altered his style somewhat to give most of the poems a surface simplicity. He also reduced the frequency of his "learned" allusions and changed in general the pitch of his poems from the rhetorical restlessness of much of his previous work—especially the war poems—to quieter speech, more subtle rhythms, which to the unobservant ear may sometimes seem like prose.

As Watson notes, Jarrell had much the same problem as did Schwartz with regard to the reception of his later work:

> Since many of these poems seem so deceptively easy in comparison with the early poems, his last poems have occasionally been dismissed with nods and sad faces which say, "How could such an intellectual giant go against the grain of his mental powers to write such simple, prosy, sentimental poems? Poor Jarrell. Such a falling off."[8]

Watson to the contrary, the learned allusions, difficult language, and rhetorical restlessness did not disappear from Jarrell's poetry between *Washington Zoo* and *The Lost World*, but between *The Seven-League Crutches* and *Washington Zoo*. What could be more stylistically straightforward than "The Lonely Man," a typical poem from the 1960 volume? It begins, "A cat sits on the pavement by the house. / It lets itself be touched, then slides away." Thereupon the poem proceeds to describe, in a flat, neutral tone, the cat's motionlessness, its restrained way of relating to the speaker, and to contrast this with a collie's bounding, unsubtle friendliness. This *Washington Zoo* poem is certainly not rhetorically restless or pretentiously allusive; indeed, it fits Watson's description of the poems of *The Lost World* almost perfectly; as much as any poem in that last volume, this poem contains "quieter speech" than Jarrell's earlier work. It is true, though, that while we can find some poems in *Washington Zoo* whose rhythms are suggestive of prose, "Nestus Gurley" for instance, there is more rhythmic freedom, as well as more blatant subjectivity, in *The Lost World* than in its immediate predecessor.

What really sets *The Lost World* apart from all of Jarrell's previous work is its blatant subjectivity. His poems about his childhood are all from this volume; for the first time, in reading Jarrell's work, we get into the habit of assuming that "this really happened." The names of places and books in these lines are not calculated for effect, drawn out of some Eliotic guide to allusions, but are there simply because of their personal significance to Jarrell. He does not set the poem in Hollywood, near Sunset Boulevard, because the place symbolizes fame or the faded American dream, but because he lived there as a child. He does not mention *Amazing Stories* because the science fiction magazine of the 1920s and 1930s suggests the poet's thematic concern with the contrast between the fantasies of an innocent past and the horrid realities of the nuclear age, but because it is a magazine he read as a child.

Yet even in *The Lost World* there are several poems in which Jarrell employs a female speaker. These women are, however, in Lowell's words, "intentionally . . . very close to the author."[10] The speaker of "Next Day" could very well be the same woman who wandered about the Washington Zoo musing about mortality. The only difference is the setting. Rather than roaming around the zoo, moaning to herself that "The world goes by my cage and never sees me," she meanders through the supermarket, wishing that the boxboy would notice her. As the woman at the zoo is obsessed with her coming death, so the woman at the supermarket stands, in her mind, beside her grave, "Confused with my life, that is commonplace and solitary." She has just been at her friend's funeral and says that the friend's face and body were her own. Two other poems in *The Lost World* also concern themselves with people who have recently attended funerals, "The Well-to-Do Invalid" and "The One Who Was Different." "In Montecito" is also about someone who has lately died. The poem is notable for its Symbolistic imagery. The speaker says that in Montecito, the wealthy suburb of Santa Barbara, she was visited one night by "a scream with breasts."[11] There a rich woman named Greenie Taliaferro has died, leaving behind a safety-deposit box, a Bentley, a seat at the cricket matches, and a girdle.[12] The scream is an interesting device, which prompts one to observe that Jarrell's later poetry never reaches the anxious, even hysterical tone that characterizes most of Schwartz's later poetry and is easy to find in Berryman and Lowell's. Jarrell never quite relinquishes conscious control of the flow of feelings and images in his poetry to the extent that the other Middle Generation poets do. He does not, in other works, allow himself to scream in his later poems; the closest he can come is to write about screams, odd, unreal screams which come out of the darkness, and to which, in the manner of a Symbolist poet, Jarrell gives a fantastic corporeal presence: "A scream hangs there in the night."

While the unrestrained tone of Schwartz's later poetry reminds one of Whitman, the restrained tone of Jarrell's later poetry reminds one of Robert Frost. At least one reviewer of *The Lost World*, John Fuller, noted its "Frostean speaking tone."[13] Indeed, not only Jarrell's controlled tone but his continuing, if unslavish, adherence to form, his unpretentious personal voice, and his concern with the individual human life are all reminiscent of Frost. One might well expect such an influence to assert itself in Jarrell's later poetry; for in his criticism of the period we find him extolling that great New England poet with an enthusiasm he reserved for those he considered the very best. In an essay called "Fifty Years of American Poetry," he congratulates Frost for writing poetry that seems to consist of "things merely put down and left to speak for themselves." This, incidentally, is a good way to describe the quality we find in Jarrell's most characteristic later poetry. "How little Frost's poems seem performances, no matter how brilliant or magical," writes Jarrell; "how little things made primarily of words, and how much things made out of lives and the world that the lives inhabit." How much, one might add, Jarrell has changed. For having begun as a poet who saw poems as performances made of words, he now sees poems as things made of lives and the real world. Finally, Jarrell writes that "Frost is that rare thing, a complete or representative poet."[14] Jarrell had once seen Eliot as the complete poet, but now his definition of "complete" has changed. The complete poet is the poet who captures completely not the spirit of the age or of the species but the essence of the individual; he is not Picasso creating his *Guernica* but a portraitist capturing to perfection the turn of the lip, the glint in the eye.

In learning from his new stylistic master, Frost, Jarrell did not forget his old one, Auden. In his poem "The Old and the New Masters," Jarrell comments upon Auden's famous poem "Musée des Beaux Arts." Auden's poem is about the fact that the tragic events of the world take place "While someone else is eating or opening a window or just walking dully along," a fact which, in Auden's eyes, the great painters understood. "About suffering they were never wrong, / The Old Masters." Jarrell responds: "About suffering, about adoration, the old masters / Disagree." He notes that when a figure in a painting suffers, all action—eating, walking, breathing—ceases.

In the works of the early masters, Jarrell says, everything in the world—past, present, future—is focused on the "small, helpless, human center." Yet eventually the masters paint the crucifixion at the edge of their canvases, put dogs at the feet of Christ, however they please; the earth is just a small planet in a large universe. Later, both Christ and the dogs disappear from the paintings, and the new masters slap colors onto their canvases "without adoration," drawing paintings in which the earth is a mere "bright spot" in a corner of the universe.[15] Jarrell is criticizing the tendency not only of art, but of literature, over the centuries, to remove its concern from the "small, helpless, human center" to abstraction, to generalization. To him, Auden is an example of such an artist, whose poem "Musée des Beaux Arts" presents what is, to him, an unwarranted generalization, and seems to endorse the notion that human suffering should not be at the center of art. Jarrell disagrees. His admiration is clearly not for the masters Auden speaks of, but for the earlier ones who are absorbed not in attempting to amalgamate the disparate details of the world but in the single suffering human soul.

The difference between the style of Jarrell's early Auden-influenced work, and that of his later, more straightforward and personal pieces, is indicated dramatically by the alterations Jarrell made, or planned to make, in his early poems during his later years. These changes, made in the 1960s, are indicated in his copy of *Blood for a Stranger*. Two examples will suffice to illustrate the type of revision Jarrell made. The published version of "The Head of Wisdom" carries the epigraph, "The head is Beethoven." In his copy of the book, Jarrell crossed the epigraph out, clearly an attempt to reduce the number of learned allusions by one. Then there is the poem, "Che Faro Senza Eurydice." The title is from Dante, and it is clearly the work of a young poet who wants to be like Eliot, whose first major poem carries an epigraph from the *Divine Comedy* and who dedicated his major work to "il miglior fabbro." An older Jarrell, freed from Eliot and the habit of literary allusion, crossed the title out and replaced it with a simple, unimpressive one in English. The two small strokes of the pen by which Jarrell made these alterations in a faded copy of his first book of poems are simple but telling indications of the great distance Jarrell had traveled between his early and late poetry.[16]

Dreams and Delusions:
Berryman's Later Poetry

In a 1960 introduction to *The Unfortunate Traveller*, John Berryman leaves the subject of Thomas Nashe briefly in order to comment on another Thomas. With pointed sarcasm, he refers to "T. S. Eliot's intolerable and perverse theory of the impersonality of the artist."[1] The remark can leave no doubt that by 1960 Berryman had left Eliot, and his own early impersonal poetry, far behind.

Indeed, in the mid-fifties Berryman had begun writing *The Dream Songs*, that long personal poem which the early, Eliotic Berryman would never have written, and which, far more than anything else, was to establish Berryman's reputation as a major American poet. Appropriately, many American works of poetry served as models for the *Songs*. Pound's *Cantos* provided an example of the sort of twentieth-century autobiography in verse which Berryman was interested in doing. "Does any reader who is familiar with Pound's poetry really not see that its subject is the life of the modern poet?" writes Berryman in an essay titled "The Poetry of Ezra Pound." "It is," asserts Berryman, "the experience and fate of this writer that concern him."[2] The Pound essay was written in 1949, when Berryman was engaged in the composition of his transitional poem, *Homage to Mistress Bradstreet*; it is interesting to notice that, during this crucial period, as he was turning away from the impersonality of Eliot, the personal poetry of Ezra Pound was much on his mind. Berryman has one fascinating *Dream Song*, number 224, which is about Pound at Eliot's funeral.[3] The song is, of course, based on the literal event, Eliot's funeral, but it can also be read metaphorically. For when Eliot, as an influence, died for Berryman, the old, lonely Pound was standing there waiting. "Ripe with pain, busy with loss," Pound's poetry constituted the perfect model for the long poem of pain and loss which Berryman wanted to write.

For *The Dream Songs* is primarily a poem about loss. Conarroe writes that Henry, Berryman's alter ego,

has suffered an "irreversible loss," we learn in the note to *His Toy, His Dream, His Rest,* and though we never find out exactly what this is, the evidence suggests that it is related to his father's suicide, the loss that "wiped out" his childhood and filled his adult life with dread and rage. Henry himself is suicidal, often so anxious and depressed that he can barely make it through the night.

Arpin concurs: "Henry's father's suicide provides the pattern for the other losses of the poem." Henry, Arpin observes, is attracted to death yet scared of it. "Death," writes Linebarger, "is the major cause of loss in Henry's life." Linebarger notes not only that Henry is preoccupied with suicide but that he is obsessed with the deaths of his friends, family, and such great writers as Yeats, Thomas, Hemingway, Frost, Faulkner, Williams, and Stevens. These deaths, notes Linebarger, have helped make Henry "a fragmented personality." Not only does Henry mourn these deaths, but he is also "in mourning for his own disorderly life," writes Conarroe.[4] Like Pound, he cannot make it cohere.

Other influences besides Pound are at work in *The Dream Songs.* Emily Dickinson's poetry, for instance, may well have helped Berryman to work out his baroque, eccentric, highly personal *Dream Songs* style, and to conceive of his long poem as a series of short, intense lyrics which followed a form uniquely his. The line breaks, the half-rhymes, the odd capitalization, the self-dramatizing tone, the strange combination, of blasphemy and piety, and the sardonic humor of Berryman's *Dream Songs* are all reminiscent of Dickinson's poetry. Moreover, like her poetry, *The Dream Songs* have the feeling of an extended foray into the poet's heart; they give one the sense that one is rummaging around in a soul.

Then there are the Symbolists. Berryman had in his early period written a series of negligible poems called "The Nervous Songs," which derived from Rilke.[5] The notion of *The Dream Songs* may well have developed, to some extent, out of these "Nervous Songs." Gary Arpin notes further that Berryman's speaker, Henry, who is "an imaginary Negro," is "a descendent of Rimbaud's 'nigger,' a metaphysical slave, one of 'the race that sang under torture.'" We find the relevant passage in Rimbaud's *A Season in Hell:*

. . . to me debauch and the comradeship of women were denied. Not even a companion. I saw myself before an infuriated mob, facing the firing-squad, weeping out of pity for the evil they could not understand, and forgiving!—like Jeanne D'Arc!—"Priests, professors, masters, you are making a mistake in turning me over to the law. I have never belonged to this people; I have never been a Christian; I am of the race that sang under torture; laws I have never understood; I have no moral sense, I am a brute: you are making a mistake."

Yes, my eyes are closed to your light. I am a beast, a nigger. But I can be saved. You are sham niggers, you, maniacs, fiends, misers. Merchant, you are a nigger; Judge, you are a nigger; General, you are a nigger; Emperor, old itch, you are a nigger: you have drunk of the untaxed liquor of Satan's still. —Fever and cancer inspire this people. Cripples and old men are so respectable that they are fit to be boiled. —The smartest thing would be to leave this continent where madness stalks to provide hostages for these wretches. I enter the true kingdom of the children of Ham.[6]

One need not be familiar with the context in order to get the general idea here, nor to appreciate what this passage meant to Berryman. The essential point is that the black man became, for Berryman, a symbol for the alien in his own land, tortured, abused, misunderstood by the powers that be. Clearly, this is an even more powerful and meaningful symbology for an American poet than for a French poet.

Berryman may have adopted not only Rimbaud's characterization of poet-as-black-man but his vision of life-as-farce. "For Henry, as for Rimbaud," writes Arpin, " 'life is the farce we all have to lead,' and the farce is painful as well as comically absurd."[7] Moreover, as Arpin observes, Berryman shares "the Symbolists' concern with the creation of a new language." Huysmans' description of Corbière is surprisingly applicable to Berryman; the poet is

talking negro, using a sort of telegram language, passing all bounds in the suppression of verbs, affecting a ribald humor, condescending to quips and quibbles only worthy of a commercial traveler of the baser sort; then, in a moment, in this tangle of ludicrous conceits, of smirking affectation, would rise a cry of acute pain, like a violoncello string breaking.[8]

But the most important influence on *The Dream Songs* is Walt Whitman, whose own epic personal poem Berryman examined in detail in a 1957 essay, "*Song of Myself*: Intention and Substance." "I like or love Whitman unreservedly," he writes; "he operates with great power and beauty over a very wide range." Berryman goes on to describe *Song of Myself* as "the greatest poem so far written by an American."[9]

Knowing what we do about the way the Middle Generation poets operated, we should consider these remarks of Berryman's quite important. For what they signify is that, in Berryman's mind, *Song of Myself* had displaced *The Waste Land* as the poem to beat. Thus, as he and his contemporaries, in their early years, had studied Eliot's poetry and critical theories, so Berryman, in his later period, carefully examined not only *Song of Myself* but the conceptions of poetry which had brought it into being. What he found, in perusing Whitman's last preface to *Leaves of Grass*, "A Backward Glance o'er Travel'd Roads," was a set of motives, on Whitman's part, which jibed almost perfectly with the reasons why he himself had so recently rebelled against Eliot's impersonal approach.

The first motive for writing poetry which Whitman mentions in "A Backward Glance" is "to be spiritual and heroic." In his essay, Berryman comments, "Nothing could be more comprehensible and explicit, and nothing more incomprehensible or repugnant to most cultivated readers a century later: though not, as it happens, to me." Are *The Dream Songs* heroic? Berryman would have said yes. As Conarroe writes,

> Our lives are all potentially disastrous, and artists like Berryman and Lowell who live perilously close to the abyss make it possible for us to journey over threatening terrain, to experience its terror, and to return intact. Literature does not tell us anything; it permits us to participate in a life, to share an angle of vision, and often to make some crucial personal discoveries. In courting certain kinds of disaster, Henry spares us the necessity of doing so for ourselves, overpowering as the attractions sometimes are.[10]

Whether such poetry as *The Dream Songs* actually does spare its readers the necessity of learning certain things for themselves is debatable; the important thing is that that is part of the idea behind them. We may well find this heroic. At the same time, we may agree with Arpin, who writes that Henry "is a mixture of heroism and cowardice: he's *there*, but very reluctantly, and scared to death." Heroism appears to be often on Berryman's mind. "Of what heroic stuff was warlike Henry made?" runs a line in one of the *Opus Posthumous* songs.[11]

Whitman's second motive is "the Religion purpose." Berryman, of course, was capable of intense religious devotion. Though he spent most of his life circling around Roman Catholicism, Berryman was interested in other faiths as well, and sometimes evinces a pantheism of sorts which reminds one of Whitman. But can we say that *The Dream Songs* are religious? As Henry is at once hero and coward, so his *Songs* are simultaneously devout and blasphemous. Henry is constantly thinking of God. "There is a great deal of Christian imagery in *The Dream Songs*," writes Arpin,

> but such imagery is generally used in the negative, as it were: Henry cannot find Christ, he cannot come to terms with the notion of a benevolent God. Despite Berryman's later conversion—or return to Christianity, *The Dream Songs* is the work, not of a man with a sense of religion, but of a man who lacks such a sense and is tormented by that lack.[12]

Sometimes, as in "Dream Song 26," Henry prays; but generally one gets the sense from *The Dream Songs* that if there is a God he is not a benevolent one: "God's Henry's enemy."[13]

Whitman's third motive is to deal with the nature of time, which is of course the Middle Generation poets' major theme. Finally, and apparently most importantly, Whitman's aim is "to put a *Person*, a human being (myself, in the latter half of the Nineteenth Century, in America,) freely, fully and truly on record." Berryman follows this quotation with these remarks:

> I call your attention to an incongruity of this formulation with Eliot's amusing theory of the impersonality of the artist, and a contrast between the mere *putting-on-record* and the well-nigh universal current notion of *creation*, or making things up. You will see that, as Whitman looks more arrogant than Eliot in the Personality, he looks less pretentious in the recording—the mere recording—poet not as *maker* but as spiritual historian—only the history must be, as we'll see in a moment, of the Present— and inquirer (characteristically; Eliot's word in the Quartets, "explorer," is more ambitious and charged than "inquirer"). Small wonder—I finish with the arbiters—if they resent Whitman: he has sold the profession short. The poet as creator plays no part in Whitman's scheme at all.
>
> For Whitman the poet is a *voice*. Not solely his own—let us settle this problem quickly: a poet's first personal pronoun is nearly always ambiguous, but we have the plain declaration from Whitman that "the trunk and centre where the answer was to radiate . . . must be an identical soul and body, a personality—which personality, after many considerings and ponderings I deliberately settled should be myself—indeed could not be any other."

It is fascinating that Berryman's early Eliotic critical prose style has here given way to a more robust, idiosyncratic style which sounds almost exactly like the Whitman excerpts that he is quoting: lively, spontaneous, full of parentheses and dashes and italics. Clearly, what Berryman says here about *Song of Myself* applies as well to *The Dream Songs*. His long poem, like Whitman's, is an attempt to put a person on record; it is not the product of a maker but of what Berryman calls a "spiritual historian."

How, one might ask, can it be said that *The Dream Songs* is a spiritual history in the manner of *Song of Myself* when it purports to be not about Berryman but about Henry, this character in blackface who, Berryman tells us, is "not the poet, not me"? Our answer to this must be that the evidence to the contrary is simply too formidable to be easily nullified by the poet's disclaimers. "I think that anyone who reads the songs carefully will reject the assertion that they are about an imaginary character," writes Conarroe; "some details, of course, are invented, but the sequence adheres closely to the facts of the poet's life and mind." Linebarger agrees: "the informing personality of John Berryman is behind [Henry], despite his tongue-in-cheek disclaimer. . . . Henry is an 'imaginary character' only in the sense that all characters are in literature—or, more exactly, in autobiography."[14]

Why, then, does Berryman present himself as Henry? Partly for the same reason that Jarrell presents himself as a housewife hanging out the wash, or a woman ambling through the zoo; Henry, like these speakers, is the lingering symptom of a long history of devotion to what Berryman calls "Eliot's amusing theory of the impersonality of the artist." The Henry persona, however, also serves a useful purpose for the poet of the moment which Berryman, like his fellow Middle Generation poets, had become. Linebarger notes that the Henry mask allows the expression of opinions that "Berryman himself would never condone beyond a moment. For example, Henry's statement that we should bomb Red China is a view that Berryman would almost certainly have been unwilling to state except as a passing thought born out of a sense of helplessness."[15]

Like Whitman, Berryman wanted to write a poem which was not merely about himself but about his suffering. In his essay on *Song of Myself*, Berryman pauses to admire these lines:

> All this I swallow, it tastes good, I like it well, it becomes mine,
> I am the man, I suffer'd, I was there.

He also shares Whitman's obsession with sex, and, to some degree, his sexual inclinations. He sees men not, in an Eliotic way, as "intelligences or whatever," but, in a Whitmanesque way, as "lovers."

Berryman, then, found in Whitman an antecedent whose poetic motives and goals were strikingly similar to his own. This simularity drew Berryman, in his later period, to the nineteenth-century poet, and made the bard of Paumanok a unique influence upon Berryman's later work. Whitman did not influence Berryman's later style as he did Schwartz's, but what he did give the poet of *The Dream Songs* was a working method. It is perhaps difficult to appreciate what a difference this made. For five years, Berryman had worked on *Homage to Mistress Bradstreet*, a poem of some 456 lines, thus producing an average of one line every four days. He had aimed for perfection in that poem, laboring incessantly over every word. Indeed, it had been a "nearly symmetrical" work, carefully structured from the very beginning. In *The Dream Songs*, his method was precisely the opposite. Conarroe writes that

> The poems emerged, were uttered, bloomed, almost spontaneously over a period of many years. Sitting all night in his green chair, puffing on Tareytons and drinking either bourbon or coffee, Berryman brought forth songs the way a tree produces leaves, in the process scattering pages, and ashes, all over the rug. Only much later did he take on the tasks of selection, revision, and rejection, finally gathering the "parts" into the order that makes up the completed sequence.[16]

Even when he did put the songs in order, there was no real plan. As Berryman said, "The placement of the Dream Songs is purely personal." Adrienne Rich says much the same thing when she writes that "it is the identity of Henry . . . which holds the book together." The difference between the rigorously planned and carefully written *Homage* and the spontaneous, instinctively organized *Dream Songs* is Whitman. The example of Whitman, who boasted "spontaneous me," made it possible for Berryman to write poems for years without a thought to the way they fit together, and to have confidence that they would indeed fit together. Paul Ramsey writes of *The Dream Songs* that "almost every poem is badly flawed in one way or another," yet he is excited by Berryman's fresh use of language, his syntactic innovations, his shifts in thought, and his humor.[17] Ramsey's dichotomous view of *The Dream Songs* is typical, and reminds us of the way many critics feel about *Song of Myself*: when it is good, it is very, very good, and when it is bad, it is horrid. There is a reason for this similarity. It is that Berryman, in *The Dream Songs*, makes the same bargain with the Muse that Whitman makes in *Song of Myself*. In *The Dream Songs* Berryman risks being badly flawed; he aims not to create the perfect aesthetic object but to capture his own momentary feelings, however eccentric and seemingly unpoetic. Like Whitman, Berryman aims for a poem which is sui generis. If sometimes the poetry is severely flawed—the language inappropriate, the syntactic innovations pointless and confusing, the humor unfunny—no matter. Those instances, however few, in which he manages to capture the self make the whole enterprise, to his mind, worthwhile. The contrast between this approach and the one Berryman follows in *Homage* could hardly be greater.

There are, of course, differences between Berryman and Whitman. As Roger Pooley notes, "In the work of containing everything in his writing Whitman also claims to be reconciling everything. Berryman and his Henry find that act of reconciliation impossible."[18] Berryman, like Pound, cannot make the world coherent in his poetry.

Another difference between Berryman and Whitman is the mask of Henry. This mask, however insubstantial it may be in the first place, disappears altogether in Berryman's poetry after *The Dream Songs*. The poems in *Love and Fame* (1970) are "clearer, simpler, more direct" than *The Dream Songs*, writes Linebarger. They were written even more quickly, the book being completed within six weeks of its conception. The subject of the poems, as Berryman himself observes, is "solely and simply myself. Nothing else. . . . the subject on which I am a real authority is me, so I wiped out all the disguises and went to work."[19]

What he did when he went to work was to write some very revealing personal poems. Like *The Dream Songs*, the poems of *Love and Fame* could be considered parts of a single long poem, even more explicitly autobiographical than *The Dream Songs*. The first part of the book covers Berryman's years at school and college in America; the second part deals with his student days at Cambridge University; the third part concentrates on the year or two before the composition of *Love and Fame*; and the fourth part consists of religious poems. As the title suggests, the poems in *Love and Fame* are about Berryman's sexual affairs and the advancement of his career. Some of the poems are discomfortingly candid. In "Thank You, Christine," Berryman reveals how many women he has slept with; in "Her and It," he informs the reader that he has fathered an illegitimate child. Linebarger comments on one typical *Love and Fame* poem: "There is nothing in this poem to indicate that the scene is an hallucination or nightmare; if it recalls actuality, as it seems to do, the poem is unpleasantly revealing."[20]

Why did Berryman leave Henry behind? Mainly it is a matter of developing further away from impersonality, of allowing the rudimentary characteristics of Eliotic poetry which remained with him to atrophy and fall away. Just as Jarrell gained the confidence between *The Woman at the Washington Zoo* and *The Lost World* to bring himself undisguised into his poetry, so Berryman, between *The Dream Songs* and *Love and Fame*, gained the confidence to drop Henry. Moreover, by the time of *Love and Fame*, Lowell, perhaps the most visible poet of the day, had published some very revealing poems in *Notebook*, which may have convinced Berryman that it was time to "wipe out the disguises." There was also the likely influence of the other most visible poet of the day. Conarroe writes of *Love and Fame* that Berryman "takes his cue from a later Columbia man, Allen Ginsberg, whose aim was 'tell it all. Poets! . . . Lovers & secrets!' "[21]

In *Love and Fame*, Berryman does seem to tell it all. He goes nearly as far as one can in the direction of personal poetry. If in *The Dream Songs* there is the slightest vestige of an intention to make some universal statement about man and art, or life and death, Berryman has in *Love and Fame* managed the difficult art of writing poems in which such a motive is well-nigh inconceivable. It is very difficult to make anything more of these poems than we find on the page. A poem like "Crisis," for example, which records a conflict with Professor Emery Neff during Berryman's college years, is pure autobiography, an anecdote about Berryman's own experience with no universal relevance whatever.[22] The allusions in the poem are purely personal. One senses that the poet has not manipulated them in the slightest. Wordsworth and Robinson are mentioned here not because something in their work bears some complex and impressive relation to Berryman's theme, but because in real life they played a part in this story. The same is true of the names dropped in the other *Love and Fame* poems. Saul Bellow, Allen Tate, and other appear, but not for any objective reason; all they had to do to get into these poems was to cross Berryman's path. Whereas in his early poems Hegel might be mentioned in order to invoke the theories of the state, in these poems Hegel is mentioned only in connection with Berryman's personal memories—a person mentioned in the poems was "the only man in college who understood Hegel."[23]

Similarly, there are poems in *Love and Fame,* among them "The Soviet Union," "The Minnesota 8 and the Letter-Writers," and "Regents' Professor Berryman's Crack on Race," which may appear at first glance to be objective political poems. However, they are in reality not about politics but about a state of mind. Berryman is no Robert Bly, offering a comment upon world affairs which he hopes will be influential; rather, he is expressing his own confusion and irresolution in the face of current events. "Nobody *knows anything,*" Berryman writes in one of these poems; and indeed, that seems to be the point. Berryman cannot make things cohere on the level of international politics any more than he can on the level of his own life. If in one poem he seems to be expressing concern for the plight of the blacks, accusing white America of having "murdered Martin Luther King," in another poem he is a raving bigot, saying "Let's confront, Blackie!" and referring to "nigger-lovers."[24] The same irresolution can be found in the religious poems. Berryman purports to have found his faith again, but he does not seem to have profited much from it. His confusion and uncertainty in the world remain, and are as much in evidence as his devotion. Doubt and perplexity fill his "Eleven Addresses to the Lord."

> I have no idea whether we live again.
>
> Whatever your end may be, accept my amazement.
>
> If I say Thy name, art Thou there? It may be so.[25]

For the most part, the style of *Love and Fame* is similar to that of *The Dream Songs.* The "colloquial voice, the mixed levels of diction, the experimentation with parts of speech, the inversions, the conscious cliches" that Linebarger observes in *The Dream Songs* are present as well in *Love and Fame.*[26] But the tone is, as Linebarger notes, "calmer, quieter." In *Delusions, Etc.* (1972) and *Henry's Fate and Other Poems* (1977), the tone grows even more sedate. Of the poems in the 1972 volume, John Thompson says that

> on the far side of his breakthrough—or his breakdown—everything was flat. Henry, that blithe and desperate spirit, came no longer with his fractured dreamy songs, his soft-shoe shuffle, his baby-talk that frightened the grown-ups with its naked infantilism. Without him, the world was small and orderly like a room made of cement blocks.[27]

The poems in all of these post–*Dream Songs* volumes are concerned, like *The Dream Songs,* with loss. In *Love and Fame,* the theme is developed in "Of Suicide," wherein "Reflexions on suicide, & on my father, possess me," and his wife threatens to leave him. In *Delusions, Etc.* we find the poem "He Resigns," with its references to age, death, ghosts, a woman departed "in spirit from me."[28] Conarroe finds that in *Delusions, Etc.* Berryman has reached "that state of terminal desolation where suicide began to seem to him not merely possible but inevitable."[29] The religious poems in this volume are, if anything, more pathetic and confused than those in *Love and Fame.* "I pray hard," Berryman writes, "I come Your child to You."[30] As Schwartz's later poems profess joy and yet sound desperate, so the religious poems of these last Berryman volumes profess faith and yet sound like the work of a man who has decided that he is living in a godless, senseless universe. Berryman's last poem, written shortly before he jumped to his death from a Minneapolis bridge, appears in *Henry's Fate.*[31] It is as personal a poem as anyone can write, the poet's scenario for his suicide. That Berryman wrote this intensely personal poem in the *Dream Song* form illustrates dramatically the degree to which Berryman was Henry. The poem is also testimony to Berryman's devotion to Whitman. For clearly, up to the last moments of his life, Berryman's premier poetic principle was the one he had learned from Whitman: "I am the man, I suffer'd, I was there."

"Yet why not say what happened?": Lowell's Later Poetry

In *The Mills of the Kavanaughs* (1951), the last poetry collection of his early period, Lowell began to incorporate more personal references than he had in previous volumes. He was still masked, however. "My husband was a fool," he has a speaker say in the title poem, "To run out from the Navy."[1] The inspiration here is clearly Lowell's bitterness over his father's decision to cut short his naval career. But unless one knew the poet's personal history, it would be impossible to guess what special meaning those lines had to him. Lowell had yet to break free of the bonds of impersonality and make his own life and feelings the subjects of his poetry. In writing *Mills*, he was still, as Jarrell wrote in his review of the book, more a poet of the will than of imagination.

Indeed, as Burton Raffel observes, Lowell was, in *Mills*, "boxed in by borrowed attitudes . . . that could no longer serve him and which, in my view, never did serve him. Lowell's comparative triumph in *Lord Weary's Castle* is in a sense a triumph over himself." In fact, it is a triumph of his mind over his self, of his impersonal, amalgamating intellect, his ordering will, over his private anguish, his acute sense of disorder. And the highly objective subject matter of his early poems goes hand in hand with a highly rigorous form in which one can hardly imagine a personality expressing itself. In order to break free of the impersonal themes of his early poems, Lowell had also to break out of the rigid lines. William Carlos Williams seems to have recognized as much. "Mr. Lowell appears to be restrained by the lines," he wrote in his review of *Mills*; "he appears to *want* to break them."[2]

In 1959 the break came, and it was called *Life Studies*. This book, the culmination of what Rosenthal called "a long struggle to remove the mask," is as much a keynote volume for the Middle Generation poets' late period as *In Dreams Begin Responsibilities* is for their early period. *Life Studies,* comments Rosenthal,

> is the volume in which the poet at last "finds himself." He does so literally, for in most of the poems he and his family are at the center, and his object is to catch himself in the process of becoming him. Equally important, in fact more so, he finds himself as a stylist. For the first time he can be casual, simple, and direct throughout a poem, and at the same time he can strike home more tellingly than ever when he wishes.[3]

Simple and direct, yes, but casual? Raffel would seem to agree with this assessment of *Life Studies.* "He can be relaxed now, he can be ironic, he can be everyday and conversational and real."[4] The Lowell of *Life Studies* is honest and real, but is he relaxed? Admittedly, *Life Studies* evinces none of the manufactured stress and deliberately tortured syntax of *Lord Weary's Castle;* but these elements are replaced by the genuine strain of real life. When we read *Life Studies,* we are not struck, as in *Lord Weary's Castle,* by the worked-up feverishness of words on a page; rather, we are struck by the uncluttered, searingly real emotional situation of a suffering human being. Is a poem like "Skunk Hour," with its confession that "My mind's not right," or a poem like "Sailing Home from Rapallo," in which Lowell escorts his mother's body home from Italy, casual and relaxed?[5] Clearly, what Rosenthal and Raffel are describing by these words is the form of the poems. Certainly there is less tension in the form. But there is a reason for that; the tension is now in the material. The revolution in form that *Life Studies* represents, and to which Rosenthal and Raffel are so very attentive, is but the corollary to a revolution in content. These two critics are not alone in emphasizing the formal revolution at the expense of the substantive one. Vivian Smith, for one, fails to recognize any real change in Lowell's poetry apart from his simplification of manner. The change in Lowell's poetry represented by *Life Studies,* she writes, "is essentially one of style rather than of preoccupation."[6] Yet even Lowell, while working on the *Life Studies* poems, wrote Jarrell that "I've been loosening up the meter, as you'll see and hosing out all the old theology and symbolism and *verbal* violence."[7] It is his emphasis, but mine as well. For what I want to underline is that *Life Studies* represents, to put it simply, a transfer of the "violence" of Lowell's poetry from the form to the content. The power of the poems now lies not in the poet's manipulation of words but in his expression of profound personal feelings. Two years after *Life Studies,* Lowell commented on the type of difficult, nervous style that characterizes his early poetry:

> Poets of my generation and particularly younger ones have gotten terribly proficient at these forms. They write a very musical, difficult poem with tremendous skill, perhaps there's never been such skill. Yet the writing seems divorced from culture somehow. It's become too much something specialized that can't handle much experience. It's become a craft, purely a craft, and there must be some *breakthrough back into life.*[8]

The essential fact about *Life Studies,* then, is that the poems are, as Lowell described them in a letter written to Jarrell during their composition, "all very direct and personal."[9] As Ehrenpreis puts it, "the reader finds himself in touch with the real author and not a mask."[10] The simplified style is subordinate to the altered sensibility, the new thematic emphasis. Lowell would later recall that

> when I was writing *Life Studies,* a good number of the poems were started in very strict meter, and I found that, more than the rhymes, the regular beat was what I didn't want. I have a long poem in there about my father, called "Commander Lowell," which actually is largely in couplets, but I originally wrote perfectly strict four-foot couplets. . . . That regularity just seemed to ruin the honesty of sentiment, and became rhetorical; it said, "I'm a poem". . . .[11]

This is not the first time we have seen a Middle Generation poet opposing "rhetoric" to "honesty of sentiment." Vendler's observation regarding the unrhymed sonnets Lowell wrote in his later period applies, to an extent, to all late Middle Generation poetry:

> His sonnets throw up nearly indigestible fragments of experience, unprefaced by explanation, unexplained by cause or result. . . . the whole litter and debris and detritus of a mind absorptive for fifty years. His free association, irritating at first, hovering always dangerously toward the point where unpleasure replaces pleasure, nonetheless becomes bearable, and then even deeply satisfying, on repeated reading. . . . The pressure of the familiar, and the genuineness of its note, act to assure the genuineness of the rest.[12]

Genuineness is a criterion which, although it would have been meaningless to the Middle Generation during their early period, becomes a paramount consideration in their later poetry. Vendler's word "indigestible" is worth commenting upon also. Louis Simpson has written of American poetry that it must be able, like the shark, to digest extremely diverse substances—"Rubber, coal, uranium, moons, poems."[13] In a sense, the later poetry of the Middle Generation bears witness to the four writers' agreement upon the principle that poetry cannot take in everything that America tosses its way, like some omnivorous shark. All it can do is utter cries, cries which arise from the poet's tortured awareness of the chaos of his life in the contemporary world, and of the inability of even the most dedicated poet to rise above it in his art.

This, in fact, is the admission which Lowell makes in the first poem of *Life Studies*, "Beyond the Alps."[14] The poem, as Crick observes, chronicles "a journey across both a modern Waste Land and a landscape of the mind." The train trip, in other words, is in part a metaphor for Lowell's pilgrimage from the poetics of *Lord Weary's Castle* and *The Mills of the Kavanaughs* to that of *Life Studies*. The city of Rome symbolizes all that the Lowell of *Life Studies* has left behind; it represents not only the principles of Catholicism which ruled his life during much of his early period, but the Eliotic precepts which dictated the type of poetry he wrote during those years. Rome is, as Crick says, "tradition, mind, authority, and the ice-like blockage of the poem about Eisenhower's inauguration." It is thus associated with everything that Eliot, in Lowell's mind, is associated with; and, like Eliot, it represents stasis, stability. Paris, on the other hand, represents those values to which the Eliotic poetic, in Lowell's mind, stands opposed: "individualism, freedom, imagination, and flux"; it stands for an exposure "to the darker reaches of the spirit."[15] The poem's trip from Rome to Paris, then, symbolizes Lowell's farewell to a type of poetry that is rooted in tradition, formed by the amalgamating mind, and founded upon the notion of the poet as an impersonal authority who speaks as if from a mountaintop. This is not the first time we have seen Eliot's poetic perspective compared to the view from the top of a mountain; Schwartz does so in "T. S. Eliot as the International Hero." In saying that the "mountain-climbing train" of Lowell's poetry has "come to earth," Lowell is rejecting the notion that he can speak as if with the voice of a god, and is embracing his common humanity, and with it a type of poetry that allows him to speak with the voice of a human being. To say that in making this change in his poetry he is acting "Much against my will" is to say that his need to express his anguish at the world's disorder has overcome his ability to surmount that anguish in poetry through an act of the ordering will.

Thus, while "Beyond the Alps" informs us, in the words of

Burton Raffel, "that religion is no longer dogma, no longer some all-pervading pillar to which the poet desperately clings, praying loudly for support and comfort," it tells us at the same time that T. S. Eliot is no longer dogma, no longer a pillar of Lowell's poetry.[16] If the doctrines of Catholicism no longer guide Lowell's life, those of Eliot no longer guide his art. Lowell as a poet no longer identifies with Minerva, the goddess of wisdom, and thus by extension of "intellectual poetry," but rather with Apollo, the god of music and art, and therefore patron of the poetry of feeling, of the spirit. One nice touch in "Beyond the Alps" is Lowell's allusion to *The Golden Bough*, the famous anthropological text which is one of the keys to *The Waste Land*; Lowell associates it in his poem with the Eliotic mountaintop that he has left behind him, as if to say that his days of intricate, calculated literary allusions are behind him.

At the same time, though, as the Frazer allusion suggests, "Beyond the Alps" is written pretty much in the manner of his early poetry; it bears little resemblance to the direct, informal poetry which makes up the bulk of *Life Studies*. Indeed, though "Beyond the Alps" may be our doorway into *Life Studies*, we must go beyond it in order to find characteristic *Life Studies* poetry. For "Beyond the Alps" is Lowell's goodbye to the Old Country delivered, as it were, in the Old Country's native language.

The New Country is one which Lowell describes succinctly in the penultimate line of "Beyond the Alps": "Now Paris, our black classic, breaking up." Yenser notes that "This vision of the sundering of the modern world epitomizes the concerns of [this] volume."[17] The terrain of *Life Studies* is indeed a disjointed, fragmented one, for it is primarily populated by the poet's memories of the deaths of those closest to him, and its climate is one of horror and helplessness in the face of the specter of mortality. As we read through *Life Studies* from beginning to end, we move slowly toward the darker reaches of Lowell's spirit, the heart of his psychic darkness. Thus "Beyond the Alps" and the three poems that follow it are relatively impersonal constructions in an Eliotic manner. "The Banker's Daughter" is about Marie de Medici; "Inauguration Day: January 1953" is a reaction to President Eisenhower's election. "A Mad Negro Soldier Confined at Munich" is a monologue, enclosed entirely in quotation marks, spoken in iambic couplets by the individual named in the title. As it happens, the voice in the poem sounds nothing at all like that of a real human being, particularly a mad Negro soldier: "the zoo's rubble fumes with cats; / hoydens with air-guns prowl the Koenigsplatz."[18] This is not a man speaking, but a Platonic mad Negro soldier, whose like exists nowhere in this world. The poem is not primarily about him or his feelings, but about the poet's thoughts on a weighty intellectual theme, the tragedy of war. The poem is not an expression of the poet's feelings about life, but is rather a highly contrived, consummately cerebral commentary upon it. The poem is actually strikingly reminiscent of many of Jarrell's early war poems. Indeed, it bears more of a resemblance to the early Jarrell than to the early Lowell. It may be that Lowell had this poem in mind when he wrote Jarrell late in 1957 about the *Life Studies* poetry that he was writing and added: "I suppose we shouldn't swap too many compliments, but I am heavily in your debt. I've been going through your selected poems quite a lot, and marvel again at how supple, scientific and personal they are."[19] Though "A Mad Negro Soldier" does not look particularly supple or personal alongside most of Lowell's later po- etry, it is certainly ahead of most of his early poems in those respects. Unlike most of Lowell's early work, "A Mad Negro Soldier" does have a clearly defined speaker, setting, and situation. This neatness, the nicely-rounded "case study" aspect of the poem that makes it so similar to such early Jarrell poems as "The Soldier" and "Jews at Haifa," may be what Lowell is referring to when he uses the word "scientific." The subject of prisoners of war is certainly one that a reading of Jarrell's *Selected Poems* would have brought to Lowell's attention; poems concerned with war prisoners, among them "Stalag Luft" and "A Camp in the Prussian Forest," are plentiful in that volume.

These four poems in the first part of *Life Studies* provide the reader with a reminder of what Lowell is rebelling against. By starting with these relatively impersonal, formal poems, Lowell endows his book with a sense of movement, of altering perspective, that gives it body and dimension, places its later poems into a context, and, most importantly, heightens one's awareness of the achievement that those later poems of *Life Studies* represent. All the same, the first poems in *Life Studies* are not pure Eliotic poems. Although written in the style of Lowell's early poetry, they serve to adumbrate the themes of his later poetry. "Inauguration Day," for example, ends with an image of the contemporary world as lifeless and disordered; the U.S. is a Republic with a "mausoleum in her heart."[20]

Part 2 of *Life Studies* is an autobiographical memoir in prose, "91

Revere Street." To include such a thing in a book of poetry was unusual in 1959; Lowell may have been influenced by Schwartz's *In Dreams Begin Responsibilities,* which included a story, and (even more likely) by *Vaudeville for a Princess,* which included several personal, semiautobiographical essays. At any rate, "91 Revere Street" provides a brief history of Lowell's early years and portraits of those members of his family who populate the poems of part 4. Besides providing a useful background to the poems that follow, this essay also serves as a stylistic bridge. For the poems that follow it are written more in the style of "91 Revere Street" than in the style of the four poems of part 1. To read the poems in conjunction with the essay is to be reminded how close their style is to that of Lowell's prose.

Part 3 of *Life Studies* consists of four tributes to literary figures with whom Lowell empathized: Ford Madox Ford, George Santayana, Delmore Schwartz, and Hart Crane. In this section we are moving closer to the heart of things. Part 4 takes us even nearer. It consists of two sections, the first of them containing the poems about Lowell's family. "My Last Afternoon with Uncle Devereux Winslow" is about an uncle who "was dying at twenty-nine." "Grandparents" is about Lowell's grandparents, who have "all gone into the world of light; the farm's my own." The poems about Lowell's parents are also here. Among them is "Sailing Home from Rapallo," based on the voyage on which Lowell brought his mother's body home from Italy after her death. The poem's major device is a contrast between the foreign things of Charlotte's death site and death-ship—the *"Golfo di Genova,"* the "nurse who could only speak Italian," the "spumante-bubbling wake of our liner," the *"Risorgimento* black and gold casket," the "Italian tinfoil" in which the corpse was wrapped "like panetone"—and the things of home: the "family cemetery in Dunbarton / . . . under the White Mountains," with "its mostly Colonial grave-slates," marking the burial places of dozens of Winslows and Starks. The significance of this pattern of contrasts lies in the fact that the poem commemorates not one journey but three: the journey from Rapallo to Dunbarton made by Lowell and his mother's body; the "journey to oblivion," in Lawrence's words, made by Charlotte Lowell's spirit; and, third, the journey to self-discovery made by Lowell. For he too, in a sense, has "crossed the bar," turning away, with his mother's death, from his former deep involvement with foreign cultures and foreign literatures, and has at last come to terms with himself as an American, as a New Englander, and as a member of the Winslow clan. The thrust of the poem seems to be that Lowell's journey of self-discovery was made possible only by his mother's journey from this world, that his mind so strongly identified his parents with America and American culture that only after both parents were dead could he reconcile himself to that country and culture.

In the second section of part 4 the focus is at last not on Lowell's family but on Lowell, the adult, who is adrift in a sea "of lost connections."[21] The poems in this section include "Memories of West Street and Lepke" and "Man and Wife." The last poem in the book is "Skunk Hour," perhaps the most celebrated poem by any member of the Middle Generation. If *Life Studies* rehearses, in miniature, Lowell's sojourn from impersonal to personal poetry, "Skunk Hour" does the same thing in an even smaller scale. The first half of the poem is about other people whose lives, almost like those in *The Waste Land*, exemplify for Lowell the sterility and senselessness of contemporary life: "Nautilus Island's hermit heiress," her bishop son, her farmer, the "summer millionaire," the "fairy decorator."[22] The latter half of the poem stuns with its sudden subjectivity, its force of feeling, its perfect rendering of the anguish of an "ill-spirit." If "Beyond the Alps" reminds the reader where Lowell has been, "Skunk Hour" shows where the poet is going. It is a précis of sorts for the poetry that will follow *Life Studies.*

For the Union Dead (1964) and *Near the Ocean* (1967) consist essentially of poems which, in both style and content, closely resemble those of *Life Studies*. Like Berryman's post–*Dream Songs* volumes, these post–*Life Studies* books have been criticized for a slackness, a lack of energy and originality. *"For the Union Dead,"* writes Raffel, "is not a bad book so much as a tired one." Vendler says that *For the Union Dead* and *Near the Ocean*, which she calls Lowell's weakest books, "warned us that Lowell had to find a new impulse of energy or die as a poet."[23] They are succeeded by a series of books written in a similar voice, but a different form. *Notebook 1967–68* (1969) consists of poems which are as subjective and colloquial as the most innovative poems of *Life Studies* but which are all unrhymed sonnets. Lowell revised the poems of *Notebook 1967–68* and republished them in 1970 as *Notebook*. Then in 1973 he revised them again and republished them in two books, *For Lizzie and Harriet* and *History*. In the same year he published *The Dolphin*, a collection of poems in the same unrhymed sonnet form. Not until his last book, *Day by Day* (1977), did

Lowell give up the unrhymed sonnet and again write poems that looked as if they might have come out of *Life Studies*. Just as Eliot critics may be broken down into the pro-*Quartets* and anti-*Quartets* camps, so Lowell critics can be divided into two factions: those, like Vendler, who feel that Lowell's greatest triumph after *Life Studies* consists in his sonnet-form poems; and those, like Burton Raffel, who prize *Day by Day* as a "final triumph" over the "prolific mediocrity" of the sonnets.[24]

Whether we admire the *Notebook*-style poems or not, we may well wonder why Lowell turned to the unrhymed sonnet form and remained loyal to it for so many years. The answer, I believe, is John Berryman. Indeed, just as the French Symbolists carried the influence of Edgar Allan Poe into twentieth-century American poetry, so I believe that Berryman forms a crucial link between the Lowell of *Life Studies* and the Lowell of the sonnet volumes. It seems very likely, in spite of the protests of Berryman's biographer, that reading *Life Studies*, either in progress or in print, must have helped Berryman, who began writing Dream Songs in 1955 but did not publish *77 Dream Songs* till 1964, five years after *Life Studies*, to find his personal voice for that long poem. In turn, Berryman's commitment in *The Dream Songs* to a single form, his concept of book-as-poem, and his decision not to sweat over each song for weeks but to allow them to pour out of him, several at one clip, clearly influenced Lowell, who tossed off his unrhymed sonnets in much the same manner. Crick agrees: "The immediate literary inspiration behind *Notebook* seems to have been John Berryman's *Dream Songs*." And upon finishing *Notebook 1967–68*, Lowell wrote to Berryman: "I think I am in your debt. . . . I've just completed a long poem, *Notebook of a Year*." Near the end of that book, Lowell acknowledges in verse Berryman's influence upon its form: "John, we used the language as if we made it."[25]

In spite of their strict adherence to the sonnet form, the poems of *Notebook 1967–68* and its progeny, if anything, offer even more matter with even less art than *Life Studies* and its companion volumes. Crick, commenting on *Notebook*, asks the same question other critics have asked of *The Dream Songs:* "Is the only unity in the character of the poet himself?" As with the late poetry of all four Middle Generation poets, the character of the poet is certainly the most important unifying factor in this book. Crick further observes of *Notebook* that "the demarcation line between art and life is constantly fluid." Raffel says of *Notebook:* "What Lowell has begun to learn, it seems to me, is that words are enough, have power to say what they are given to say. There is no need to pile layers and then still more layers of over-wrought action and thought on top of the bare, sufficient reality." It is this recognition on Lowell's part that seems to dictate most of the revisions in the *Notebook* sequence. In one poem, for example, Lowell changes Wien to Vienna, Milano to Milan; the difference between *Notebook 1967–68* and its children is made up largely of hundreds of such small but telling alterations.[26]

Many of the poems in the *Notebook* group are concerned with such historical figures as Caligula, Alexander the Great, Mohammed, Anne Boleyn, and Peter the Great. There are also poems about such contemporary public figures as Che Guevara, Doctor Spock, and Norman Mailer, and the political events in which they participated. Thus we have late Lowell poems with such titles as "Liberty and Revolution, Buenos Aires," "Statue of Liberty," "The March 1," "Pacification at Columbia," "Leader of the Left," "Small College Riot," and "The Revolution." All of these poems eventually found their way into *History*, while the poems which do not make reference to public events were shunted into *For Lizzie and Harriet*. It is primarily because of the so-called political poems in *History*, and because of such other late Lowell poems as "Memories of West Street and Lepke," that Lowell is thought of by some critics as a fundamentally political poet, a "public" poet, as one critic puts it in the title of a book-length study of Lowell's work. But what such critics fail to recognize is that the organizing principle throughout all of the late poems remains a deliberately subjective one. "Lowell feels the thread of self as a perpetual clue," writes Vendler of Lowell's late poetry. Lowell, in other words, is not a public but a private poet. Whereas the early Middle Generation poems borrow from established mythical systems, and make use of other poets' catalogues of symbols and allusions, the Middle Generation poets in their later poems generate their own systems of reference. What makes a reference to Mo-hammed in a later Lowell poem different from a reference to King Herod in an early poem is what Vendler would call its "genuineness." Mohammed is there, not because the Encyclopedia of Literary Tradi-tion which Lowell has in his head tells him that Mohammed is the received symbol for this or that, or because he means something to Eliot; he is there because he means something to Lowell. To under-stand his place in the later Lowell poem is to understand Lowell's mind a bit better than one would otherwise. By comparison, a complete understanding of the place of the Hostenwall in Lowell's early poem "The Exile's Return," the meaning of which depends wholly on Mann's "Tonio Kruger" and a handful of Eliot's major poems, tells us nothing about the young man who wrote the poem beyond what we already know: that he is a confirmed disciple of Eliot. What Vendler says of some of Lowell's later volumes is relevant here. "There are morals that can be quoted or deduced from the poems in *History* and its companion volumes," she writes, "but they are not what vivifies them. These poems live neither on ideology nor on logic—props thought to be the mainstays of an earlier Lowell; instead, they yield to the lawless free associations of the rocked and dangerous mind."[27] Louis Simpson says the same thing a bit more succinctly: "The life presented in *History* was only Robert Lowell's."

As Simpson has noted, Lowell's activist audiences often failed to recognize that his "political" poems did not really say what the audiences thought they were hearing. Simpson quotes a piece of "classic . . . resignation" (including lines like "Pity the planet, all joy gone") and comments: "It is difficult to see what the crowd at the Pentagon could have heard in this to encourage them. A poem that said it was resigned to having children die in wars around the globe— what could this have to say to war protestors, Civil Rights marchers, and other political activists? This was counsel of despair, if ever there was. Moreover, with its carefully tuned couplets the poem was listening to itself and indifferent to their existence."[28]

Exactly. Indeed, none of Lowell's later poetry is really political poetry in the sense that we usually mean. It is not poetry that forcefully expresses the position of a group of people on some issue or another. Lowell was too solipsistic to write anthems. He could not, for example, have written a poem like Simpson's "American Dreams." History and politics are always present in his poetry in the same way they are in Whitman's poetry; they are not part of an escape from the self, but are rather a means to self-knowledge. Crick notes that in *Notebook* "there is a kind of innocence in the face of reality of a kind similar to that which inspired another long American poem, Whitman's *Song of Myself*, and the poetry of Whitman's successor, William Carlos Williams." Lowell himself, in *For Lizzie and Harriet*, wrote: "I am learning to live in history."[29] The simple truth is that he was too busy learning to teach.

That the name of William Carlos Williams has come up in this context is not incidental. The poet was an obvious influence on

Lowell's later poetry. In the early fifties Lowell wrote Williams, "I wish rather in vain that I could absorb something of your way of writing into mine." In the late fifties he began writing the *Life Studies* poems, and wrote again to Williams, "I feel more and more technically indebted to you!" In 1961, two years after *Life Studies*, Lowell wrote, "It's as if no poet except Williams had really seen America or heard its language."[30]

Steven Gould Axelrod has summarized the Williams-Lowell connection succinctly. He notes that during the late forties, Lowell "praised Elizabeth Bishop and William Carlos Williams for the plainness of their language and condemned Dylan Thomas (whose style rather resembled Lowell's own) for his excessive 'rhetoric.' " This is not the first time we have seen a Middle Generation poet on the threshold of his later period take rhetoric to task. Axelrod says that

> Lowell's growing personal and artistic affinities with Williams during the 1950s made his *Life Studies* 'revolution' possible. For several seasons Lowell periodically visited Williams in Rutherford, bearing bottles of bourbon and set to 'wallow in prosody.' His poetry running dry, Lowell sensed that Williams's ideas of prosody spoke to his problem. After all, Williams's primary goal, as he wrote in "The Poem as a Field of Action" (1948), was a technique to "let our feelings through."

Not only Lowell's personal contacts with Williams, but the older poet's reviews of the younger poet's work, served to establish Williams as an important influence upon Lowell's poetry. Interestingly, in 1957, before Rosenthal coined the term "confessional poetry" to describe *Life Studies*, Lowell anticipated it by describing a Williams poem as "a triumph of simple confession." Axelrod writes that "Lowell did not specifically adopt Williams's own triadic stanza. Rather, he took from him the idea of freedom: the idea that form is only 'an arrangement of the words for the effect, not *the* arrangement, fixed and unalterable.' "

Axelrod sums up by saying that Lowell learned "three different but closely related lessons from Williams's poetry." These lessons involved, respectively, form, style, and content. They were, first, Williams's notion of the "variable foot," which helped Lowell to create the form he used in *Life Studies;* second, Williams's plain-speaking, ambiguity-free "American Idiom," which influenced Lowell's clear, colloquial *Life Studies* style; and third, Williams's notion of poetry as a means of depicting "the reality of his own life history."[31]

The Symbolists, an important early influence on Lowell, remain important in his later poetry. In 1957, while writing the *Life Studies* poems, Lowell wrote to Jarrell, "I think the French poets from Baudelaire to Apollinaire have really renewed poetry, they are modern poetry (except for Hardy and Hopkins) And Rilke and Yeats and all our best people (except Frost) have come from them."[32] If in his early poetry, the patterns of symbols which he adapted from the Symbolists helped him to forge a system of order, in his late poetry, a Symbolistic "baring of the anguished soul" and "an unremitting self-examination" reminiscent of Baudelaire possessed his work. Crick notes that Lowell's late poems are Baudelairean in that they "take the exposure of the tormented self further than ever before." Smith compares "Home After Three Months Away," a *Life Studies* poem, to Baudelaire's "L'Ennemi." In both poems, she writes, "the poet's sense of his own life is inseparable from his creativity as an artist." In Lowell's poem he has come home from the mental hospital, temporarily cured of his illness, but also cured of the drive to write poetry. The poem ends with the line: "Cured, I am frizzled, stale and small."[33]

But of course Lowell was never cured; none of the Middle Generation poets was ever cured. To have been cured of their common ailment would have been tantamount to being cured of their vocation. The story of each of their careers is, in a sense, the story of a poet's discovery and acceptance of—or, to put it otherwise, his ultimate inability to evade—the ineradicable nexus among his poetry, his personality, and his psychopathology. This growing recognition on their parts results in striking similarities among the reviews of the works of their last years. Just as Jarrell's *The Lost World* brought criticism of the too-simple form and too-personal content, and Berryman's *Love and Fame* evoked cries of "unpleasantly revealing," so Lowell's *The Dolphin*, which contained excerpts from letters his second wife, Elizabeth Hardwick, had written him during their recent divorce, drew flak: "*The Dolphin* is more gossip than gospel," ran a typical notice.[34] *Day by Day* was, like Berryman's *Delusions, Etc.*, somewhat less sensational, but perhaps more introspective, than its predecessor. Its last poem, "Epilogue," may well serve as an appropriate abstract of the Middle Generation poets' later period. For it is a *précis*, of sorts, of everything they had come to believe since their descent from the Eliotic mountain.

> Those blessed structures, plot and rhyme—
> why are they no help to me now
> I want to make
> something imagined, not recalled?

I hear the noise of my own voice:
The painter's vision is not a lens,
it trembles to caress the light.
But sometimes everything I write
with the threadbare art of my eye
seems a snapshot,
lurid, rapid, garish, grouped,
heightened from life,
yet paralyzed by fact.
All's misalliance.
Yet why not say what happened?
Pray for the grace of accuracy
Vermeer gave to the sun's illumination
stealing like the tide across a map
to his girl solid with yearning.
We are poor passing facts,
warned by that to give
each figure in the photograph
his living name.[35]

Notes

PROLOGUE

1. Some critics also consider Theodore Roethke to be a member of this group. I do not. His poetry is very different, and so is his attitude toward poetry. This I hope will become clear in the course of my study.
2. Clayton Eshleman, "A Braggart, Boozer, Brute—and Poet," *Los Angeles Times*, 10 October 1982, book review section, 2. A review of John Haffenden, *The Life of John Berryman* (Boston: Routledge and Kegan Paul, 1982).
3. James Atlas, *Delmore Schwartz: The Life of an American Poet* (New York: Farrar, Straus and Giroux, 1977), 137.

CHAPTER 1

1. Atlas, *Schwartz*, 8. Unless otherwise noted, all the biographical information about Schwartz is from this book.
2. Ibid., 10.
3. Quoted in ibid., 33.
4. Ibid., 152.
5. Ibid., 366. As Atlas further notes (p. 369), Schwartz, toward the end of his life, penned a marginal note in his copy of *Genesis:* "Don't be like me, Hershey—forgive & live." *Genesis: Book One* (New York: New Directions, 1943) itself opens with an epigraph from Dante which ends "Such grew I, who, without power to speak, wished to beg forgiveness—" (v).
6. Schwartz, *Genesis*, 104.
7. Haffenden, *Life*, 14. The biographical information about Berryman in this chapter is from this book, from Eileen Simpson, *Poets in their Youth* (New York: Random House, 1982), and from Joel Conarroe, *John Berryman: An Introduction to the Poetry* (New York: Columbia University Press, 1977).
8. Simpson, *Poets*, 36.
9. Ibid., 60.
10. Haffenden, *Life*, 29.
11. John Berryman, "Dream Song 384," in *His Toy, His Dream, His Rest* (New York: Farrar, Straus and Giroux, 1968), 316. Eileen Simpson notes (p. 236) that when Berryman was dismissed from a teaching position at the

University of Iowa in 1954, he called on Allen Tate—far from his closest friend—for help. "My first thought," writes Simpson, "was: He's gone in search of his father. John Allyn Smith came from Minnesota."

12. Haffenden, *Life*, 49.

13. Simpson, *Poets*, 64.

14. Haffenden, *Life*, 33.

15. Simpson, *Poets*, 68; Haffenden, *Life*, 61.

16. John Berryman, "Dream Song 145," in *His Toy*, 72.

17. Ian Hamilton, *Robert Lowell* (New York: Random House, 1982), 4–13. Most of the biographical information about Lowell in this chapter is from this book; additional information is from Louis Simpson, *A Revolution in Taste* (New York: Macmillan, 1978), 150.

18. Robert Lowell, "Commander Lowell," in *Life Studies* (New York: Farrar, Straus and Cudahy, 1959), 70–72.

19. Robert Lowell, "Dunbarton," in *Life Studies*, 65.

20. Hamilton, *Lowell*, 102, 198.

21. Robert Lowell, "Middle Age," in *For the Union Dead* (New York: Farrar, Straus and Giroux, 1964), 7.

22. I have left Jarrell for last because, although the facts available about his childhood indicate that he had essentially the same experience as the three other poets, those facts are in relatively short supply, and so my conclusions about Jarrell's childhood must be more tentative. One reason is Jarrell's reticence with would-be biographers and compilers of reference books. Another is the unreliability of one of the major sources of biographical information on Jarrell, Sister Bernetta Quinn, *Randall Jarrell* (Boston: Twayne Publishers, 1981). Quinn's information not only contradicts information in other places, but also facts that appear elsewhere in her own book. Moreover, Quinn's Catholicism, one suspects, may be responsible for her twisting of biographical information to make it more acceptable in philosophical or moral terms. She refuses to acknowledge the cause of Jarrell's death as suicide, for example. She also engages in careless biographical readings of Jarrell's poems.

   In chronicling Jarrell's childhood relocations, I follow Mary von Schrader Jarrell, "The Group of Two," in *Randall Jarrell: 1914–1965*, ed. Robert Lowell, Peter Taylor, and Robert Penn Warren (New York: Farrar, Straus and Giroux, 1966), 278, rather than Quinn. Quinn confuses Long Beach with Hollywood, and leaves the impression that the separation between Jarrell's parents took place in Tennessee, after which Jarrell was sent out alone to California. Mrs. Jarrell makes it clear that this was not the case.

   Donald Barlow Stauffer, in *A Short History of American Poetry* (New York: Dutton, 1974), 371, refers to this period as Jarrell's "strange, half-real, half-make-believe boyhood years in Hollywood," but Mrs. Jarrell says that her late husband only lived in Hollywood for one year.

23. Randall Jarrell, "The Lost World," in *The Lost World* (New York: Macmillan, 1965), 18.

24. Robert Lowell, "Unwanted," in *Day by Day* (New York: Farrar, Straus and Giroux, 1973), 121.

25. A. Alvarez, *The Savage God: A Study of Suicide* (New York: Knopf, 1972), 108–27.

CHAPTER 2

1. Delmore Schwartz, "The Repetitive Heart: VI," in *In Dreams Begin Responsibilities* (New York: New Directions, 1939), 97. This poem, retitled "Do the Others Speak of Me Mockingly, Maliciously?," appears also in Delmore Schwartz, *Summer Knowledge* (New York: Doubleday, 1959), reprinted as *Selected Poems: Summer Knowledge* (New York: New Directions, 1967). Most of the *In Dreams* poems are available in the latter volume, which is by far the easiest to obtain. Since many of the poems are known by their 1959 titles, I will hereafter indicate these alternate titles in addition to the original ones.
2. John Berryman, "Dream Song 74," in *77 Dream Songs* (New York: Farrar, Straus and Giroux, 1967), 81.
3. Randall Jarrell, "The Knight, Death, and the Devil," in *The Seven-League Crutches* (New York: Harcourt, Brace and Company, 1951), 24.
4. Delmore Schwartz, "The Repetitive Heart: IX," in *In Dreams*, 101. 1959 title: "The Heavy Bear Who Goes With Me."
5. John Berryman, "From the Middle and Senior Generations," in *The Freedom of the Poet* (New York: Farrar, Straus and Giroux, 1976), 311.
6. Randall Jarrell, "The Obscurity of the Poet," in *Poetry and the Age* (New York: Knopf, 1953), 17–18.
7. Delmore Schwartz, "The Vocation of the Poet in the Modern World," *Poetry* 78 (July 1951), 228.
8. "Our Country and Our Culture," *Partisan Review* 19 (1952), 284, 596–97.
9. Robert Lowell, "Memories of West Street and Lepke," in *Life Studies*, 86.
10. Simpson, *Revolution*, 86.
11. R. K. Meiners, "The Way Out: The Poetry of Delmore Schwartz and Others," *Southern Review* N.S. 7 (1971), 317. (Emphasis added.)
12. Randall Jarrell, "The Woman at the Washington Zoo," in *The Woman at the Washington Zoo* (New York: Atheneum, 1960), 2; and "Next Day," in *The Lost World*, 3. Lowell's speakers often feel caged as well; see, for example, "For the Union Dead," in *For the Union Dead*, 70–72. In a poem on Jarrell, Lowell compares Jarrell to a "caged squirrel on its wheel," as Marjorie Perloff notes in *The Poetic Art of Robert Lowell* (Ithaca: Cornell University Press, 1973), 27. Robert Watson, in "Randall Jarrell," in *Randall Jarrell: 1914–1965*, 272, writes "few poets can capture man's feelings of loneliness and loss as poignantly as Jarrell."
13. Hamilton, *Lowell*, 45.
14. Schwartz, *Genesis*, 19, 10.
15. James F. Knapp, "Delmore Schwartz: Poet of the Orphic Journey," *Sewanee Review* 78 (1970), 516. In 1957, during an internment at Bellevue, Schwartz wrote these lines: "I am the major poet D[elmore] S[chwartz] / America ignores my inmost thoughts" (Schwartz papers, Beinecke Library, Yale University).
16. Atlas, *Schwartz*, 310, 367; Saul Bellow, *Humboldt's Gift* (New York: Viking

Press, 1975), 32. See also John Berryman, "Dream Song 23: The Lay of Ike," in *77 Dream Songs*, 25.

17. Hamilton, *Lowell*, 197. See also Robert Lowell, "Inauguration Day," in *Life Studies*, 7. Hamilton, in *Lowell*, 301, records that, like Schwartz, Lowell engaged in manic oneway correspondences with political figures. In Lowell's case, the letters went not to Stevenson but to Eisenhower and the Pope.

18. Karl Shapiro, *The Poetry Wreck* (New York: Random House, 1975), 268; Hamilton, *Lowell*, 193, 306; Atlas, *Schwartz*, 366; and interview with Leonard Gross, 15 December 1982.

19. Norman Mailer, *The Armies of the Night* (New York: New American Library, 1968), 51.

20. William Barrett, *The Truants* (New York: Anchor, 1982), 138. Barrett attributes Schwartz's hostility toward Trilling to Schwartz's belief that Trilling had prevented him from getting a job at Columbia (p. 163). But this unfounded idea seems to be the result of a paranoid fixation on Trilling, rather than its cause. Aside from this, Barrett makes a number of the same points I have made about Schwartz's attitude toward Trilling (pp. 166-68); he also makes some observations about Schwartz's acute consciousness of his Jewishness (pp. 44, 214). See also Atlas, *Schwartz*, 162–66, 172, 370.

21. Atlas, *Schwartz*, 311–12. See also Delmore Schwartz, "The Duchess' Red Shoes," *Partisan Review* 21 (1953), 60.

22. Simpson, *Revolution*, 138, quoting Robert Lowell, "Christ for Sale," in *Land of Unlikeness* (Cummington, Mass.: Cummington Press, 1944), n.p. Suzanne Ferguson, *The Poetry of Randall Jarrell* (Baton Rouge: Louisiana State University Press, 1971), 10, discusses Jarrell's poem "For an Emigrant," whose child protagonist, a victim of Hitler, identifies with his victimizer. Berryman's interest in Judaism is discussed in Haffenden, *Life*, 383. See also Berryman's story "The Imaginary Jew," in *The Freedom of the Poet*, 359–66, which is based on a real incident in Berryman's life. That Berryman identified with another minority as well, blacks, would seem to be indicated by the fact that Henry, his *Dream Songs* persona, appears "in blackface" (*His Toy*, ix).

23. John Berryman, "Dream Song 152," in *His Toy*, 81.

24. Barrett, *Truants*, 219; Hamilton, *Lowell*, 334. Berryman, for his part, reacted to the news of Frost's death by asking his informant, "Who's number one? Who's number one? Cal is number one, isn't he?" (Haffenden, *Life*, 319).

25. John Berryman, "Dream Song 133," in *His Toy*, 60.

26. Haffenden, *Life*, 106; John Berryman, "Dream Song 192," in *His Toy*, 121; Hamilton, *Lowell*, 241; Robert Lowell, "Exorcism," in *The Dolphin* (New York: Farrar, Straus and Giroux, 1973), 48; Delmore Schwartz, "The First Morning of the Second World," in *Summer Knowledge*, 154; Jay L. Halio, "Delmore Schwartz's Felt Abstractions," *Southern Review* N.S. 1 (1965), 812; Delmore Schwartz, "In the Silent Ripple, the Mind Perceives the Heart," in *In Dreams*, 134. Moreover, "Love is more exciting / Than

precocious early success" (Schwartz papers, Beinecke Library, Yale University).

27. John Berryman, "Dream Song 4," in *77 Dream Songs*, 6; "Dream Song 48," in ibid., 52; Delmore Schwartz, "The Repetitive Heart: VIII," in *In Dreams* (1959 title: "Abraham and Orpheus, Be With Me Now"); Robert Lowell, "Skunk Hour," in *Life Studies*, 90; Randall Jarrell, untitled poem ("Falling in love is never as simple"), in *The Complete Poems* (New York: Farrar, Straus and Giroux, 1969), 426; John Berryman, "Sonnet 73," in *Berryman's Sonnets* (New York: Farrar, Straus and Giroux, 1969), 73; Delmore Schwartz, "The Repetitive Heart: I," in *In Dreams*, 91 (1959 title: "All of Us Always Turning Away for Solace").

28. Atlas, *Schwartz*, 223; Hamilton, *Lowell*, 126.

29. Atlas, *Schwartz*, 117. Berryman's first marriage is discussed in Haffenden, *Life*, 138–39; Schwartz's in Atlas, *Schwartz*, 115. Jarrell's Hamlet remark is reported by Quinn, *Jarrell*, 146. Lowell himself wrote to Jarrell, on the occasion of the latter's divorce from his first wife, that "we all envied you and Mackie because your difficulties seemed to have nothing in common with the difficulties of other marriages, none of the open deliberate unkindnesses, scenes etc." (Robert Lowell, letter to Randall Jarrell, 24 February 1952, Berg Collection, New York Public Library).

30. Hamilton, *Lowell*, 154.

31. Atlas, *Schwartz*, 61, 115, 148.

32. Ibid., 61–62.

33. Haffenden, *Life*, 375.

34. Robert Lowell, "First Love," in *Selected Poems* (New York: Farrar, Straus and Giroux, 1976), 181.

35. Hamilton, *Lowell*, 135, 157, 301, 431; Haffenden, *Life*, 243.

36. A. A. Brill, *Lectures on Psychoanalytic Psychiatry* (New York: Knopf, 1947), 259. What causes homosexuality is still an open question, but classic Freudian theory posits an inextricable connection among paranoia and narcissism—both of which have, of course, figured prominently in these pages—and homosexuality. Brill, who introduced Freudian psychoanalysis into the United States, would clearly have known what to make of the Middle Generation poets; he wrote that "the delusion of persecution is always a reaction to a repressed homosexual wish-phantasy" (p. 252), and said that "milder forms of homosexuality and paranoia . . . are neither psychotic nor inverted but manifest throughout life a strong struggle with mother fixations" (p. 253). Haffenden, in *Life*, 240, quotes Berryman as follows: "Writers are likely to have more masked-homosexual-component around than other people; and heading for friends' wives or girls is really a way of getting closer to friends." M. L. Rosenthal, in his study *Randall Jarrell* (Minneapolis: University of Minnesota Press, 1972), 39, detects massive evidence of "sexual repression" in Jarrell's work.

It is hardly possible to go overboard in attributing aspects of the Middle Generation poets' lives and writings to their sexuality. Indeed, the poets themselves were in the habit of basing their interpretations of other writers' work on those writers' sexual histories, as if they, the

Middle Generation poets, knew that sexual motives were in fact at the bottom of everything. Schwartz, for example, read all of Eliot's work—perhaps the single most important oeuvre for him—as "sexual confession" (Atlas, *Schwartz*, 365). Berryman did the same thing for Stephen Crane.

37. Haffenden, *Life*, 240.
38. Atlas, *Schwartz*, 37.
39. John Berryman, "Dream Song 90: Op. posth. no. 13," in *His Toy*, 15.
40. John Berryman, "Dream Song 127," in *His Toy*, 54.
41. Robert Lowell, "Randall Jarrell," in *History* (New York: Farrar, Straus and Giroux, 1973), 135. Lowell has an essay by the same name in *Randall Jarrell: 1914–1965*.
42. Hamilton, *Lowell*, 351. This is similar to the last paragraph of a letter Lowell wrote to Jarrell early in 1965, after the latter's hospitalization for a nervous breakdown: "Please let me tell you how much I admire you and your work and thank you for the many times when you have given me the strength to continue. Let me know if there's anything I can do. And courage, old friend! Affectionately," (Robert Lowell, letter to Randall Jarrell, 29 April 1965, Berg Collection, New York Public Library).
43. Hamilton, *Lowell*, 349–50.
44. Robert Lowell, "Our Dead Poets," in *History*, 137.
45. John Berryman, "Dream Song 147," in *His Toy*, 76.
46. Hamilton, *Lowell*, 438; Robert Lowell, "Death and the Bridge," in *History*, 205; and "For John Berryman," in *Day by Day*, 27.
47. John Berryman, "Dream Song 149," in *His Toy*, 78. Lowell wrote to Jarrell in similar terms: "hardly a day goes by when I do not wish you were here to talk to" (Robert Lowell, letter to Randall Jarrell, 24 February 1952, Berg Collection, New York Public Library).
48. John Berryman, "Dream Song 155," in *His Toy*, 84; Robert Lowell, "For John Berryman I," in *History*, 203. Lowell wrote similarly to Jarrell: "You know about everything about me that I do" (Robert Lowell, letter to Randall Jarrell, 15 February 1959, Berg Collection, New York Public Library).
49. Robert Lowell, "To Delmore Schwartz," in *Life Studies*, 54.
50. Barrett, *Truants*, 217.
51. John Berryman, "At Chinese Checkers," in *The Dispossessed* (New York: William Sloane Associates, 1948), 42.
52. Atlas, *Schwartz*, 210.
53. John Berryman, "Dream Song 137," in *His Toy*, 64.
54. Randall Jarrell, "Eine Kleine Nachtmusik," in *The Rage for the Lost Penny*, in *Five Young American Poets*, ed. James Laughlin (Norfolk, Conn.: New Directions, 1940), 110–11; Robert Lowell, "Myopia: A Night," in *For the Union Dead*, 31–33.

CHAPTER 3

1. Atlas, *Schwartz*, 378; Hamilton, *Lowell*, 69; Alfred Kazin, *New York Jew*, (New York: Knopf, 1978), 201.

2. Randall Jarrell, *Selected Poems* (New York: Atheneum, 1964), xi.
3. Atlas, *Schwartz*, 51.
4. Ibid., 50. Schwartz's essay, "A Note on the Nature of Art," *Marxist Quarterly* (January-March 1937), 305–9 gives a good indication of his attitude toward Marxism.
5. Atlas, *Schwartz*, 82.
6. Delmore Schwartz, "The Two Audens," *Kenyon Review* 1 (1939), 34–35.
7. Barrett, *Truants*, 230.
8. Delmore Schwartz, "Narcissus: The Mind is an Ancient and Famous Capital," in *Summer Knowledge*, 226.
9. Ferguson, *Jarrell*, 64.
10. Quinn, *Jarrell*, 28.
11. Simpson, *Poets*, 111.
12. Haffenden, *Life*, 41. We may well doubt this; Berryman felt guilty all his life for taking his stepfather's name, because he felt he'd rejected his father; abandoning Catholicism may indeed have intensified his feeling of guilt, for it seems likely that a Catholic boy would feel, in such a situation, that he was rejecting his spiritual Father—who, as I have already observed, is in Freudian terms symbolically identical with his actual father.
13. Ibid., 202. See also 383, 385, 391–92, 399, 407, 415. I do not understand how Haffenden, who chronicles these waverings, can say as he does that Berryman "scarcely ever doubted God" (p. 382). The poet's persistent doubts about God are one of the most characteristic aspects of his adult life. "My doubts fight my faith," he writes in an untitled poem in *Henry's Fate and Other Poems, 1967–1972* (New York: Farrar, Straus and Giroux, 1977), 57.
14. Haffenden, *Life*, 184.
15. Among the condemnatory critics were Graham Greene, "The Badge of Courage," *New Statesman and Nation* 41 (1951), 627–28; Claude Jones, "Stephen Crane," *Nineteenth Century Fiction* 6 (June 1951), 74–76; Orville Prescott, "Books of the Times," *New York Times*, 12 December 1950, 31; Andrews Wanning, "A Portrait of Stephen Crane," *Partisan Review* 18 (1951), 358–61. One reviewer who said that the Freudian interpretations in *Stephen Crane* were shaky but could not be dismissed out of hand was Edmund Wilson, who wrote in the *New Yorker*, 6 January 1951, 77–85. Patricia Ann Brenner has written a dissertation, "John Berryman's *Dream Songs*: Manner and Matter" (Kent State University, 1970), which is largely devoted to the influence of Freud on the songs.
16. Hamilton, *Lowell*, 78.
17. Hamilton, *Lowell*, 95. Schwartz was also "profoundly affected" (during his years as a student at New York University) by neo-Thomism. To him as to Lowell, it seems to have been a form of "intellectual independence"—a way of rebelling. Sidney Hook, "Imaginary Enemies, Real Terror," *American Scholar* 47 (1978), 408.
18. Hamilton, *Lowell*, 201.
19. Delmore Schwartz, "The Graveyard by the Sea," in *Last and Lost Poems of Delmore Schwartz*, ed. Robert Phillips (New York, Vanguard, 1979), 31.

20. Robert Lowell, "Dream," in *The Dolphin*, 34; John Berryman, "Dream Song 101," in *His Toy*, 28.
21. Robert Lowell, "The Couple," in *The Dolphin*, 50.
22. Hamilton, *Lowell*, 85; Haffenden, *Life*, 167; Randall Jarrell, "A Conversation with the Devil," in *The Seven-League Crutches*, 45.
23. Ferguson, *Jarrell*, 95.
24. Delmore Schwartz, "O Child Do Not Fear the Night and Sleep's Dark Possession," in *Summer Knowledge*, 162.
25. John Berryman, "Dream Song 132," in *His Toy*, 59; "Dream Song 178," in *His Toy*, 107. To at least three of the poets, the images of movies and dreams were interchangeable; both movies, in their day, and dreams represented wish-fulfillments. See Schwartz, "Metro-Goldwyn-Mayer," in *Last and Lost Poems*, 22; "In Dreams Begin Responsibilities," in *In Dreams*, 11–20; Jarrell, "The Truth," in *The Seven-League Crutches*, 28; Berryman, "Dream Song 109," in *His Toy*, 36.
26. "Waking dream": Delmore Schwartz, "Sonnet: The Ghosts of James and Peirce in Harvard Yard," in *In Dreams*, 137; John Berryman, "Dream Song 109," in *His Toy*, 36. "Dream of life": Randall Jarrell, "The Death of the Ball Turret Gunner," in *Little Friend, Little Friend* (New York: Dial Press, 1945), 58. Arnold lines: Robert Lowell, *The Mills of the Kavanaughs* (New York: Harcourt, Brace and World, 1951), 1. "Sick dream": Randall Jarrell, "Eine Kleine Nachtmusik," in *The Rage for the Lost Penny*, in *Five Young American Poets*, 110. "When I saw": John Berryman, "Dream Song 130," in *His Toy*, 57. "We live while": Delmore Schwartz, "Kilroy's Carnival: A Poetic Prologue for TV," in *Last and Lost Poems*, 96. "The lights": Randall Jarrell, "Absent without Official Leave," in *Little Friend*, 33. Jarrell also refers to the "sleep of life" in "A Girl in a Library," in *The Seven-League Crutches*, 72. Quinn discusses the life-as-a-dream motif in Jarrell in "Randall Jarrell," in *Randall Jarrell: 1914–1965*, 149–51. In a letter to Jarrell, Lowell refers to the world as "a murderer's nightmare" (Robert Lowell, letter to Randall Jarrell, 7 November 1961, Berg Collection, New York Public Library).
27. Randall Jarrell, "Hohensalzburg: Fantastic Variations on a Theme of Romantic Character," in *The Seven-League Crutches*, 17; Delmore Schwartz, "Now He Knows All There Is to Know: Now He Is Acquainted With the Day and Night," in *Last and Lost Poems*, 3; Delmore Schwartz, "This Is a Poem I Wrote at Night, Before the Dawn," in *Last and Lost Poems*, 3; Robert Lowell, "Home," in *Day by Day*, 114; John Haffenden, Introduction, in John Berryman, *Henry's Fate*, xv. Berryman's more well-known statement along these lines is, of course, the one in the introductory note to *His Toy*; the same remarks are repeated in the introductory note to *The Dream Songs*. "The poem . . . is essentially about an imaginary character (not the poet, not me) named Henry . . . he has a friend, never named, who addresses him as Mr Bones and variants thereof" (*His Toy*, ix).
28. Delmore Schwartz, "All Night, All Night," in *Last and Lost Poems*, 6; Randall Jarrell, "The End of the Rainbow," in *The Woman at the Washington Zoo*, 9.

29. Robert Lowell, "Another Summer," in *The Dolphin*, 63; Robert Lowell, "David and Bathsheba in the Public Garden," in *The Mills of the Kavanaughs*, 44; Randall Jarrell, "The Emancipators," in *Little Friend*, 14; John Berryman, "Dream Song 123," in *His Toy*, 50; Delmore Schwartz, "Father and Son," in *In Dreams*, 110; Schwartz, "The Repetitive Heart: XI," in ibid., 104 (1959 title: "Time's Dedication").

30. Delmore Schwartz, "Father and Son," in *In Dreams*, 112. Lowell's remark about the fear of death is from "During a Transatlantic Call," in *The Dolphin*, 47.

31. Delmore Schwartz, "Concerning the Synthetic Unity of Apperception," in *In Dreams*, 126.

32. Robert Lowell, "For John Berryman," in *Day by Day*, 27.

33. Hamilton, *Lowell*, 423.

34. Simpson, *Poets*, 127.

35. John Crowe Ransom, "The Rugged Way of Genius," in *Randall Jarrell: 1914–1965*, 155; Delmore Schwartz, "On Poetry and the Age," in ibid., 189–90.

36. Atlas, *Schwartz*, 357.

37. Barrett, *Truants*, 71.

CHAPTER 4

1. Omitted from this list are all works of fiction, criticism, drama, and translation, including Schwartz's *Shenandoah*, a verse play, and his translation of Rimbaud's *Une saison en enfer*. Both works are of interest but are not relevant to the present topic. I have also omitted Lowell's *Poems 1938–49*. Published in Britain in 1950, it contains work already present in his American volumes. *Berryman's Sonnets*, published in 1967, is included because the poems in it were all written in 1947.

2. T. S. Eliot, "Tradition and the Individual Talent," in *Selected Essays* (New York: Harcourt, Brace and Company, 1932), 3–11.

3. T. S. Eliot, "Hamlet and His Problems," in *Selected Essays*, 121–26.

4. T. S. Eliot, "The Metaphysical Poets," in *Selected Essays*, 241–50.

5. Barrett, *Truants*, 28; Rosenthal, *Jarrell*, 6; Richard Eberhart, quoted in Hamilton, *Lowell*, 181; Sidney Hook, "Imaginary Enemies, Real Terror," 408; Haffenden, *Life*, 77. In Lowell's case the rebellion I speak of in this paragraph may have been intensified by the fact that Frost was a hero of his parents and the New England poets included among them his forebear James Russell Lowell.

6. Quoted in Hamilton, *Lowell*, 85.

7. Geoffrey Thurley, *The American Moment: American Poetry in the Mid-Century* (New York: St. Martin's Press, 1977), 53. The Wordsworth line is from *The Prelude 11*, line 108.

8. Delmore Schwartz, "Father and Son," in *In Dreams*, 111.

9. Delmore Schwartz, "The Ghosts of James and Peirce in Harvard Yard," in *In Dreams*, 137.

10. Randall Jarrell, "On the Railway Platform," in *The Rage for the Lost Penny*, in *Five Young American Poets*, 91. Lowell too sees "The past / Is cities from

a train," in "At the Altar," in *Lord Weary's Castle* (New York: Harcourt, Brace and World, 1946), 45. The line from Donne is from *Devotions* 17.

11. John Berryman, "The Statue," in *Twenty Poems*, in *Five Young American Poets*, 49–50. It may be significant that the younger Humboldt sought in *Kosmos* "to formulate a concept of unity amid the complexity of nature." "Humboldt, Alexander, Freiherr von," *The New Columbia Encyclopedia*, 1975.

12. Conarroe, *Berryman*, 27.

13. Delmore Schwartz, "The Ballad of the Children of the Czar," in *In Dreams*, 113–16.

14. Randall Jarrell, "Eine Kleine Nachtmusik," in *The Rage for the Lost Penny*, in *Five Young American Poets*, 110–11.

15. John Berryman, "The Ball Poem," in *The Dispossessed*, 14.

16. Robert Lowell, "The Ferris Wheel," in *Lord Weary's Castle*, 16.

CHAPTER 5

1. Allen Tate, letter to Delmore Schwartz, 5 January 1939, quoted in Atlas, *Schwartz*, 129; Mark Van Doren, "Music of a Mind," *Kenyon Review* 1 (1939), 208; Louise Bogan, "Young Modern," *Nation*, 25 March 1939, 353; George Marion O'Donnell, "Delmore Schwartz's Achievement," *Poetry* 52 (May, 1939), 105.

2. Delmore Schwartz, "Coriolanus and His Mother," in *In Dreams*, 23, 66.

3. T. S. Eliot, "Hamlet and His Problems," in *Selected Essays*, 124.

4. Delmore Schwartz, "In the Naked Bed, in Plato's Cave," in *In Dreams*, 134.

5. T. S. Eliot, *The Waste Land*, in *The Complete Poems and Plays* (New York: Harcourt, Brace and World, 1971), 38.

6. T. S. Eliot, "Gerontion," in *The Complete Poems and Plays*, 22.

7. T. S. Eliot, "Preludes," in *The Complete Poems and Plays*, 12–13.

8. Atlas, *Schwartz*, 27, 40, 55, 127, 244.

9. Delmore Schwartz, "T. S. Eliot as the International Hero," *Partisan Review* 12 (1945), 199–201.

10. Delmore Schwartz, "The Literary Dictatorship of T. S. Eliot," *Partisan Review* 16 (1949), 121, 137. Schwartz's review of *Four Quartets*, "Anywhere Out of the World," *Nation*, 24 July 1943, 102, reflects the same resentment of Eliot's "new" style, the conviction that Eliot has betrayed Eliot.

11. Schwartz papers, Beinecke Library, Yale University.

12. T. S. Eliot, "The Love Song of J. Alfred Prufrock," in *The Complete Poems and Plays*, 3.

13. Schwartz papers, Beinecke Library, Yale University; T. S. Eliot, "The Love Song of J. Alfred Prufrock," in *The Complete Poems and Plays*, 5; Eliot, "Ash Wednesday," in ibid., 60.

14. Delmore Schwartz, "To the Reader," in *Genesis*, vii–ix.

15. Delmore Schwartz, *Genesis*, 78, 192, 208.

16. *Vaudeville for a Princess and Other Poems* (New York: New Directions,

1950), although an early volume, contains some transitional elements which are enlightening in the context of the later poetry; thus it will be discussed in part 3.

CHAPTER 6

1. Randall Jarrell, "When You and I Were All," in *The Rage for the Lost Penny*, in *Five Young American Poets*, 97; Jarrell, "The Soldier," in *Little Friend*, 50; Jarrell, "Because of Me, Because of You . . . ," in *The Rage for the Lost Penny*, in *Five Young American Poets*, 113.
2. Randall Jarrell, "Port of Embarkation," in *Little Friend*, 30; Jarrell, "A Lullaby," in ibid., 49; Jarrell, "Sears Roebuck," in *Losses* (New York: Harcourt, Brace and Company, 1948), 31.
3. Randall Jarrell, "the Head of Wisdom," in *Blood for a Stranger* (New York: Harcourt, Brace and Company, 1942), 65; Jarrell, "The See-er of Cities," in *The Rage for the Lost Penny*, in *Five Young American Poets*, 95.
4. Conrad Aiken, "Poetry: What Direction?", *New Republic*, 12 May 1941, 670–72; James Laughlin, quoted in Atlas, *Schwartz*, 103-4; Rosenthal, *Jarrell*, 7.
5. W. H. Auden and John Garrett, Introduction, *The Poet's Tongue* (London: G. Bell and Sons, 1935), ix.
6. Atlas, *Schwartz*, 50.
7. W. H. Auden, "Authority in America," *The Griffin* (March 1955), quoted in Monroe K. Spears, *The Poetry of W. H. Auden: The Disenchanted Island* (New York: Oxford University Press, 1963), 86.
8. W. H. Auden, "Another Time," in *Collected Poems*, ed. Edward Mendelson (New York: Random House, 1976), 218.
9. W. H. Auden, "Refugee Blues," in *Selected Poems of W. H. Auden*, "new edition," ed. Edward Mendelson (New York: Vintage, 1979), 83–84. The poem appears in the *Collected Poems*, as the first of a series of ten "songs"; it is untitled and indexed under its first line: "Say this city has ten million souls."
10. Randall Jarrell, "The Refugees," in *The Rage for the Lost Penny*, in *Five Young American Poets*, 106.
11. There is a handful of exceptions to the rule that early Middle Generation poetry does not make political comments. The most blatant exception is perhaps Berryman's "Communist."
12. Schwartz, "The Two Audens," 35; Randall Jarrell, "Poetry in a Dry Season," in *Kipling, Auden & Co.* (New York: Farrar, Straus and Giroux, 1980), Jarrell, "Recent Poetry," in ibid., 226.
13. Justin Replogle, *Auden's Poetry* (Seattle: University of Washington Press, 1969), 190.
14. Delmore Schwartz, "The Repetitive Heart: VII," in *In Dreams*, 99 (1959 title: "I Am to My Own Heart Merely a Serf"); Schwartz, "The Repetitive Heart: VIII," in ibid., 100 (1959 title: "Abraham and Orpheus, Be With Me Now"); Randall Jarrell, "On the Railway Platform," in *The Rage for the Lost Penny*, in *Five Young American Poets*, 91; John Berryman, "Love in Its

Separate Being," in *Twenty Poems,* in *Five Young American Poets,* 93; Jarrell, "When You and I Were All," in *The Rage for the Lost Penny,* in *Five Young American Poets,* 96; Berryman, "Ancestor," in *The Dispossessed,* 35; Berryman, "The Long Home," in ibid., 92; Robert Lowell, "The Exile's Return," in *Lord Weary's Castle,* 3; Lowell, "Colloquy in Black Rock," in ibid., 5; Lowell, "The Quaker Graveyard in Nantucket," in ibid., 8.

15. Replogle, *Auden,* 194; W. H. Auden, "Oxford," in *Collected Poetry,* 81; Auden, "The Walking-Tour," in ibid., 146; Auden," "So from the years the gifts were showered; each," in ibid., 319; Replogle, *Auden,* 195. "Oxford" appears in *Collected Poems,* 124; "The Walking-Tour" in ibid., as part of the play "Paid on Both Sides," 21–35; and "So from the years" in ibid., as the first of a series of "Sonnets from China," 149.

16. Delmore Schwartz, "The Ballad of the Children of the Czar," in *In Dreams,* 115; Schwartz, "Prothalamion," in ibid., 108; Schwartz, "Socrates' Ghost Must Haunt Me Now," in ibid., 118; Randall Jarrell, "The Winter's Tale," in *The Rage for the Lost Penny,* in *Five Young American Poets,* 104; Jarrell, "The Head of Wisdom," in ibid., 65; John Berryman, "The Ball Poem," in *The Dispossessed,* 14; Berryman, "The Statue," in *Twenty Poems,* in *Five Young American Poets,* 49; Berryman, "A Point of Age," in *The Dispossessed,* 8.

17. W. H. Auden, "The chimneys are smoking, the crocus is out in the border," in *Look, Stranger!* (London: Faber and Faber, 1936), 40; Randall Jarrell, "The Bad Music," in *The Rage for the Lost Penny,* in *Five Young American Poets,* 115; John Berryman, "Caravan," in *Twenty Poems,* in ibid., 80.

18. Replogle, *Auden,* 180–81; W. H. Auden, "Musée des Beaux Arts," in *Collected Poetry,* 3; Auden, "The Cave of Making," in *About the House* (New York: Random House, 1965), 8. "Musée" appears in the *Collected Poems,* 126–27.

19. Replogle, *Auden,* 180; Delmore Schwartz, "Someone is Harshly Coughing as Before," in *Summer Knowledge,* 37; Randall Jarrell, "The Winter's Tale," in *The Rage for the Lost Penny,* in *Five Young American Poets,* p. 104; John Berryman, "Meditation," in *Twenty Poems,* in ibid., 59; Robert Lowell, "The Exile's Return," in *Lord Weary's Castle,* 3.

20. W. H. Auden, "O what is that sound which so thrills the ear," in *Selected Poems of W. H. Auden,* 26. The poem appears in the *Collected Poems,* 105, under the title "O What Is That Sound." There are slight differences between the two versions.

21. W. H. Auden, " 'O where are you going?' said reader to rider," in *Selected Poems of W. H. Auden,* 20; Auden, "O Love, the interest itself in thoughtless Heaven," in ibid., 25; Auden, "O for doors to be open and an invite with gilded edges," in ibid., 42. "O where" appears in the *Collected Poems,* 60, as the fifth of five "songs"; "O for doors" appears in ibid., 116, under the title "Song of the Beggars" and in a somewhat different version.

22. Replogle, *Auden,* 131, 205.

23. Delmore Schwartz, "The Ballad of the Children of the Czar," in *In*

Dreams, 113; Randall Jarrell, "London," in *Blood for a Stranger*, 4; John Berryman, "Fare Well," in *The Dispossessed*, 15; Robert Lowell, "The Drunken Fisherman," in *Lord Weary's Castle*, 31.

24. Delmore Schwartz, "Coriolanus and His Mother," in *In Dreams*, 72; Randall Jarrell, "Song: Not There," in *Blood for a Stranger*, 73; John Berryman, "Boston Common: A Meditation upon the Hero," in *The Dispossessed*, 67; Robert Lowell, "New Year's Day," in *Lord Weary's Castle*, 7.

25. Delmore Schwartz, "Cambridge, Spring 1937," in *Summer Knowledge*, 57.

CHAPTER 7

1. John Berryman, "A Note on Poetry," in *Twenty Poems*, in *Five Young American Poets*, 45–48.

2. T. S. Eliot, "The Metaphysical Poets," in *Selected Essays*, 241; Eliot, "The Music of Poetry," in *Selected Prose*, ed. John Hayward (London: Penguin, 1953), 56; Eliot, "Dante," in *Selected Essays*, 199.

3. John Berryman, "Monkhood," in *Love and Fame* (New York: Farrar, Straus and Giroux, 1970), 144.

4. Haffenden, *Life*, 82–83.

5. See, for example, R. P. Blackmur, "Twelve Poets," *Southern Review* 7 (1941), 197–213; Allen Tate, "The Last Omnibus," *Partisan Review* 8 (1941), 241–44; Babette Deutsch, "Poets—Timely and Timeless," *New Republic*, 29 March 1943, 420–21; and Frank Jones, "Skilled Workers," *Nation*, 17 April 1943, 569–70.

6. Winfield Townley Scott, "The New Intellectualism: Two Views. I: The Dry Reaction," *Poetry* 58 (May 1941), 86.

7. John Berryman, "The Disciple," in *Twenty Poems*, in *Five Young American Poets*, 63–64.

8. Among the Middle Generation poems that refer to "the State" are Jarrell's "The Death of the Ball Turret Gunner," in *Little Friend*, 58; Berryman's "Rock Study with Wanderer," in *The Dispossessed*, 87–89; Schwartz's "Coriolanus and His Mother," in *In Dreams*, 24; Lowell's "At the Indian Killer's Grave," in *Lord Weary's Castle*, 56.

9. W. B. Yeats, "The Dolls," in *The Collected Poems of W. B. Yeats* (New York: Macmillan, 1956), 124.

10. Richard Ellmann, *The Identity of Yeats* (New York: Oxford University Press, 1964), 127, 130, 132, 134, 136–38, 140–41.

11. W. B. Yeats, "The Magi," in *The Collected Poems of W. B. Yeats*, 124. Note the echo of Yeats's first line in the last stanza of Berryman's poem: "now that I'm / Old I behold it as a young man yet."

12. John Unterecker, *A Reader's Guide to William Butler Yeats* (New York: Farrar, Straus and Giroux, 1959), 128.

13. See, for example, J. M. Linebarger, *John Berryman* (New York: Twayne Publishers, 1974), 43; Ian Hamilton, "John Berryman," *London Magazine*, February 1965, 94.

14. T. S. Eliot, "The Journey of the Magi," in *The Complete Poems and Plays*, 68–69.

15. W. B. Yeats, "A General Introduction for My Work," in *Essays and Introductions* (New York: Collier, 1968), 509.

16. John Berryman, "Rock Study with Wanderer," in *The Dispossessed*, 87–89.

17. Linebarger, *Berryman*, 50.

18. T. S. Eliot, *The Waste Land*, in *The Complete Poems and Plays*, 38–39.

19. Cleanth Brooks, "T. S. Eliot: Thinker and Artist," in *A Shaping Joy* (New York: Harcourt Brace Jovanovich, 1971), 41.

20. Berryman's opening note in *The Dispossessed*, vii, tells us that the line "occurs in Pirandello's *Six Characters*."

21. W. B. Yeats, "The Second Coming," in *The Collected Poems of W. B. Yeats*, 185.

22. T. S. Eliot, "East Coker," in *The Complete Poems and Plays*, 123; Eliot, "Gerontion," in ibid., 21; Eliot, "The Hollow Men," in ibid., 56.

23. John Berryman, "Letter to His Brother," in *Twenty Poems*, in *Five Young American Poets*, 55.

24. Linebarger, *Berryman*, 32; Gary Q. Arpin, *The Poetry of John Berryman* (Port Washington, N.Y.: Kennikat Press, 1978), 17.

25. Conarroe, *Berryman*, 29.

26. This is a fact to which Conarroe seems inattentive. Quoting such phrases from the early Berryman canon as "Disfigurement is general," "none of us is well," "the violent world," "the world's decay," "bitter and exhausted ground," and "a dying race," Conarroe cites them as indications of "the intensity and dimension of Berryman's political despair." Again, Conarroe is eager to extend Auden's stylistic domination of Berryman into a thematic domination as well. Yet, we may well ask, how can anyone mistake the spiritual despair that these phrases express—a spiritual despair that is, in accordance with the principles of Eliot, filtered through the intellect and treated impersonally—as political?

    Conarroe also writes: "Yeats saved Berryman from the overwhelming influences of Eliot and Pound" (Conarroe, *Berryman*, 28). This misguided statement proves to be nothing more than a paraphrase from the poet himself: "Yeats somehow saved me from the then-crushing influences of Ezra Pound and T. S. Eliot" ("One Answer to a Question: Changes," in *The Freedom of the Poet*, 324). If nothing else, this demonstrates the error of taking a poet's remarks about himself at face value. Linebarger too makes this mistake. Berryman, he remarks in his chapter on Berryman's early poetry, "disagreed with Eliot's view that poetry should be impersonal" (Linebarger, *Berryman*, 50). His sources for this contention, however, are a 1949 essay by Berryman about Ezra Pound in which Berryman expresses no such disagreement, and a 1969 interview with the *Harvard Advocate* in which he does indeed disagree with Eliot. But this attitude toward Eliot is to be expected in 1969, when Berryman was in his later period; his attitude toward Eliot twenty-five years earlier was quite different.

27. W. H. Auden, "September 1, 1939," in *Selected Poems of W. H. Auden*, 86.

28. John Berryman, "1 September 1939," in *The Dispossessed*, 51.

29. W. B. Yeats, "Death," in *The Collected Poems of W. B. Yeats*, 230.

30. Delmore Schwartz, "O Love, Sweet Animal," in *In Dreams*, 122.

31. John Berryman, "On the London Train," in *Twenty Poems*, in *Five Young American Poets*, 96.

32. Randall Jarrell, "When You and I Were All," in *The Rage for the Lost Penny*, in *Five Young American Poets*, 96. The Yeats line is from "A Prayer for My Son," in *Collected Poems of W. B. Yeats*, 209.

33. John Berryman, "Sonnet 18," in *Berryman's Sonnets*, 18.

34. John Berryman, "Sonnet 5," in ibid., 5.

35. Haffenden, *Life*, 175–76.

36. This information comes from Marius Bewley, "Poetry Chronicle," *Hudson Review* 20 (1967), 500–504. "The Curse" and "The Apparition" in *Five Young American Poets* are also based upon Donne poems.

37. Haffenden, *Life*, 176–77.

CHAPTER 8

1. Leslie Fiedler, "The Believing Poet and the Infidel Reader," *New Leader*, 10 May 1947, 18.

2. T. S. Eliot, Preface, *For Lancelot Andrewes: Essays on Style and Order* (Garden City: Doubleday and Doran, 1929), vii.

3. Irvin Ehrenpreis, "The Age of Lowell," in *Robert Lowell: A Portrait of the Artist in His Time*, ed., Michael London and Robert Boyers (New York: David Lewis, 1970), 45.

4. Jean Stafford wryly commented that Lowell meant *"literary* purpose"; but he clearly also meant "psychological purpose."

5. Randall Jarrell, "From the Kingdom of Necessity," in *Poetry and the Age*, 212.

6. Herbert Leibowitz, "Robert Lowell: Ancestral Voices," in *Robert Lowell: A Portrait of the Artist in His Time*, 201.

7. Christ is, for example, present in the Hanged Man. F. R. Leavis, "The Waste Land," in *T. S. Eliot: A Collection of Critical Essays*, ed. Hugh Kenner (Englewood Cliffs, N.J.: Prentice-Hall, 1962), 94.

8. Stephen Yenser, *Circle to Circle: The Poetry of Robert Lowell* (Berkeley: University of California Press, 1975), 30.

9. Robert Lowell, "The Exile's Return," in *Lord Weary's Castle*, 3.

10. T. S. Eliot, *The Waste Land*, in *The Complete Poems and Plays*, 37.

11. Yenser, *Circle to Circle*, 73.

12. Burton Raffel, *Robert Lowell* (New York: Frederick Ungar, 1981), 18.

13. Yenser, *Circle to Circle*, 31.

14. Raffel, *Lowell*, 15.

15. Alan Williamson, *Pity the Monsters: The Political Vision of Robert Lowell* (New Haven: Yale University Press, 1974), 16.

16. Robert Lowell, "New Year's Day," in *Lord Weary's Castle*, 5; Lowell, "In Memory of Arthur Winslow," in ibid., 19; Lowell, "At the Indian Killer's

Grave," in ibid., 57. "In Memory of Arthur Winslow" first appeared in *Land of Unlikeness*, n.p.

17. Robert Lowell, "On the Eve of the Feast of the Immaculate Conception," in *Land of Unlikeness*, n.p.; Yenser, *Circle to Circle*, 22.

18. Ehrenpreis, "The Age of Lowell," 163.

19. Robert Lowell, "Salem," in *Lord Weary's Castle*, 26. The poem first appeared in *Land of Unlikeness*, n.p.

20. Williamson, *Pity the Monsters*, 43ff.

21. Haffenden, *Life*, 86; Atlas, *Schwartz*, 40. Actually Schwartz's hallucinations occurred a few years before Berryman's.

22. Much of this biographical information comes from Geoffrey Brereton, *An Introduction to the French Poets* (London: Methuen, 1956), 191–92, 196–97.

23. Edward Engelberg, *The Symbolist Poem* (New York: Dutton, 1967), 31, 35; Simpson, *Revolution*, 154; Perloff, *Lowell*, 57–59; Brereton, *French Poets*, 196–97.

24. Brereton, *French Poets*, 196, 225; Ehrenpreis, "The Age of Lowell," 179.

25. Engelberg, *Symbolist Poem*, 25–26.

26. Charles Baudelaire, "The Swan" ("Le Cygne"), trans, F. P. Sturm, in Engelberg, *Symbolist Poem*, 131; Arthur Rimbaud, "Sensation" ("Sensation"), trans. John Gray, in ibid., 179; Jules Laforgue, "Lightning of the Abyss" ("Éclair de Gouffre"), trans. Vernon Watkins, in ibid., 190.

27. Delmore Schwartz, "Out of the Watercolored Window, When You Look," in *Summer Knowledge*, 36.

28. Engelberg, *Symbolist Poem*, 32.

29. John Berryman, "A Poem for Bhain," in *Poems* (Norfolk, Conn.: New Directions, 1942), 24; Randall Jarrell, "Moving," in *Losses*, 48.

30. Robert Lowell, "In the Cage," in *Lord Weary's Castle*, 53; Hugh B. Staples, *Robert Lowell: The First Twenty Years* (New York: Farrar, Straus and Cudahy, 1962), 38.

31. T. S. Eliot, "The Metaphysical Poets," in *Selected Essays*, 248–49.

CHAPTER 9

1. I have left a number of volumes out of this list, including all fiction, criticism, drama, and translations. *Berryman's Sonnets,* published in 1967, has been considered with the early poetry because all the sonnets were written in 1947. The same author's *Short Poems* is omitted because the poems in that volume were all published previously in book form. I have omitted volumes of *Selected Poems* by Lowell and Jarrell, as well as Berryman's *Dream Songs,* for similar reasons. Several volumes by Lowell—*Notebook 1967–68, Notebook, History,* and *For Lizzie and Harriet*—are more or less reshuffled versions of one another; but I have included all four on this list because each book contains a few poems, or versions of poems, which the others do not.

2. T. S. Eliot, *After Strange Gods: A Primer of Modern Heresy* (London: Faber and Faber, 1934), 64.

3. Delmore Schwartz, "Poem" ("Remember midsummer: the fragrance of box, or white roses"), in *Last and Lost Poems*, 12–13.

4. Ezra Pound, "Canto CXVI," in *The Cantos of Ezra Pound* (New York: New Directions, 1970), 796.

5. Harry Levin, "Ezra Pound, T. S. Eliot and the European Horizon," in *Memories of the Moderns* (New York: New Directions, 1982), 19.

6. Delmore Schwartz, "T. S. Eliot as the International Hero," 205.

7. Robert Penn Warren, "The Present State of Poetry: III: In the United States," *Kenyon Review* 1 (1939), 384–98.

8. Simpson, *Revolution*, xv. He quotes Wallace Stevens, "To Richard Eberhart. . . . Jan. 20, 1954," in *Letters of Wallace Stevens*, ed. Holly Stevens (New York: Knopf, 1967), 815.

9. Samuel Taylor Coleridge, "Notes on Herbert's *Temple* and Harvey's *Synagogue*," ed. Thomas Middleton Raysor (London: Constable & Co., 1936), 244.

10. Hamilton, *Lowell*, 231.

11. M. L. Rosenthal, of course, coined the term "confessional poetry" to describe *Life Studies* in his review, "Poetry as Confession," published in the *Nation*, 19 September 1959. But, like many critics, I find the term limiting, particularly when applied to such a poet as Robert Lowell. If "confessional poetry" has any meaning at all, it is, to me, defined by the obvious limitations in the poetry of Plath, Sexton, and Snodgrass, and not by the work of such poets as Lowell and Berryman, who strike me as essentially different from Plath, Sexton, and Snodgrass, in ways which I hope to make clear.

12. Robert Lowell, letter to Randall Jarrell, 24 October, 1957, Berg Collection, New York Public Library. Interestingly, like Snodgrass, Lowell would write a series of poems addressed to his young daughter after his estrangement from her mother.

13. M. L. Rosenthal, *The New Poets: American and British Poetry Since World War Two* (New York: Oxford University Press, 1967), 79, 130; Robert Phillips, *The Confessional Poets* (Carbondale: Southern Illinois University Press, 1973), 4–5.

14. This and the characterizations of confessional poetry which follow are from Phillips, *Confessional Poets*, 8–9, 14.

15. Robert Lowell, "For Sale," in *Life Studies*, 76; Delmore Schwartz, "Vivaldi," in *Summer Knowledge*, 177.

16. "Hate poems": Anne Sexton, interviewed by Barbara Kevles, in *Writers at Work: The Paris Review Interviews*, 4th series, ed. George Plimpton (New York: Viking Press, 1976), 408. "O ho alas": John Berryman, "Dream Song 384," in *His Toy*, 316. "Daddy, you bastard": Sylvia Plath, "Daddy," in *The Collected Poems* (New York: Harper and Row, 1981), 224.

17. Rosenthal, *The New Poets*, 82. Patrick Cosgrave, in his study *The Public Poetry of Robert Lowell* (New York: Taplinger, 1972), 111–12, says that Lowell's late poems were less "direct" than Plath's. I would say that this is true of most late Middle Generation poetry in comparison with confessional poetry. Also, Laurence Lieberman, in "The Expansional Poet: A Return to Personality," *Yale Review* 57 (1968), 258–71, contrasts Berryman, an "expansionist" poet who conveys "the sum total of a vivid personality," with the confessional poets, who specialized in "mere

autobiography." Anne Sexton may be making much the same comparison when, in the *Writers at Work* interview, p. 403, she compares her friend Maxine Kumin, "an intellectual," to herself, "a primitive."

18. Quoted in Conarroe, *Berryman*, 70.
19. John Berryman, *Homage to Mistress Bradstreet* (New York: Farrar, Straus and Giroux, 1956), n.p.
20. Linebarger, *Berryman*, 72–73.
21. Arpin, *Berryman*, 48.
22. John Haffenden, *John Berryman: A Critical Commentary* (New York: New York University Press, 1980), 10.
23. Helen Vendler, "Savage, Rueful, Irrespressible Henry," *New York Times Book Review*, 3 November 1968, 1, 58; Linebarger, *Berryman*, 74.
24. Linebarger, *Berryman*, 75; John Ciardi, "The Researched Mistress," *Saturday Review*, 23 March 1957, 36.
25. John Berryman, quoted in Dorothy Strudwick, "Homage to Mr. Berryman," *Minnesota Daily*, 5 November 1956, 6; quoted in Conarroe, *Berryman*, 81.
26. Delmore Schwartz, "On a Sentence by Pascal," in *Vaudeville for a Princess*, 3.
27. But of course this is generally true of all Schwartz's early imaginative prose. His first published story, "In Dreams Begin Responsibilities," expresses his feelings about personal experiences more simply and directly than any of his early poems. Critics have noted with puzzlement that many of Schwartz's later stories, particularly those in *Successful Love*, seem completely unrelated to his personal life, and are, as Atlas remarks, about "the sexual education of a typical adolescent girl in the 1950's, the fortunes of a brilliant scholar whose idiosyncrasies include a refusal to sleep with his young wife, or an idealistic college girl who kidnaps a baby adopted by her liberal parents and then rejected because it has a trace of Negro blood." Atlas wonders why the stories are so detached from Schwartz's own experience, and radiate "the benevolence and bland tolerance of the Eisenhower era at the very moment when he was enduring his most profound agony." (Atlas, *Schwartz*, 348). The explanation appears obvious; Schwartz's agony, which in his early years he had poured into his stories, while producing poems which were models of impersonality, in his later years informed his poems. Having finally learned to be a subjective poet, this man who had always been a poet first and a story writer second lost the need to bare his soul in prose, and fell into the habit of writing stories only when he came up with "story ideas" of the type that people who write for *Redbook* store in their card files. And so, while his early stories are anguished and real, his later stories are often contrived potboilers.
28. Delmore Schwartz, "Hamlet, or There is Something Wrong with Everyone," in *Vaudeville, for a Princess*, 18–19.
29. Atlas, *Schwartz*, 292.
30. Sir Edward Dyer, "The Mind to Me a Kingdom Is"; Delmore Schwartz, " 'The Mind to Me a Kingdom Is,' " in *Vaudeville for a Princess*, 7.

31. Delmore Schwartz, "I Did not Know the Spoils of Joy," in ibid., 13–14.
32. Delmore Schwartz, "True Recognition Often is Refused," in ibid., 20.
33. Delmore Schwartz, "The Passionate Shepherd to His Love," in ibid., 27.
34. Delmore Schwartz, "Most Things at Second Hand Through Gloves We Touch," in ibid., 62.
35. Delmore Schwartz, "Starlight Like Intuition Pierced the Twelve," in ibid., 49.
36. Randall Jarrell, "The Woman at the Washington Zoo," in *The Woman at the Washington Zoo*, 3.
37. John Berryman, "Dream Song 7," in *77 Dream Songs*, 9.
38. Robert Lowell, "For Sheridan," in *Day by Day*, 82.
39. Arthur Rimbaud, *A Season in Hell*, trans. Louise Varese (New York: New Directions, 1951), 87, 89.

CHAPTER 10

1. Delmore Schwartz, "Christmas Poem for Nancy," in *Last and Lost Poems*, 19. "Deathless present": Schwartz, "Vivaldi," in *Summer Knowledge*, 179. "Eternity is now": Schwartz, "Hölderlin," in ibid., 184.
2. Delmore Schwartz, "Phoenix Lyrics: I," in *Last and Lost Poems*, 9.
3. Delmore Schwartz, "The Foggy, Foggy Blue," in *Summer Knowledge*, 206.
4. Richard McDougall, *Delmore Schwartz* (New York: Twayne Publishers, 1974), 115.
5. Atlas, *Schwartz*, 326.
6. Delmore Schwartz, "Seurat's Sunday Afternoon along the Seine," in *Summer Knowledge*, 192.
7. John Keats, "Ode on a Grecian Urn."
8. Delmore Schwartz, " 'I Am Cherry Alive,' the Little Girl Sang," in *Summer Knowledge*, 161.
9. Delmore Schwartz, "Summer Knowledge," in ibid., 157–58.
10. Delmore Schwartz, "T. S. Eliot as the International Hero," 199.
11. T. S. Eliot, "Burnt Norton," in *The Complete Poems and Plays*, 117–18.
12. Delmore Schwartz, "America, America," in *Last and Lost Poems*, 4.
13. Delmore Schwartz, "A Dream of Whitman Paraphrased, Recognized and Made More Vivid by Renoir," in ibid., 48.
14. Delmore Schwartz, "Now He Knows All There Is to Know: Now He Is Acquainted With the Day and Night," in ibid., 46.
15. Delmore Schwartz, "Darkling Summer, Ominous Dusk, Rumorous Rain," in *Summer Knowledge*, 149.
16. Arpin, *Berryman*, 7; Atlas, *Schwartz*, 132.
17. Atlas, *Schwartz*, 326.
18. Robert Phillips, Foreword, *Last and Lost Poems*, xiv–xv.

CHAPTER 11

1. Randall Jarrell, "Aging," in *The Woman at the Washington Zoo*, 22.
2. Alfred Kazin, "Randall: His Kingdom," in *Randall Jarrell: 1914–1965*, 88.

3. Randall Jarrell, "The Elementary Scene," in *The Woman at the Washington Zoo*, 19; Jarrell, "Windows," in ibid., 21; Jarrell, "Nestus Gurley," in ibid., 24.

4. Ferguson, *Jarrell*, 161.

5. Randall Jarrell, "Deutsche Durch Freud," in *The Woman at the Washington Zoo*, 56.

6. Charlotte Beck, "Unicorn to Eland: The Rilkean Spirit in the Poetry of Randall Jarrell," *Southern Literary Journal* 12 (1979), 6.

7. Randall Jarrell, "Childhood," in *The Woman at the Washington Zoo*, 56.

8. Robert Watson, "Randall Jarrell: The Last Years," in *Randall Jarrell: 1914–1965*, 267.

9. Randall Jarrell, "The Lonely Man," in *The Woman at the Washington Zoo*, 48.

10. Robert Lowell, "Randall Jarrell," in *Randall Jarrell: 1914–1965*, 109.

11. Randall Jarrell, "Next Day," in *The Lost World*, 4.

12. Randall Jarrell, "In Montecito," in ibid., 7.

13. John Fuller, review of *The Lost World*, in *The Review*, no. 16 (October 1966), 5.

14. Randall Jarrell, "Fifty Years of American Poetry," in *The Third Book of Criticism* (New York: Farrar, Straus and Giroux, 1969), 300–302.

15. W. H. Auden, "Musée des Beaux Arts," in *Collected Poems*, 126; Randall Jarrell, "The Old and the New Masters," in *The Lost World*, 62.

16. Randall Jarrell papers, Berg Collection, New York Public Library.

CHAPTER 12

1. John Berryman, "Thomas Nashe and *The Unfortunate Traveller*," in *The Freedom of the Poet*, 12.

2. John Berryman, "The Poetry of Ezra Pound," in ibid., 263.

3. John Berryman, "Dream Song 224: Eighty," in *His Toy*, 153.

4. Conarroe, *Berryman*, 93; Arpin, *Berryman*, 63–64; Linebarger, *Berryman*, 80, 115.

5. See Linebarger, *Berryman*, 119. The only important connection between *The Dream Songs* and *The Nervous Songs* is the similarity of names and of stanzaic patterns.

6. Arpin, *Berryman*, 75; Rimbaud, *Season*, 17.

7. Arpin, *Berryman*, 75.

8. Arpin, *Berryman*, 76–77; Huysmans, *Against the Grain*, quoted in ibid., 76.

9. John Berryman, "*Song of Myself*: Intention and Substance," in *The Freedom of the Poet*, 227–28.

10. Conarroe, *Berryman*, 96.

11. Arpin, *Berryman*, 69; John Berryman, "Dream Song 79: Op. posth. no. 2," in *His Toy*, 4.

12. Arpin, *Berryman*, 70.

13. John Berryman, "Dream Song 13," in *77 Dream Songs*, 15.

14. John Berryman, *His Toy*, ix; Conarroe, *Berryman*, 95; Linebarger, *Berryman*, 80.

15. Linebarger, *Berryman*, 80.

16. Conarroe, *Berryman*, 86–87.

17. John Berryman, interviewed by Peter Stitt, in *Writers at Work*, 300; Adrienne Rich, "Mr. Bones, He Lives," *Nation*, 25 May 1964, 538; Paul Ramsey, review, of *77 Dream Songs*, *Sewanee Review* 74 (1966), 936.

18. Roger Pooley, "Berryman's Last Poems: Plain Style and Christian Style," *Modern Language Review* 76 (1981), 291.

19. Linebarger, *Berryman*, 126; John Berryman, interviewed by Peter Stitt, in *Writers at Work*, 298.

20. Linebarger, *Berryman*, 129.

21. Conarroe, *Berryman*, 154.

22. John Berryman, "Crises," in *Love and Fame*, 27–29.

23. John Berryman, "In & Out," in ibid., 24.

24. "Nobody knows": John Berryman, "Have a Genuine American Horror-&-Mist on the Rocks," in ibid., 65. "Murdered Martin Luther King": Berryman, "The Soviet Union," in ibid., 60. "Let's confront": Berryman, "Regents' Professor Berryman's Crack on Race," in ibid., 63.

25. John Berryman, "Eleven Addresses to the Lord," in ibid., 85–89. The first two excerpts are from the first address, the last from the fourth.

26. Linebarger, *Berryman*, 127.

27. John Thompson, "Last Testament," in *New York Review of Books*, 9 April 1973, 4.

28. John Berryman, "Of Suicide," in *Love and Fame*, 69–70; Berryman, "He Resigns," in *Delusions, Etc.* (New York: Farrar, Straus and Giroux, 1972), 40.

29. Conarroe, *Berryman*, 180.

30. John Berryman, "A Prayer After All," in *Delusions, Etc.*, 46; Berryman, "Somber Prayer," in ibid., 59; Berryman, "Amos," in ibid., 64.

31. John Berryman, "I didn't. And I didn't. Sharp the Spanish blade," in *Henry's Fate*, 93.

CHAPTER 13

1. Robert Lowell, "The Mills of the Kavanaughs," in *The Mills of the Kavanaughs*, 83.

2. Randall Jarrell, "Three Books," in *Poetry and the Age*, 260; Raffel, *Lowell*, 41; William Carlos Williams, "In a Mood of Tragedy: *The Mills of the Kavanaughs*," in *Selected Essays of William Carlos Williams* (New York: New Directions, 1951), 36.

3. M. L. Rosenthal, "Robert Lowell and the Poetry of Confession," in *Robert Lowell: A Portrait of the the Artist in His Time*, 45.

4. Raffel, *Lowell*, 45.

5. Robert Lowell, "The Holy Innocents," in *Lord Weary's Castle*, 10; Lowell, "The Quaker Graveyard in Nantucket," in ibid., 18; Lowell, "Sailing Home from Rapallo," in *Life Studies*, 77; Lowell, "Terminal Days at Beverly Farms," in ibid., 74; Lowell, "Skunk Hour," in ibid., 90.

6. Vivian Smith, *The Poetry of Robert Lowell* (Sydney: Sydney University Press, 1974), 52.

7. Robert Lowell, letter to Randall Jarrell, 11 October 1957, Berg Collection, New York Public Library.
8. Robert Lowell, interviewed by Frederick Seidel, "An Interview with Robert Lowell," in *Robert Lowell: A Portrait of the Artist in His Time*, 269–70.
9. Robert Lowell, letter to Randall Jarrell, 24 October 1957, Berg Collection, New York Public Library.
10. Ehrenpreis, "The Age of Lowell," 174.
11. Robert Lowell, interviewed by Frederick Seidel, in *Robert Lowell: A Portrait of the Artist in His Time*, 269.
12. Helen Vendler, "Robert Lowell: A Difficult Grandeur," in *Part of Nature, Part of Us: Modern American Poets* (Cambridge, Mass.: Harvard University Press, 1980), 126.
13. Louis Simpson, "American Poetry," in *At the End of the Open Road* (Middletown, Conn.: Wesleyan University Press, 1963), 55.
14. Robert Lowell, "Beyond the Alps," in *Life Studies*, 3–4.
15. John Crick, *Robert Lowell* (Edinburgh: Oliver and Boyd, 1974), 57, 61.
16. Raffel, *Lowell*, 45.
17. Yenser, *Circle to Circle*, 122.
18. Robert Lowell, "A Mad Negro Soldier Confined at Munich," in *Life Studies*, 8.
19. Robert Lowell, letter to Randall Jarrell, 11 October 1957, Berg Collection, New York Public Library.
20. Robert Lowell, "Inauguration Day: January 1953," in *Life Studies*, 7.
21. Robert Lowell, "My Last Afternoon with Uncle Devereux Wilson," in ibid., 23; Lowell, "Grandparents," in ibid., 68; Lowell, "Memories of West Street and Lepke," in ibid., 86.
22. Robert Lowell, "Skunk Hour," in ibid., 89–90.
23. Raffel, *Lowell*, 59; Vendler, *Part of Nature*, 133.
24. Raffel, *Lowell*, 81–82.
25. Crick, *Lowell*, 125; Haffenden, *Life*, 2; Robert Lowell, "For John Berryman I," in *History*, 203.
26. Crick, *Lowell*, 130; Raffel, *Lowell*, 87; Robert Lowell, "Elisabeth Schwartzkopf in New York," in *History*, 167.
27. Vendler, *Part of Nature*, 132.
28. Simpson, *Revolution*, 160, 167. Even Vendler, who loves *History* and all the sonnet-volumes, says that "The compulsion to rewrite history, to afford privileged glimpses of the hidden moments of intimacy in public lives, to insert in the book of history the commentaries of poets—Horace, DuBellay, Góngora, Heine, Baudelaire, Bécquer, Leopardi, Rilke, Rimbaud—to modernize relentlessly in laconic colloquialisms, to assume familiarity, to impute motive—all this rules more of *History* than perhaps it should." *Part of Nature*, 130.
29. Crick, *Lowell*, 124; Robert Lowell, "Mexico: 1," in *For Lizzie and Harriet* (New York: Farrar, Straus and Giroux, 1973), 31.
30. "I wish": quoted in Hamilton, *Lowell*, 181. "I feel more": quoted in ibid., 234; the date of the letter is 30 September 1957. "It's as if": Robert Lowell, "William Carlos Williams," *Hudson Review* 14 (1961), 534.

31. Steven Gould Axelrod, *Robert Lowell: Life and Art* (Princeton: Princeton University Press, 1978), 84–97.
32. Robert Lowell, letter to Randall Jarrell, 24 October 1957, Berg Collection, New York Public Library.
33. Crick, *Lowell*, 55, 99; Smith, *Lowell*, 71; Robert Lowell, "Home After Three Months Away," in *Life Studies*, 83–84.
34. Stephen Yenser, "Half Legible Bronze?", *Poetry* 123 (1974), 308.
35. Robert Lowell, "Epilogue," in *Day by Day*, 127.

Bibliography

Alvarez, A. *The Savage God: A Study of Suicide*. New York: Knopf, 1972.

Arpin, Gary Q. *The Poetry of John Berryman*. Port Washington, N.Y.: Kennikat Press, 1978.

Atlas, James. *Delmore Schwartz: The Life of an American Poet*. New York: Farrar, Straus and Giroux, 1977.

———. "Unsentimental Education." *Atlantic*, June 1983, 78–92.

Auden, W. H. *About the House*. New York: Random House, 1965.

———. *Collected Poems*. Ed. Edward Mendelson. New York: Random House, 1976.

———. *Collected Poetry*. New York: Random House, 1945.

———. *Look, Stranger!* London: Faber and Faber, 1936.

———. *Selected Poems of W. H. Auden*. "New edition." Ed. Edward Mendelson. New York: Vintage, 1979.

———. *Selected Poetry of W. H. Auden*. 2nd ed. New York: Vintage, 1971.

Auden, W. H. and John Garrett, eds. *The Poet's Tongue*. London: G. Bell and Sons, 1935.

Axelrod, Steven Gould. *Robert Lowell: Life and Art*. Princeton: Princeton University Press, 1978.

Barrett, William. *The Truants*. New York: Anchor, 1982.

Barzun, Jacques. *Classic, Romantic and Modern*. Boston: Little, Brown, 1961.

Beck, Charlotte. "Unicorn to Eland: The Rilkean Spirit in the Poetry of Randall Jarrell." *Southern Literary Journal*, 12 (1979), 3–17.

Bellow, Saul. *Humboldt's Gift*. New York: Viking Press, 1975.

Berryman, John. *Berryman's Sonnets*. New York: Farrar, Straus and Giroux, 1967.

———. *Delusions, Etc*. New York: Farrar, Straus and Giroux, 1972.

———. *The Dispossessed*. New York: William Sloane Associates, 1948.

———. *The Dream Songs*. New York: Farrar, Straus and Giroux, 1969.

———. *The Freedom of the Poet*. New York: Farrar, Straus and Giroux, 1976.

———. *Henry's Fate and Other Poems, 1967-1972*. New York: Farrar, Straus and Giroux, 1977.

———. *His Thought Made Pockets and the Plane Buckt*. Pawlet, Vt.: Claude Fredericks, 1958.

————. *His Toy, His Dream, His Rest*. New York: Farrar, Straus and Giroux, 1968.

————. *Homage to Mistress Bradstreet*. New York: Farrar, Straus and Giroux, 1956.

————. *Love and Fame*. New York: Farrar, Straus and Giroux, 1970.

————. *Poems*. Norfolk, Conn.: New Directions, 1942.

————. *Recovery*. New York: Farrar, Straus and Giroux, 1973.

————. *77 Dream Songs*. New York: Farrar, Straus and Giroux, 1967.

————. *Short Poems*. New York: Farrar, Straus and Giroux, 1967.

————. *Stephen Crane*. New York: William Sloane Associates, 1950.

————. *Twenty Poems*. In *Five Young American Poets*. Ed. James Laughlin. Norfolk, Conn.: New Directions, 1940.

Bewley, Marius. "Poetry Chronicle." *Hudson Review* 20 (1967), 500–504.

Blackmur, R. P. "Twelve Poets." *Southern Review* 7 (1941), 197–213.

Bogan, Louise. "Young Modern." *Nation*, 25 March 1939, 353.

Bowra, C. M. *Heritage of Symbolism*. London: Macmillan, 1947.

Brenner, Patricia Ann. "John Berryman's *Dream Songs:* Manner and Matter." Ph.D. Diss.: Kent State University, 1970.

Brereton, Geoffrey. *An Introduction to the French Poets*. London: Methuen, 1956.

Brill, A. A. *Lectures on Psychoanalytic Psychiatry*. New York: Knopf, 1947.

Brooks, Cleanth. *A Shaping Joy*. New York: Harcourt Brace Jovanovich, 1971.

Ciardi, John. "The Researched Mistress." *Saturday Review*, 23 March 1957, 36–37.

Conarroe, Joel. *John Berryman: An Introduction to the Poetry*. New York: Columbia University Press, 1977.

Cooper, Phillip. *The Autobiographical Myth of Robert Lowell*. Chapel Hill: University of North Carolina Press, 1970.

Cosgrave, Patrick. *The Public Poetry of Robert Lowell*. New York: Taplinger, 1972.

Crick, John. *Robert Lowell*. Edinburgh: Oliver and Boyd, 1974.

Deutsch, Babette. "Poets—Timely and Timeless." *New Republic*, 29 March 1943, 420–21.

Deutsch, R. H. "Poetry and Belief in Delmore Schwartz." *Sewanee Review* 74 (1966), 915–24.

Eliot, T. S. *After Strange Gods: A Primer of Modern Heresy*. London: Faber and Faber, 1934.

————. *The Complete Poems and Plays*. New York: Harcourt, Brace and World, 1971.

————. *For Lancelot Andrewes: Essays on Style and Order*. Garden City: Doubleday and Doran, 1929.

————. *Selected Essays*. New York: Harcourt, Brace and Company, 1932.

Ellmann, Richard. *The Identity of Yeats*. New York: Oxford University Press, 1964.

Engelberg, Edward. *The Symbolist Poem*. New York: Dutton, 1967.

Eshleman, Clayton. "A Braggart, Boozer, Brute—and Poet." *Los Angeles Times*, 10 October 1982, book review section, 2.

Ferguson, Suzanne. *The Poetry of Randall Jarrell.* Baton Rouge: Louisiana State University Press, 1971.

Fiedler, Leslie. "The Believing Poet and the Infidel Reader." *New Leader,* 10 May 1947, 18.

Fuller, John. Review of *The Lost World. The Review,* no. 16 (October 1966), 5.

Greene, Graham. "The Badge of Courage." *New Statesman and Nation* 41 (1951), 627–28.

Gross, Leonard. Personal interview. 15 December 1982.

Haffenden, John. *John Berryman: A Critical Commentary.* New York: New York University Press, 1980.

———. *The Life of John Berryman.* Boston: Routledge and Kegan Paul, 1982.

Halio, Jay L. "Delmore Schwartz's Felt Abstractions." *Southern Review,* n.s. 1 (1965), 803–19.

Hamilton, Ian. "John Berryman." *London Magazine,* February 1965, 93–100.

———. *Robert Lowell.* New York: Random House, 1982.

Hook, Sidney. "Imaginary Enemies, Real Terror." *American Scholar* 47 (1978), 406–12.

Jarrell, Randall. *Blood for a Stranger.* New York: Harcourt, Brace and Company, 1942.

———. *The Complete Poems.* New York: Farrar, Straus and Giroux, 1969.

———. *Jerome: The Making of a Poem.* New York: Grossman, 1971.

———. *Kipling, Auden & Co.* New York: Farrar, Straus and Giroux, 1980.

———. *Little Friend, Little Friend.* New York: Dial Press, 1945.

———. *Losses.* New York: Harcourt, Brace and Company, 1948.

———. *The Lost World.* New York: Macmillan, 1965.

———. *Poetry and the Age.* New York: Knopf, 1953.

———. *The Rage for the Lost Penny.* In *Five Young American Poets.* Ed. James Laughlin. Norfolk, Conn.: New Directions, 1940.

———. *A Sad Heart at the Supermarket.* New York: Atheneum, 1962.

———. *Selected Poems.* New York: Atheneum, 1964.

———. *The Seven-League Crutches.* New York: Harcourt, Brace and Company, 1951.

———. *The Third Book of Criticism.* New York: Farrar, Straus and Giroux, 1969.

———. *The Woman at the Washington Zoo.* New York: Atheneum, 1960.

Jones, Claude. "Stephen Crane." *Nineteenth Century Fiction* 6 (1951), 74–76.

Jones, Frank. "Skilled Workers." *Nation,* 17 April 1943, 569–70.

Kazin, Alfred. *New York Jew.* New York: Knopf, 1978.

Kenner, Hugh. *T. S. Eliot: A Collection of Critical Essays.* Englewood Cliffs, N.J.: Prentice-Hall, 1962.

Knapp, James F. "Delmore Schwartz: Poet of the Orphic Journey." *Sewanee Review* 78 (1970), 506–16.

Levin, Harry. *Memories of the Moderns.* New York: New Directions, 1982.

Lieberman, Laurence. "The Expansional Poet: A Return to Personality." *Yale Review* 57 (1968), 258–71.

Linebarger, J. M. *John Berryman.* New York: Twayne Publishers, 1974.

London, Michael and Robert Boyers. *Robert Lowell: A Portrait of the Artist in His Time.* New York: David Lewis, 1970.

Lowell, Robert. *Day by Day*. New York: Farrar, Straus and Giroux, 1977.
———. *The Dolphin*. New York: Farrar, Straus and Giroux, 1973.
———. *For Lizzie and Harriet*. New York: Farrar, Straus and Giroux, 1973.
———. *For the Union Dead*. New York: Farrar, Straus and Giroux, 1964.
———. *History*. New York: Farrar, Straus and Giroux, 1973.
———. *Imitations*. New York: Noonday / Farrar, Straus and Giroux, 1961.
———. *Land of Unlikeness*. Cummington, Mass.: The Cummington Press, 1944.
———. *Life Studies*. New York: Farrar, Straus and Cudahy, 1959.
———. *Lord Weary's Castle*. New York: Harcourt, Brace and World, 1946.
———. *The Mills of the Kavanaughs*. New York: Harcourt, Brace and World, 1951.
———. *Near the Ocean*. New York: Farrar, Straus and Giroux, 1967.
———. *Notebook*. New York: Farrar, Straus and Giroux, 1970.
———. *Notebook 1967-68*. New York: Farrar, Straus and Giroux, 1969.
———. *Selected Poems*. New York: Farrar, Straus and Giroux, 1976.
———. "William Carlos Williams." *Hudson Review* 14 (1961), 534.
Lowell, Robert, Peter Taylor, and Robert Penn Warren, eds. *Randall Jarrell: 1914–1965*. New York: Farrar, Straus and Giroux, 1966.
Mailer, Norman. *The Armies of the Night*. New York: New American Library, 1968.
Matthiessen, F. O. *The Achievement of T. S. Eliot*. New York: Oxford University Press, 1959.
McDougall, Richard. *Delmore Schwartz*. New York: Twayne Publishers, 1974.
Meiners, R. K. "The Way Out: The Poetry of Delmore Schwartz and Others." *Southern Review* n.s. 7 (1971), 314–37.
O'Donnell, George Marion. "Delmore Schwartz's Achievement." *Poetry* 52 (May 1939), 105–8.
"Our Country and Our Culture." *Partisan Review* 19 (1952), 282–326, 420–50, 562–97.
Parkinson, Thomas, ed. *Robert Lowell: A Collection of Critical Essays*. Englewood Cliffs, N.J.: Prentice-Hall, 1968.
Perloff, Marjorie. *The Poetic Art of Robert Lowell*. Ithaca: Cornell University Press, 1973.
Phillips, Robert. *The Confessional Poets*. Carbondale: Southern Illinois University Press, 1973.
Plath, Sylvia. *The Collected Poems*. New York: Harper and Row, 1981.
Plimpton, George, ed. *Writers at Work: The Paris Review Interviews* 4th series (New York: Viking Press, 1976).
Pooley, Roger. "Berryman's Last Poems: Plain Style and Christian Style." *Modern Language Review* 76 (April 1981), 291–97.
Pound, Ezra. *The Cantos of Ezra Pound*. New York: New Directions. 1970.
Price, Jonathan, ed. *Critics on Robert Lowell*. Coral Gables: University of Miami Press, 1972.
Quinn, Sister Bernetta. *Randall Jarrell*. Boston: Twayne Publishers, 1981.
Raffel, Burton. *Robert Lowell*. New York: Frederick Ungar, 1981.
Ramsey, Paul. "In Exasperation and Gratitude." *Sewanee Review* 74 (1966), 930–45.

Replogle, Justin. *Auden's Poetry.* Seattle: University of Washington Press, 1969.

Rich, Adrienne. "Mr. Bones, He Lives." *Nation,* 25 May 1964, 538, 540.

Rimbaud, Arthur. *A Season in Hell.* Trans. Louise Varèse. New York: New Directions, 1951.

Rosenthal, M. L. *The New Poets: American and British Poetry Since World War Two.* New York: Oxford University Press, 1967.

———. *Randall Jarrell.* Minneapolis: University of Minnesota Press, 1972.

Schwartz, Delmore. "Anywhere Out of the World." *Nation,* 24 July 1943, 102.

———. "The Duchess' Red Shoes." *Partisan Review* 21 (1953), 55–73.

———. *Genesis: Book One.* New York: New Directions, 1943.

———. *In Dreams Begin Responsibilities.* New York: New Directions, 1939.

———. *Last and Lost Poems of Delmore Schwartz.* Ed. Robert Phillips. New York: Vanguard, 1979.

———. "The Literary Dictatorship of T. S. Eliot." *Partisan Review* 16 (1949), 119–37.

———. "A Note on the Nature of Art." *Marxist Quarterly,* January–March 1937, 305–9.

———. *Summer Knowledge.* New York: Doubleday, 1959; reprinted as *Selected Poems: Summer Knowledge* (New York: New Directions, 1967).

———. "T. S. Eliot as the International Hero." *Partisan Review* 12 (1945), 119–206.

———. "The Two Audens." *Kenyon Review* 1 (1939), 34–45.

———. *Vaudeville for a Princess and Other Poems.* New York: New Directions, 1950.

———. "The Vocation of the Poet in the Modern World." *Poetry* 78 (July 1951), 223–32.

Scott, Winfield Townley. "The New Intellectualism: Two Views. I: The Dry Reaction." *Poetry* 58 (May 1941), 86.

Shapiro, Karl. *The Poetry Wreck.* New York: Random House, 1975.

Simpson, Eileen. *Poets in their Youth.* New York: Random House, 1982.

Simpson, Louis. *A Revolution in Taste.* New York: Macmillan, 1978.

———. *At the End of the Open Road.* Middletown, Conn.; Wesleyan University Press, 1963.

Smith, Vivian. *The Poetry of Robert Lowell.* Sydney: Sydney University Press, 1974.

Spears, Monroe K. *The Poetry of W. H. Auden: The Disenchanted Island.* New York: Oxford University Press, 1963.

Staples, Hugh. B. *Robert Lowell: The First Twenty Years.* New York: Farrar, Straus and Cudahy, 1962.

Stauffer, Donald Barlow. *A Short History of American Poetry.* New York: Dutton, 1974.

Stevens, Wallace. *Letters of Wallace Stevens.* Ed. Holly Stevens. New York: Knopf, 1967.

Strudwick, Dorothy. "Homage to Mr. Berryman." *Minnesota Daily,* 5 November 1956, 6.

Tate, Allen. "The Last Omnibus." *Partisan Review* 8 (1941), 241–44.

Thompson, John. "Last Testament." *New York Review of Books,* 9 April 1973, 4.

Thurley, Geoffrey. *The American Moment: American Poetry in the Mid-Century.* New York: St. Martin's Press, 1977.

Trilling, Lionel. *The Liberal Imagination.* New York: Viking Press, 1950.

Unterecker, John. *A Reader's Guide to William Butler Yeats.* New York: Farrar, Straus and Giroux, 1959.

Van Doren, Mark. "Music of a Mind." *Kenyon Review* 1 (1939), 208–11.

Vendler, Helen. *Part of Nature, Part of Us: Modern American Poets.* Cambridge, Mass.: Harvard University Press, 1980.

————. "Savage, Rueful, Irrepressible Henry." *New York Times Book Review,* 3 November 1968, 1, 58.

Wanning, Andrews. "A Portrait of Stephen Crane." *Partisan Review* 18 (1951), 358–61.

Warren, Robert Penn. "The Present State of Poetry: III: In the United States." *Kenyon Review* 1 (1939), 384–98.

Williams, William Carlos. *Selected Essays of William Carlos Williams.* New York: New Directions, 1951.

Williamson, Alan. *Pity the Monsters: The Political Vision of Robert Lowell.* New Haven: Yale University Press, 1974.

Wilson, Edmund. *Letters on Literature and Politics.* Ed. Elena Wilson. New York: Farrar, Straus and Giroux, 1977.

————. Review of *Stephen Crane. New Yorker,* 6 January 1951, 77–85.

Yeats, W. B. *The Collected Poems of W. B. Yeats.* New York: Macmillan, 1956.

————. *Essays and Introductions.* New York: Collier, 1968.

Yenser, Stephen. *Circle to Circle.* Berkeley: University of California Press, 1975.

————. "Half Legible Bronze." *Poetry* 113 (1974), pp. 304–09.

Index